P9-DVC-456

Tools of Critical Thinking

Metathoughts for Psychology

David A. Levy

Pepperdine University

Foreword by Thomas Szasz

Allyn and Bacon

Boston • London • Toronto • Sydney • Tokyo • Singapore

Dedication

To my family—past, present, and future

Vice President and Editor-in-Chief, Social Sciences: Sean W. Wakely
Editorial Assistant: Erika Stuart
Marketing Manager: Joyce Nilsen
Editorial/Production Service: Chestnut Hill Enterprises, Inc.
Manufacturing Buyer: Suzanne Lareau
Cover Administrator: Suzanne Harbison

Copyright © 1997 by Allyn & Bacon
A Viacom Company
Needham Heights, MA 02194

All rights reserved. No part of the material protected by this copyright notice may be reproduced or utilized in any form or by any means, electronic or mechanical, including photocopying, recording, or by any information storage and retrieval system, without written permission from the copyright holder.

Library of Congress Cataloging-in Publication Data

Levy, David A., (Date)
   Tools of critical thinking : metathoughts for psychology / David
A. Levy.
     p. cm.
   Includes bibliographical references (p.   ) and indexes.
  ISBN 0-205-26083-7 (pbk.)
   1. Critical thinking.   2. Problem solving.   3. Thought and
thinking.   I. Title.
BF441.L484   1997
150'.01—dc20   96-27649
                                         CIP

Printed in the United States of America

10 9 8 7 6 5 4   01 00 98

Contents

Foreword

David Levy follows in the footsteps of classical philosophers who believed that knowledge of the Other begins with self-knowledge. Their perspective led to the grand humanist maxim, "Nothing human is alien to me."

Levy asks the readers to think, about thinking, and that they do so for themselves. He deviates from the dogma of psychological scientism that dictates studying the Other as a defective object, a perspective that generates the grand psychodiagnostic maxim, "Nothing alien is human to me." The fruits of this folly are now widely regarded as scientific progress. I think Ogden Nash's formula (made in a different context) applies: "We're making great progress, but we are headed in the wrong direction."

To be sure, accepting the invitation to think critically entails assuming the risk of living dangerously, the extent of the danger depending on what the thinker does as a result of, and with, his or her thoughts. Socrates thought for himself—and, for sharing his thoughts with others, was condemned as a criminal by the Athenian authorities. Zola thought for himself—and, for thinking and saying that Dreyfus was innocent, had to flee France. Official protestations to the contrary notwithstanding, we are not supposed to think. We are supposed to believe what the Authorities think, and define as Truth and Justice.

Lest we delude ourselves that that way lies security, we had better remember F. Scott Fitzgerald's fine insight in *Tender Is the Night*. "Either you think," he warned, "or else others have to think for you and take power from you, pervert and discipline your natural tastes, civilize and sterilize you." Unaware or unmindful of this risk, most people choose to abuse thinking or to avoid it altogether. According to Voltaire, "[People] use thought only to justify their injustices, and speech only to disguise their thoughts." And according to Aldous Huxley, "Most of one's life is one prolonged effort to prevent oneself thinking."

Because thinking is an arduous process of self-challenging, we are inclined to think only until we arrive at an understanding with which we are satisfied, that we call "explanation" and use as justification for ceasing to think further about the matter. Keeping our minds open to new explanations requires tolerating uncertainty, which, ironically is precisely the mental vexation we try to relieve by thinking.

Levy's style combines erudition with simplicity and earnestness with humor. *Tools of Critical Thinking* is devoid of psychobabble and avoids the pitfall of treating psychology as the pretentious demeaning of the Other by enrobing him in diagnostic deformations. The result is a clear and compelling book, accessible to lay persons and mental health professionals alike, that reaffirms Blaise Pascal's noble vision: "Man is obviously made for thinking. Therein lies all his dignity and his merit; and his whole duty is to think as he ought."

THOMAS SZASZ
Syracuse, New York

Introduction

In this era of so-called post-modernism, those of us who still try to teach enduringly useful modes of critical thinking often, in my own experience, feel themselves inundated and overwhelmed by multitudes of contemporary influences suggesting the propriety of more self-indulgent ways of rendering judgments about "the way things are." In the humanities and social sciences (the latter including the vast majority of issues relating to mental health and psychopathology), in particular, the task sometimes seems almost hopeless because the complexities and the value considerations involved routinely undercut the otherwise self-evident power of rigorous inductive and deductive logic applied to the realm of reliably established empirical observation. No less a figure than Carl Rogers, who in his appropriately revered earlier years had proclaimed "the facts are always friendly," and who was to learn otherwise in the tragic Mendota experience, eventually succumbed in his later writing to the considerable allures of a radically "humanistic" muddle-headedness.

But some help, at last, is on the way! In his *Tools of Critical Thinking: Metathoughts for Psychology,* David Levy has condensed both the wisdom of the ages and the findings of contemporary psychological science into a manageable set of principles ("Metathoughts") that will, where taken seriously, notably improve the general quality of thought not only in clinical psychology and cognate areas but across the broad expanse of scholarly and scientific endeavor. The work is remarkable in its successful reduction of certain extremely subtle and complex ideas to terms that should be accessible to and readily understood by the average college student. Indeed, the book is replete with compelling examples and suggested exercises that will be especially useful, I believe, to this level of reader.

It would not be a fair judgment, however, to suggest that the latter group is the exclusively appropriate audience for Levy's analysis. While his writing style is deceptively down-to-earth—even at times breezy—the central ideas examined are by and large profound ones, and they are engaged at an appropriately profound level. Accordingly, even "established" scholars will find much to ponder in this work, as did the present reviewer.

ROBERT C. CARSON
Professor of Psychology
Duke University

Preface

Man is only a reed, the weakest in nature, but he is a thinking reed.
—Blaise Pascal*

I think therefore I am. [Cogito ergo sum.]
—Rene Descartes**

Thinking—one of the most essential of all human characteristics. Thinking is an inexorable component of almost everything that we do. We use it to understand and control the world around us. It guides us in formulating problems and seeking solutions. It underlies our loftiest goals and our deepest fears. It is the very basis of learning and knowledge. It is fundamentally linked to language itself. In fact, it's nearly impossible to imagine any human experience that is completely void of the thinking process.

But do we ever *think* about *thinking?* Although we may focus on the content of our thoughts—that is, on *what* we think—what about the *way* we think? Or *how well* we think? Or *why* we think? In other words, how often do we subject our thinking process to critical analysis?

Educators rightfully profess that learning how to think is far more important than learning specific information, content, or facts. Throughout our schooling we are continually requested, urged, ordered, implored and harangued, coaxed and cajoled, begged and beseeched to "think critically." We are taught that critical thinking is one of the most vital and indispensable components of learning. Unfortunately, however, specific tools for critical thinking are rarely, if ever, provided to us. Thus, although we may be convinced of the value of critical thinking, we are left not knowing quite what to do about it.

Herein lies the impetus for this book, whose express purpose is to improve your thinking skills, to teach you to think critically, to help you think about thinking—in a word, to promote *metathinking*. Metathinking is not a magical, mystical, or mysterious abstraction. It is not an unattainable gift that is miraculously bestowed upon the intellectually elite. Rather, it is a *skill* (or more accurately, a series of skills) that can be successfully taught and learned. The thought principles, or *Metathoughts* (literally, "thoughts about thought") contained in this book are, in essence, cognitive tools that provide the user with specific strategies for inquiry and problem-solving. They serve, thereby, as potent antidotes to thinking that is prone to be simplistic, lethargic, myopic, biased, flawed, or otherwise just plain sloppy.

*1623–1662, *Pensées:* 200
**1596–1650, *Le Discours de la Method,* Pt. IV

For purposes of this book, each Metathought is illustrated primarily from the theory and application of contemporary social and clinical psychology.[1] Keep in mind, however, that these Metathought principles transcend the confines of any specific topic and can be utilized in a diverse array of fields, ranging from philosophy and theology to law, political science, history, sociology, anthropology, economics, journalism, business, medicine, biology, sports, the arts—in fact, in all areas of education and learning.

Acknowledgments

This book was over fifteen years in the making. It reflects a distillation and synthesis of my academic training in social psychology, my endeavors in conducting theoretical and empirical psychological research, my ventures in clinical psychology both as a therapist and a client in psychotherapy, my work as a clinical supervisor at a psychiatric hospital, my experiences teaching undergraduate and graduate psychology courses in the United States and the Soviet Union, as well as my observations of life around and within me.

Some of the ideas contained herein are centuries old, dating back to the ancient Greeks, whereas many are relatively new formulations. I am indebted to every person who has, wittingly or unwittingly, contributed to the creation, development, and illustrations of these Metathought principles. Consequently, I have made every effort throughout the book to give credit where credit is due by providing comprehensive reference citations for others' words, ideas, and research. In those instances in which I have inadvertently neglected to do so, or when I have been unable to locate a particular source, I offer in advance my apologies. For ethical reasons, in all clinical examples I have, of course, taken great care to protect the anonymity of any real persons (clients as well as therapists) involved.

I wish to take this opportunity to express my gratitude to my academic mentors at the University of California at Los Angeles for their guidance, insights, wisdom, and support. I am particularly grateful to Barry Collins, Shelley Taylor, Harold Kelley, Letitia Anne Peplau, Alex Caldwell, Bertram Raven, Christine Dunkel-Schetter, Harold Gerard, and James Coleman.

Although many authors have greatly influenced my thinking, those whose ideas I still find to be especially valuable include Thomas Szasz, R. D. Laing, Paul Meehl, Hans Eysenck, Viktor Frankl, Kurt Lewin, and Jay Haley (in my field), and Albert Einstein, Carl Sagan, Harry S Truman, and Blaise Pascal (from other fields of study and areas of life). Inspiration of a different kind was provided by the insights, humor, and wisdom of Matt Groening, Gary Larson, B. Kliban, Jules Feiffer, Jackie Mason, and "Vic."

I extend my thanks and appreciation to my esteemed colleagues, several of whom also happen to be my dearest friends, particularly Drew Erhardt

---

[1] See Epilogue for specific ideas and suggestions for students, instructors, clinicians, and researchers.

(*ontological chum extraordinaire*) and William M. Lamers. The same is true of some of my dearest friends, many of whom I wish were my colleagues, especially Vincent "Vinnie" DeStefano and Jonathan "J. P." Perpich. Thomas Greening, Elizabeth Loftus, Robert Carson, David Myers, Debora Carlin, Lynne Wetzell, Elizabeth Ann Snider, Mary J. Allen, Joseph Wolpe, Sandra Kaler, Charles Ramskov, Harold Chipman, and Eric Shiryaev also have my sincerest gratitude.

A special note of appreciation is due to Pepperdine University, an institution with which I am most proud to be affiliated and where I have consistently received the highest measure of academic freedom, respect, and courtesy. In particular, I want to thank Dean Nancy Magnusson Fagan and Associate Dean James Hedstrom for their years of encouragement and support. My gratitude goes not only to the administration and staff, but also to the truly remarkable faculty at Pepperdine's Graduate School of Education and Psychology and to my graduate students who have, over the years, supplied me with scores of fascinating examples and illustrations of these Metathoughts. In addition, Michele Nuzzo, Anre Venter, Parker Wilson, Stephen J. H. Kim, Rebecca Ishida, and Joe Lotta provided invaluable feedback and assistance on this project. I would also like to thank the therapy clients in my practice and at the hospital for teaching me more about the human experience than I ever thought possible.

To everyone at Allyn and Bacon who helped make this dream become a reality: I cannot imagine working with a finer, more dedicated, or more talented team of professionals, and I consider myself fortunate to have become a part of your first-rate organization. In particular, thank you to Laura Pearson and Alan Steinharter for the initial enthusiastic endorsements; to Bill Barke for your vote of confidence; to Sean Wakely for your input and guidance; to Joyce Nilsen for your magnificent and innovative marketing skills; to Marjorie Payne, Cynthia Newby, and Julia Penelope for your consummate professionalism and incredible attention to detail; to Suzanne Harbison for your creative contributions; to Erika Stuart for your diligence, kindness, and patience; and to Susan Badger for your extraordinary tenacity, honesty, insights, and wisdom.

My deepest appreciation goes to my immediate and extended family (especially my Mother and Father) and friends for their love, patience, and understanding, some of whom include (alphabetically): Marilee Bradford; Diana Brief; Dena Chertoff; Michael Christiansen; Lewis Colick; Kerry Hartjen; Rose Hasson; Terri Hayes-Clark; Erin Holvey; the Levy family (Allegra, Carrie, Jacob, Leon, Lucy, LuJean, Rachel, Rita, Robert, and Rosie); Anina Macchia; Brenda McKibben; Corrado Militi; J'Marie Moore; Steve Nevil; Dennis Palumbo; Nadine and Sterling Rachootin; Margot Ramirez; Bruce Shapiro; Colette Valette; and Anne Wharton. Although sheer numbers prevent me from listing everyone else by name, they all have my sincerest thanks.

I find myself virtually lost for words (a rare occurrence indeed) when it comes to expressing my heartfelt love, gratitude, and never-ending devotion to my wife, Beth. Suffice it to say, thank you Beth: "You're the One..."

DAVID A. LEVY

About the Author

Dr. David A. Levy has extensive experience as a teacher, psychotherapist, and researcher. He received his B.A. degree in theater arts at UCLA, an M.A. degree in psychology at Pepperdine University, a second M.A. degree in psychology at UCLA, and his Ph.D. in psychology at UCLA, where he specialized in social psychology, with minors in psychological assessment and personality psychology. He is an Associate Professor of Psychology at Pepperdine University, where he teaches graduate courses in Psychopathology, Theories of Personality, Clinical Practicum, and Marriage and Family Therapy. He served as a Visiting Professor of Psychology in the Soviet Union, where he delivered lectures and workshops in psychology and psychotherapy at Leningrad (now St. Petersburg) State University, the Leningrad Academy of Science, and the Bekhterev Psychoneurological Institute. He was honored as a Harriet and Charles Luckman Distinguished Teaching Fellow at Pepperdine, and was the recipient of the Shepard Ivory Franz Distinguished Teaching Award and Charles F. Scott Fellowship at UCLA.

Dr. Levy holds professional licenses both in psychology and in marriage, family, and child counseling. He conducts a private practice, supervises clinical interns, is certified in hypnotherapy, and works with the psychiatric population as a psychodrama consultant. He also served as the Executive Director of Crime Survivors Services, an agency which specializes in clinical work with victims of violent crimes. He utilizes his expertise in psychological testing (particularly the MMPI) in forensic settings, where he evaluates plaintiffs and provides legal testimony as an expert witness in cases involving allegations of emotional distress.

His numerous theoretical and empirical research studies have been published in scientific journals and presented at professional conferences. His areas of research focus include social cognition, interpersonal influence, psychopathology, and media psychology. His book, *Family Therapy: History, Theory, and Practice,* is the first complete textbook on family therapy available in Russian to clinicians, researchers and educators of that country. His *Levy Optimism-Pessimism Scale (LOPS)* has been translated into several foreign languages (including Russian, Slovak, Italian, Japanese, and Spanish) and has been utilized internationally in a wide variety of research contexts. He is also the author of numerous satirical articles, including "How to Be a Good Psychotherapy Patient," "Psychometric Infallibility Realized: The One-Size-Fits-All Psychological Profile," and "A Proposed Category for the Diagnostic and Statistical Manual of Mental Disorders (DSM): Pervasive Labeling Disorder."

Dr. Levy is a member of the Board of Editors for the *Journal of Humanistic Psychology,* he has served as a reviewer for the *Journal of Social Behavior and Personality,* he is a consultant for the Russian-American Center for International Education, and he is listed in *Who's Who in California* and in *International Leaders of Achievement.* He has appeared on over two dozen television and radio programs, where he was interviewed on his research findings, as well as on current issues, problems and trends in the fields of psychology and mental health.

Part One

Conceptualizing Phenomena

Chapter 1

I. *The Evaluative Bias of Language: To Describe Is to Prescribe*

Description is always from someone's point of view.
—RHODA KESLER UNGER*

Preferring a nonjudgmental term to a judgmental one is itself a judgment.
—THOMAS SZASZ**

Language serves many functions. Certainly one of its most common and most important purposes is to help us *describe* various phenomena, such as events, situations, and people: "What is it?" Another purpose is to *evaluate* these same phenomena: "Is it good or bad?" Typically, we consider descriptions to be objective, whereas we consider evaluations to be subjective.

But is the distinction between objective description and subjective evaluation a clear one? The answer, in the vast majority of cases, is no. Why? Because words both describe *and* evaluate. Whenever we attempt to describe something or someone, the words we use are almost invariably value laden, in that they reflect our own personal likes and dislikes. Thus, our use of any particular term serves not only to describe, but also to *prescribe* what is desirable or undesirable to us.

---

*Unger, 1983
***The Therapeutic State,* 1984

This problem is not so prevalent in the physical sciences, as compared to the social sciences. Let's take, as an illustration, the terms *cold* and *hot.* In the field of physics, both terms refer, in a relatively neutral sense, to the rate of molecular vibrations (or temperature): "That liquid is very cold," or "That liquid is very hot." When we use these same terms to describe an *individual,* however, they take on a distinctly *evaluative* connotation: "That person is very cold," or "That person is very hot."

What are the consequences of the evaluative bias of language? The words that we use can, with or without our intent, become powerful instruments of change. In those instances where we are deliberately attempting to influence others to agree with our point of view, we intentionally select words that most persuasively communicate our values. In many cases, however, the process is tacit or unintentional. Our best attempts to remain neutral are constrained by the limits of language. When it comes to describing people it is nearly impossible to find words that are devoid of evaluative connotation. Incredible as it may seem, we simply don't have neutral adjectives to describe personality characteristics. And even if such words did exist, we still would be very likely to utilize the ones that reflect our own personal preferences.

The evaluative bias of language is illustrated in the following table and accompanying exercise. Let's say that two different observers (Person A and Person B), each with a different set of values, are asked to describe the same person or event. Notice how the words they use reveal to us their own points of view.

TABLE 1-1   The Same Phenomenon as Described from Two Different Perspectives

Person A	Person B	Person A	Person B
pushy	assertive	oversensitive	vulnerable
greedy	ambitious	cowardly	self-protective
manipulative	persuasive	pushover	flexible
ruthless	driven	spineless	cooperative
stubborn	tenacious	immature	childlike
intrusive	concerned	naive	idealistic
exhibitionistic	outgoing	old	mature
reckless	brave	overly emotional	passionate
troublemaker	feisty	obsessed	committed
cheap	frugal	manic	enthusiastic
rigid	steadfast	weird	interesting
unfeeling	nerves-of-steel	wimpy	sweet

TABLE 1-1   *Continued*

Ready to try some on your own? Remember that you are to select words that best reveal Person B's personal attitudes and values, which are clearly and consistently more "positive" than Person A's. (Some suggestions appear in Appendix 2.)

Person A	Person B	Person A	Person B
obstacle	_____	rationalization	_____
problem	_____	resistance	_____
issue	_____	defense	
failure	_____	mechanism	_____
terrorist	_____	psychotherapy	_____
murder	_____	therapy patient	_____
handout	_____	psychiatric	
conformity	_____	institution	_____
hostage	_____	Dependent	
brainwashed	_____	Personality	
		Disorder	_____
perversion	_____	Avoidant	
slut	_____	Personality	
promiscuous	_____	Disorder	_____
idiot savant	_____	Paranoid	
retarded	_____	Personality	
developmentally		Disorder	_____
disabled	_____	Narcissistic	
		Personality	
anal retentive	_____	Disorder	_____
egocentricity	_____	Histrionic	
thought disordered	_____	Personality	
irresponsible	_____	Disorder	_____
psychotic	_____	Obsessive–Compulsive	
catatonic	_____	Personality	
codependent	_____	Disorder	_____

This Metathought also underscores the reciprocal influence of attitudes and language. That is, not only do our attitudes and perceptions affect our use of language, but our use of language in turn influences our attitudes and perceptions (see Metathought XI, Bi-Directional Causation).

Because of the evaluative bias of language, we must be careful both to become aware of our own personal values and to communicate these values as openly and fairly as possible. In other words, we should avoid presenting our value judgments as objective reflections of truth. It also should alert us to the value judgments inherent in *other* people's use of language, and that in many cases the words they use tell us at least as much about *them* as the events and individuals they are attempting to describe.

Glossary Terms

The following terms (or variations) are defined in the Glossary:

affect	personality
attitude	personality disorder
bias	phenomenon
connotation	physical
consequence	prescription
defense mechanism	psychosis
description	psychotherapy
disorder	rationalization
evaluation	reciprocal
event	resistance
intentionality	science
judgment	social
neutral	subjective
objective	truth
perception	value

Chapter 2

II. The Reification Error: Comparing Apples and Existentialism

The world is a unity of the given and the constructed.
—GEORG WILHELM FRIEDRICH HEGEL*

It is difficult to determine what is "given"
and what are our "constructions."
—R. D. LAING**

Mental illnesses do not exist; indeed, they cannot exist,
because the mind is not a body part or bodily organ.
—THOMAS SZASZ***

It is tempting but misleading to regard abstract concepts as if they were concrete objects. This error in thinking is called *reification*.[1] To reify is to invent a concept (or "construct"), give it a name, and then convince ourselves that such a thing objectively exists in the world.

As an example, consider the term "self-esteem." It is easy to forget that self-esteem isn't something that someone actually "has." Rather, it is nothing more than a concept which we have created to help us organize and make sense out of other people's (as well as our own) behavior. Unfortunately, however, many well-intentioned individuals persist in reifying this construct, for

---

*1770–1831
***The Politics of the Family,* 1969
****The Therapeutic State,* 1984

instance, by advising others, "You know what your problem is? You need to get a whole lot more self-esteem," (as if self-esteem were some kind of commodity that can be purchased at one's local hardware store!).

The litany of constructs that are commonly reified in the field of psychology is never-ending. To list but a few:

the mind	emotions
intelligence	complexes
motivation	archetypes
cognition	personality traits
personality	personality disorders
the unconscious	mental illnesses
the self	

In fact, the traditional usage of the term *mental* represents one of the most pervasive and chronic reification errors in the entire "mental health" (!) field. Remember that *mental* is a metaphorical construct, not an objective entity, like a tree or a stone. It is thus linguistically fallacious to pose the question, "Is the patient's problem *physical,* or is it *mental?*" To ask such a question is to compare a concrete thing to an abstract concept. The brain is a thing; the mind is a concept. Apples and oranges are things; existentialism is a concept. Thus, asking the question, "Is the patient's problem physical or mental?" is as senseless as comparing apples and existentialism.

Consider, as another illustration, Freud's depiction of the human psyche. In using the terms *id, ego,* and *superego,* Freud (1933/1964) did not mean to imply that these are concrete entities that have a specific location in the brain. Rather, they were Freud's shorthand way of designating various hypothetical personality processes. Freud *created* these constructs as "useful aids to understanding," which assisted him in depicting his view of how people work. In like fashion, the unconscious was not "discovered," it was *invented;* resistance was not "encountered," it was *conceived;* neuroses were not "detected," they were *declared.*

Exercise: Differentiating Events and Constructs

To give you some practice at honing your ability to differentiate concrete (observable) phenomena from abstract (hypothetical) phenomena, try the following exercise. For each pair of terms below, indicate which refers to a physical event (E) and which refers to a theoretical construct (C). (Answers appear in Appendix 2.)

humor: _____
laughter: _____

tearfulness: _____
sadness: _____

smiling: _____
happy: _____

nervous: _____
fidgety: _____

restless: _____
anxious: _____

energy: _____
activity: _____

talkative: _____
extraverted: _____

quiet: _____
introverted: _____

personality type: _____
blood type: _____

muscular strength: _____
ego strength: _____

disordered psyche: _____
disordered desk: _____

housing complex: _____
inferiority complex: _____

drunkenness: _____
alcoholism: _____

heartburn: _____
heartache: _____

rotten egg: _____
rotten attitude: _____

sea sickness: _____
love sickness: _____

broken dream: _____
broken nose: _____

lost toothbrush: _____
lost soul: _____

healthy outlook: _____
healthy spleen: _____

Ready for a few more?

free will: _____
motionless: _____
love: _____
disorganized: _____
heavy: _____
self-concept: _____
self-actualization: _____

deviant: _____
unseen: _____
hepatitis: _____
schizophrenia: _____
repression: _____
intuition: _____
suicide: _____

The Reification of Theory

We are also subject to committing errors of reification when it comes to creating, testing, and evaluating certain types of theories. Let us begin by defining some key terms. First, what is a theory? Briefly stated, a theory is a proposed explanation of observed phenomena. We may further differentiate two types of theory: *Event Theory* and *Construct Theory.*

Event (or "Type E") Theories provide explanations that lend themselves to direct measurement. Thus, given the proper circumstances, an Event Theory can be verified or proven. When this occurs, it is no longer a theory—it is a *fact.*

Event Theories seek to answer a wide variety of questions, ranging from the mundane to the profound. For example:

"Why does my car stall at stoplights?"
"What happened to the money in my desk drawer?"
"How did the patient acquire an infection?"
"Who is responsible for committing these serial murders?"
"How many assassins were involved in shooting President Kennedy?"
"Did human beings evolve from apes?"
"What caused dinosaurs to become extinct?"
"When did life first appear on earth?"

Under the assumption that there are actual, objective answers to all questions of this type, Event Theories are intended to ascertain these solutions, irrespective of whether or not we currently possess the methods to do so. In other words, Type E Theories are, *in principle,* confirmable.

Construct (or "Type C") Theories, by contrast, provide explanations that, by their very nature, are *not* directly measurable. As a consequence, even under ideal conditions, a Construct Theory can *never* be "proven." This is because the explanations are, in themselves, intangible abstractions.

Construct Theories abound in many areas of study. In the field of physics, for example, there are theories of gravitation, magnetism, electricity, sound, light, and energy. In psychology, we have theories that attempt to explain everything from cognition, emotion, memory, and perception to motivation, maturation, personality, and numerous forms of psychopathology, to name but a few.

In all of these instances, although the phenomena under investigation may be observable, their underlying explanations are not. An apple falling from a tree to the ground can be seen directly; "gravitation," however, cannot. Similarly, behavior can be directly measured; but "motivation," "personality," or "psychopathology" cannot.

Now, how do we go about evaluating a theory? The answer depends on the *type* of theory in question. Specifically, Event Theories should be evaluated in terms of their *accuracy.* In other words, they can be judged as true or false, right or wrong, correct or incorrect. This is because Type E Theories are, in principle, provable (and therefore refutable).

This is not the case, however, for Construct Theories, which are *never* capable of being proven directly. As such, it is pointless to subject a Construct Theory to the criterion of accuracy. How, then, are we to evaluate Construct Theories? Simply put, in terms of their *utility*. Is the theory *useful,* for example, in helping us to describe, predict, or control various phenomena? Is Einstein's theory of gravitation more *useful* than Newton's theory of gravitation in accounting for the motion of celestial bodies? Is one theory of psychopathology more *useful* than another in helping us to alleviate human suffering? To the extent that a Type C Theory is useful, it should be pursued, cultivated, and applied; to the extent that it is not useful, it should be revised, reworked or, if need be, discarded.

Why are these distinctions important? Because we create nothing but conceptual (not to mention methodological) havoc for ourselves when we confuse these two types of theory. In particular, we must be especially careful not to reify Construct Theories by treating them as if they were Event Theories. Whenever we naively set out to "prove" if a Type C Theory is true or false, our mission is doomed at the outset as we embark on a pointless journey through an impossible maze in the futile pursuit of an exit that does not exist, and encounter only one blind alley after the next. Why? Because the question we are asking is unanswerable; it is, in fact, quite meaningless.

For instance, because we can neither prove nor disprove directly the existence of the unconscious, it is inappropriate to ask whether Freudian theory is true or false. The same may be said of so-called "laws of nature." Gravity, for example, isn't an actual "law" that must be "obeyed" and never "violated." Rather, it is nothing more than a hypothetical model—a fiction—that various theorists, from Newton to Einstein, have created and re-created to assist them in explaining why every object in the universe appears to be attracted to every other object in the universe. Once again, the issue with Type C Theories isn't one of truth; rather, it is one of usefulness.

One very unfortunate consequence of this confusion is that the field of psychology is teeming with outdated and empirically unsupported theories that have long overstayed their welcome. Why do such theories persist? Perhaps the most important reason is that they have never been directly disproven, which some people mistakenly take as evidence of their veracity. Could it be that these theories are, in fact, true? Not once we realize that they are, by and large, Type C Theories and thus are not *capable* of being proven or disproven. In other words, "correctness" is an *inappropriate criterion* for evaluating these theories. They should be judged, instead, solely in terms of their usefulness (or lack thereof), an endeavor that is all too rare.

What is the lesson to be learned here? Don't make the mistake of reifying Construct Theories. Remember that Type C Theories are not objective facts "somewhere out there," just waiting to be stumbled upon. (Einstein did not *discover,* so much as he *invented,* "$E = mc^2$.") Rather, they are human-made constructions—fragile and imperfect—that represent our best attempts to explain the world around us.

Glossary Terms

The following terms (or variations) are defined in the Glossary:

abstract	intuition
assumption	judgment
attitude	measurement
behavior	mental
category	mental illness
chronic	metaphor
cognition	mind
concept	motivation
concrete	objective
consequence	perception
construct	personality
Construct (Type C) Theory	personality disorder
criterion	personality trait
description	phenomena
disorder	physical
emotion	psyche
empirical	psychology
evaluation	psychopathology
event	reification
Event (Type E) Theory	repression
existence	resistance
existentialism	theoretical
explanation	theory
extraversion	thinking
fact	truth
fallacious	unconscious
hypothetical	utility
introversion	veracity

Notes

[1] Gilbert Ryle, the British philosopher, referred to such errors as "category mistakes" (see Ryle, *The Concept of Mind,* 1949).

Chapter **3**

III. Multiple Levels of Description: The Simultaneity of Physical and Psychological Events

Body and soul are not two different things, but only two different ways of perceiving the same thing. Similarly, physics and psychology are only different attempts to link our perceptions together by way of systematic thought.
—ALBERT EINSTEIN*

Two errors: 1. to take everything literally,
2. to take everything spiritually.
—BLAISE PASCAL**

What is the relationship between mind and body? Which comes first? Does one cause the other? If so, which is the cause and which is the effect? Can one exist without the other?

These questions (and countless versions thereof) have plagued philosophers for centuries. More recently, social scientists have picked up the gaunt-

---

*1879–1955, quoted in Dukas & Hoffman, *Albert Einstein: The Human Side,* 1979
**1623–1662, *Pensées:* 252

let and grappled with new variations of this age-old theme by asking, "Are psychological events the cause or the effect of biological events?" More specifically, for example, does neurochemical activity (such as the release or inhibition of neurotransmitters) cause changes in psychological events (such as thoughts or feelings)? Or, conversely, do psychological events cause changes in neurochemical activity?

Perhaps nowhere is this debate better illustrated than in the clinical psychologist's primary diagnostic question, namely, "Is the patient's problem *physical* or *mental*?" As I pointed out in Metathought II (the Reification Error) this question is linguistically senseless because, in this context, *physical* and *mental* are noncomparable terms. It is, in other words, an error in reification to treat a theoretical construct (mental) as if it were a concrete event (physical).

An even more profound flaw, however, lies in the implication that mental events are somehow not physical. The artificial and fallacious dichotomy inherent in the "physical-or-mental" question does not take into account the principle of *multiple levels of description*.[1] By this I mean that any given event can be described at different levels of analysis. At one level, for example, events can be described in terms of physical phenomena. At another level, these same events can be described in terms of theoretical constructs.

The physical level of description refers to concrete events that are directly and objectively observable, quantifiable, or measurable.[2] With respect to human behavior, we have a multitude of terms that describe phenomena at the physical level of analysis, such as *biological, biochemical, physiological, anatomical, organic, neurological, neurochemical,* and *neurophysiological.*

By contrast, the construct level of description refers to abstract events that are *not* directly or objectively observable, quantifiable, or measurable. Rather, they involve *subjective* phenomena that are theoretical, conceptual, or metaphorical. In describing human behavior at this level of analysis, we typically use such terms as *psychological, perceptual, experiential, cognitive,* and *mental.*

What, then, is the relationship between these two levels of description? Does one cause the other? If so, which is the cause and which is the effect? Before we can address these questions, we first must take a step back and define some key terms and concepts.

In order to say that there is a cause and effect relationship between two events (let's call them Event A and Event B), two conditions must be satisfied, each of which is necessary and both of which are sufficient:

1. Event A must occur before Event B.
2. When Event A changes or is manipulated (like a switch being turned on), then Event B changes accordingly; similarly, when Event A stops changing or ceases to be manipulated (like a switch being turned off), then Event B changes accordingly.

Pay particular attention to the first condition, namely, the *temporal relationship* between the events. If Event A does not occur before Event B, then by definition A cannot cause B. Thus, if Event A occurs *after* Event B, then A does not cause B. Further, if Event A and Event B occur *simultaneously,* then A does not cause B (and, of course, B does not cause A). Again, if two events occur simultaneously, then they do not (in fact, they *cannot*) constitute a cause and effect relationship. For instance, if a biological event occurs simultaneously with a psychological event, then one does not cause the other; rather, they constitute a singular phenomenon, simply described at two different levels of analysis.

Let's take this a step further. Can a physical event occur in the absence of a psychological event? Of course. Even after death, biochemical activity exists in the deceased's body.

But is the converse also true? That is, can a psychological event occur in the absence of a physical event? This supposition is groundless. In fact, it is safe to assume that *every* mental event has some corresponding physical correlate. Thinking, happiness, and creativity, for example, are no more or less biochemical than delusions, depression, or schizophrenia. They are *all* reflected or "mapped" in some form physically, whether or not we know how to measure them. In other words, psychological and biological phenomena are linked, but not causally; rather, they occur *simultaneously* as one "psychobiological" event.

Keeping these ideas in mind, let us now return to the clinical question of determining whether a patient's problem is "physical or mental." The question rests on the assumption that disorders have causes that are *either* physical (biological, neurochemical, organic,) *or* mental (psychological, psychogenic, functional). Put another way, it assumes that physical and mental events are independent phenomena.

In one sense, the patient's problem is *always* physical, if one chooses to explain it at that level of description. In fact, the patient's problem *may* be *entirely* physical, since biological events can occur in the absence of psychological phenomena. However, if the patient's problem is mental, then by definition it is *also* physical, since all psychological events have biological correlates. Further, the patient's problem can *never* be *entirely* mental, since psychological phenomena cannot exist in the absence of biological activity. In sum, mental and physical phenomena are not independent events; rather, they are inexorably intertwined.

Where does this leave us? With a clinical pseudo-question that rests on faulty premises and that almost invariably results in misleading conclusions. Specifically, in the course of formulating a diagnosis, when clinicians are not able to locate any specific physical malfunction, they sometimes jump to the conclusion that, "Since the patient's problem isn't physical, it therefore must be mental." When we consider the simultaneity of psychological and physical phenomena, this is, as you can see, a senseless (and in fact, a patently absurd) deduction.

As an illustration of this Metathought, let us analyze the phenomenon of "anxiety" using this dual-level model of description (refer to Figure 3-1). At the biological level (B_1), anxiety involves specific neurochemical activity (namely, arousal of the sympathetic division of the autonomic nervous system along with other particular neurological configurations). *Concurrently,* at the psychological level (P_1), anxiety involves the subjective perception and experience of apprehension or fear. Thus, neurochemistry doesn't cause fear, and fear doesn't cause neurochemistry; they are *equivalent* and *simultaneous* phenomena, merely described in two different ways and at two different levels of analysis. (Put another way, B_1 doesn't cause P_1, and P_1 doesn't cause B_1; rather, they occur together as a singular P_1/B_1 event.) The same is true for *all* psychological phenomena, pathological or otherwise: the relationship between "physical" and "mental" is, by definition, not concretely causal but conceptually correlational.

To elaborate on this example, let's say that a person's anxiety (Event 1) causes him to want to feel better (Event 2). This event consists of the motivation to alleviate his emotional discomfort (P_2), which is accompanied by the biological correlate (or "map") of this psychological drive state (B_2). Event 2 then leads to Event 3, namely, the formulation of a plan of action for anxiety reduction (P_3); these cognitive strategies, again, coincide with (and are reflected in) particular neurochemical activity (B_3).

Now, let's postulate that the person decides to assuage his misery by taking an antianxiety medication. The outcome is Event 4, which consists of the occurrence of B_4 (activation of the parasympathetic division of the autonomic nervous system along with a new neurological configuration) and P_4 (subjective feelings of relief and relaxation).

Alternately, let's say that, rather than ingesting pills, the person opts to seek the assistance of a psychotherapist, who promptly offers soothing words of comfort and support. What is the outcome? Theoretically, Event 4 can be essentially *equivalent* to the one produced by taking tranquilizers. Thus, two different courses of action (tranquilizers or psychotherapy) may lead to the same (P_4/B_4) effect (see Metathought XIV, Multiple Pathways of Causation). Further, note that either course of action involves *both* biological *and* psychological phenomena. In this way, contrary to common intuition, psychotherapy is *no less biochemical* than medication.

To enhance and consolidate your understanding of these ideas—which can be somewhat elusive at first glance—try analyzing a different phenomenon (for instance, insomnia, anger, sexual arousal, depression, or any original example of your own choosing) using this dual-level model of description. You also may find it helpful to map out graphically the sequence, utilizing Figure 3-1 as a template.

Notice in the figure illustration how the causal sequences at each level of description run *parallel* to each other; the arrows do not cross diagonally between the two levels. In other words, if we choose to analyze a sequence of events purely at the conceptual level, we could say that one psychological

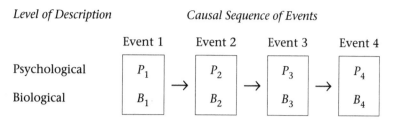

Level of Description   *Causal Sequence of Events*

(*Note:* P = Psychological; B = Biological.)

**FIGURE 3-1   A Causal Sequence of Events Analyzed
at Dual Levels of Description**

event causes another psychological event (for example, P_1 causes P_2). Similarly, if we were to analyze the same sequence solely at the physical level, we would not be mistaken in saying that one biological event causes another biological event (for example, B_1 causes B_2).

However, we must be careful not to confuse these two different levels of description. Specifically, psychological events do not, strictly speaking, cause biological events. Put another way, *a theoretical construct can't produce a physical symptom.* In like manner, biological events do not cause solely psychological events. In terms of the figure above, for example, P_1 does not cause B_2 nor does B_1 cause P_2. Once again, the key point is that psychological and biological events are linked, as a unit, in their simultaneous occurrence.

Why is all of this important? Because we must not allow ourselves to be seduced into believing that once we have located a biological *correlate* to a psychological event, we have therefore discovered its biological *cause* (see Metathought X, Correlation Does Not Prove Causation).[3] Even worse, we must not equate a biological *correlate* with a biological *disease.* To take an example, if we find neurological differences between those persons whom we diagnose as schizophrenic and those whom we consider normal, it should come as no great surprise. After all, we are also likely to discover neurological differences between those persons whom we call creative and those whom we do not. But what does this prove? Only that we've located the biological correlates for different types of psychological processes. However, this criterion alone doesn't prove that schizophrenia is a medical disease any more than it proves that creativity is not. Even if we were to find the physical correlates to *every* psychological phenomenon, it still leaves us with the formidable and complex task of defining and differentiating illness from health (see Wakefield, 1992, for the one such attempt). In other words, evidence of physical *difference* is not, *per se,* scientifically valid proof of medical *disease.*

All things considered, it isn't surprising that the "physical or mental?" question has not yet been answered. What's surprising is that it's still being *asked.*

Glossary Terms

The following terms (or variations) are defined in the Glossary:

abstract	fallacious
assumption	intuition
attitude	measure
behavior	mental
belief	metaphor
causal	mind
cause	motivation
clinical	normal
cognitive	objective
concept	pathological
concrete	perception
construct	*per se*
correlate	phenomenon
correlation	physical
criterion	premise
deduction	psychological
delusion	psychotherapy
description	quantify
diagnosis	reification
dichotomous variable	scientific
disease	social
disorder	subjective
effect	symptom
event	temporal
experience	theoretical
explanation	thinking

Notes

[1] Portions of this Metathought originally appeared in my essay, "Is the Remedicalization of Psychiatry Good for the Mental Health Field? No." (Levy, 1994), published in *Controversial Issues in Mental Health*.

[2] In stating that physical events are measurable, I am referring to all phenomena that, by definition, lend themselves to the possibility of direct measurement, irrespective of our actual ability to do so. In other words, the property of "measurability" should not be determined by the current (or even future) limits of our technology, instrumentation, or resources. By contrast, theoretical constructs (such as thoughts, attitudes, or philosophies) are, by definition, *never* capable of being measured directly.

[3] For an examination and integrative analysis of some of the principles discussed in this Metathought, see Cacioppo and Berntson's (1992) article, "Social Psychological Contributions to the Decade of the Brain: Doctrine of Multilevel Analysis."

Chapter 4

IV. The Nominal Fallacy and Tautologous Reasoning: To Name Something Isn't to Explain It

> *Just because your doctor has a name for your condition doesn't mean he knows what it is.*
> *—ARTHUR BLOCH**

> *There must be something the matter with him*
> *because he would not be acting as he does*
> *unless there was*
> *therefore he is acting as he is*
> *because there is something the matter with him*
> *—R. D. LAING***

The Nominal Fallacy

Words are so important to us that if we can find, formulate, or invent a special *name* for something, we easily fool ourselves into believing that we have *explained* it. This error is called the *Nominal Fallacy*. Given that descriptive labels are an essential component both of science and of everyday life, we need

**Murphy's Law, Book Two, 1980*
***Knots, 1970*

to be aware that *naming* any particular behavior (such as with a diagnostic label) does not, therefore, *explain* the behavior. Here are some examples of the Nominal Fallacy in action:

"Why does she have difficulty falling or staying asleep?"
　"Because she's got *Insomnia.*"

"Why is that boy chronically disobedient toward authority figures?"
　"Because he's got *Oppositional Defiant Disorder.*"

"Why does the patient have a persistent, irrational fear of heights?"
　"Because she's got *Acrophobia.*"

"Why is she completely preoccupied with the unfounded fear that she has a serious disease?"
　"Because she's got *Hypochondriasis.*"

"Why does that man get sexually aroused by rubbing up against nonconsenting people?"
　"Because he's got *Frotteurism.*"

Tautologous Reasoning

The Nominal Fallacy typically involves circular or tautological reasoning. A *tautology* is the needless repetition of an idea, statement, or word, wherein the phenomenon is true by virtue of its logical form alone. Put another way, it is circular reasoning in which one conclusion rests upon another, which in turn refers back to the first. Thus, a tautology can never be falsified.

For example: "People who hit others are aggressive; therefore, people who are aggressive hit others," or "People who display gross impairment in reality testing are psychotic; therefore, people who are psychotic display gross impairment in reality testing."

Here are some other illustrations of tautologous reasoning:

"Why is that guy so sociable?"
　"Because he's an extravert."
"How do you know that he's an extravert?"
　"Well, can't you see how sociable he is?"

"Why is she completely suspicious of everybody's motives?"
　"Because she's got Paranoid Personality Disorder."
"How do you know that she's got Paranoid Personality Disorder?"
　"By the fact that she's so suspicious of everybody's motives."

"Why did the defendant do what he did?"
　"Because he is insane."
"How do you know that he's insane?"
　"Because only an insane person would do what he did!"

These kinds of circular explanations are, of course, no explanations at all. It's like "explaining" a bright child's low grades by declaring that he or she is an "underachiever." Similarly, a diagnosis of Depression does not explain profound sadness; a diagnosis of Alcohol Dependence does not explain drinking problems; a diagnosis of Schizophrenia does not explain delusions and hallucinations; a diagnosis of Narcissistic Personality Disorder does not explain extreme grandiosity; and a diagnosis of Borderline Personality Disorder does not explain someone's severe problems in their interpersonal relationships.

As an exercise, try your hand at completing the following tautological dialogues:

"Why does she firmly cling to her false beliefs, despite obvious evidence to the contrary?"
"Because she's got Delusional Disorder."
"How do you know that she's got Delusional Disorder?"
"_____."

"Why does that man persistently have an absence of any sexual drive?"
"Because he's got Hypoactive Sexual Desire Disorder."
"How do you know that he's got Hypoactive Sexual Desire Disorder?"
"_____."

"Why does that woman have difficulties in achieving a sexual climax?"
"Because she has Inhibited Female Orgasm Disorder."
"How do you know that she has Inhibited Female Orgasm Disorder?"
"_____."

"Why is he intentionally producing symptoms for the sole purpose of assuming the patient role?"
"Because he's got Factitious Disorder."
"_____?"
"_____."

"Why does the patient have a persistent, irrational fear of train travel?"
"Because she's got Siderodromophobia."
"_____?"
"_____."

"Why does the patient have a persistent, irrational fear of the number 13?"
"Because he's got Triskaidekaphobia."
"_____?"
"_____."

For a final illustration of this Metathought, do your best to navigate through the mind-bending tautologies in the following "Catch 22"-like discourse:

The man who has just been found guilty of first-degree murder is asking for the death penalty. He must *be crazy, therefore, since only someone who is crazy would ask for the death penalty. We don't administer the death penalty to people who are crazy. Therefore, since he asked to be executed, we* cannot *have him executed. If, on the other hand, he had asked* not *to receive the death penalty, then we* could *give him the death penalty, since we only execute people who* aren't *crazy, and anybody who* doesn't *want to be executed obviously* isn't *crazy. Thus, if he requests the death penalty, that proves he's crazy, so we* can't *sentence him to death (since people who request the death penalty are crazy, and we do* not *give the death penalty to people who are crazy). But if he requests* not *to have the death penalty, that proves he* isn't *crazy, so we* can *sentence him to death (since people who request* not *to have the death penalty aren't crazy, and we do give the death penalty to people who are* not *crazy). In conclusion, if he's* not *crazy, then we* can *execute him; but if he* is *crazy, then we* cannot *execute him. Therefore, if he wants to be executed, he should say that he* doesn't *want to be executed; then we* can *sentence him to death. But if he doesn't want to be executed, he should say that he does want to be executed; then we* cannot *sentence him to death.*

In summary, be sure not to confuse a name with an explanation. Remember that labeling something does not, *per se,* explain it. Finally, learn to recognize tautologous reasoning. Remind yourself that although tautologies may have the appearance of being logical, they are, in fact, a completely invalid method of proof.

Glossary Terms

The following terms (or variations) are defined in the Glossary:

behavior	interpersonal
belief	motive
chronic	Nominal Fallacy
delusion	*per se*
description	personality disorder
diagnosis	phenomenon
disease	psychotic
disorder	reasoning
explanation	science
extraversion	symptom
fallacy	tautologous (tautological)
intentionality	reasoning

Chapter 5

V. Differentiating Dichotomous Variables and Continuous Variables: Black and White, or Shades of Grey?

In approaching the subject of mental disorder, I must empha-
size that, in my view, persons showing mental disorder do not
manifest anything specifically different in kind from what is
manifested by practically all human beings.
—HARRY STACK SULLIVAN*

Sanity is a matter of degree.
—ALDOUS HUXLEY**

Some phenomena in the world may be divided (or *bifurcated*) into two mutually exclusive or contradictory categories. These types of phenomena are
dichotomous variables. For example, when you flip a coin, it must turn up either
heads or tails—there is no middle ground. Similarly, a woman cannot be "a little bit," "somewhat," or "moderately" pregnant—she is either pregnant or not
pregnant. Here are some other examples:

A light switch is either on or off.
A toilet is either flushed or not flushed.

*Clinical Studies in Psychiatry, 1956
**1894–1963, quoted in Rowes, The Book of Quotes, 1979

A golf ball either ends up in the hole or it doesn't.

A neuron either fires or does not fire (the *all-or-none principle*).

A person is either male or female (with some rare exceptions).

Other phenomena, by contrast, consist of a theoretically infinite number of points lying between two polar opposites. These types of phenomena are *continuous variables.* For example, between the extremes of black and white there exists a middle ground consisting of innumerable shades of grey. Consider also the measurement of distance, weight, volume, motion, or temperature. In these cases, the results may fall at any point along a range, spectrum, or dimension, and are expressed in terms of quantity, magnitude, or degree.

The problem is that we often confuse these two types of variables. Specifically, we have a natural tendency to dichotomize variables that, more accurately, should be conceptualized as continuous. In particular, most person-related phenomena (especially psychological constructs) are frequently presumed to fit into one of two discrete types (*either* category A *or* category B), rather than as lying along a continuum. In the vast majority of cases, however, continuous variables are more accurate (and therefore more useful) representations of the phenomena we are attempting to describe and explain.[1]

What are some examples of continuous psychological variables that frequently are assumed to be, or treated as if they were, dichotomous?

normal–abnormal

mental health–mental illness[2]

introvert–extravert

autonomous–dependent

trust–mistrust

functional–dysfunctional

adaptive–maladaptive

therapeutic success–therapeutic failure

scientifically useful–scientifically not useful

The following exercise will give you some hands-on practice at differentiating dichotomous and continuous phenomena. For each of the terms below, indicate those that refer to dichotomous phenomena (D) and those that refer to continuous phenomena (C). (Answers appear in Appendix 2.)

conscious–unconscious: ____

feminine–masculine: ____

gun fired–not fired: ____

optimist–pessimist: ____

married–single: ____

present–absent: ____
emotionally secure–emotionally insecure: ____
published–not published: ____
airborne–grounded: ____
day–night: ____
good mood–bad mood: ____
licensed–unlicensed: ____
honest–dishonest: ____
morning person–evening person: ____
neurotic–nonneurotic: ____
mailed–unmailed: ____
subjective–objective: ____
alcoholic beverage–nonalcoholic beverage: ____
successful basketball shot–unsuccessful shot: ____
psychological trait–psychological state: ____
tenured–untenured: ____
"Type A" personality–"Type B" personality: ____
guilty verdict–not guilty verdict: ____
power on–power off: ____
addicted–not addicted: ____
therapeutic–nontherapeutic: ____

Theoretical and Clinical Applications

In terms of psychological theory, the process of false dichotomization is illustrated in the ego defense mechanism of *splitting*. In explaining early childhood development, some neo-Freudians (e.g., Klein, 1937; Mahler, Pine, & Bergman, 1975) have theorized that the child both wishes for, yet is hostile and fearful toward, the maternal object. According to these theorists, the child attempts to resolve this conflict by categorizing or "splitting" the world into good versus bad components by treating them in an all-or-none fashion. Adults, too, may manifest this same defense mechanism, which these theorists interpret as representing fixation at a more primitive level of psychological development.

This Metathought also has applications to the practice of psychotherapy. An important goal of cognitive therapy approaches, for instance, is to help clients modify their "black-or-white" thinking into seeing more "shades of grey" (see Ellis, 1984; Ellis & Bernard, 1985). A person with an eating disorder, for example, may be encouraged to recognize and to moderate such dichotomous thinking patterns as "fat *or* thin," "perfect *or* imperfect," and "mature *or* immature." By learning to view their life situation in less absolute (and therefore more realistic) terms, clients can presumably gain a greater sense of acceptance, flexibility, and control over their lives.

Glossary Terms

The following terms (or variations) are defined in the Glossary:

bifurcate	measurement
category	mental
clinical	mood
cognitive	neurotic
cognitive therapy	normal
cognitive–behavioral therapy	objective
conscious	personality
construct	phenomena
continuous variable	psychological
description	psychotherapy
dichotomous variable	scientific
dimension	splitting
disorder	subjective
dysfunction	theoretical
e.g.	theory
ego defense mechanism	thinking
explanation	trait
extraversion	unconscious
interpretation	variable
introversion	

Notes

[1] This principle is discussed in depth by the eminent social psychologist Kurt Lewin in his article, "The Conflict Between Aristotelian and Galileian Modes of Thought in Contemporary Psychology" (1931). Lewin's article is noteworthy in that it also pertains to several other Metathoughts, in particular the Belief Perseverance Effect (Metathought XXV), Deductive and Inductive Reasoning (Metathought XX), and the Nominal Fallacy and Tautologous Reasoning (Metathought IV). Lewin's essay serves as a foundation for Robert Carson's superb commentary and critical analysis of contemporary approaches to conceptualizing psychopathology, "Aristotle, Galileo, and the *DSM* Taxonomy: The Case of Schizophrenia" (in press). This Metathought is related as well to some of the ideas expressed in Bart Kosko's book, *Fuzzy Thinking: The New Science of Fuzzy Logic* (1993).

[2] This Metathought is directly relevant to the ongoing debate between *categorical* versus *dimensional* approaches to clinical assessment and diagnosis.

VI. *Consider the Opposite: To Contrast Is to Define*

There can be no reality without polarity.
*—CARL G. JUNG**

A great truth is one whose opposite is also true.
*—NIELS BOHR***

The lady doth protest too much, methinks.
*—WILLIAM SHAKESPEARE****

In order to define or understand any given phenomenon, its theoretical opposite also should, whenever possible, be addressed and explored. How can we possibly define the concept of "mental illness," for example, without also addressing what we mean by "mental health"? How can we define introversion in the absence of defining extraversion? Can we ever truly understand conformity without also understanding dissent? This same principle holds true for scores of other psychological opposites: depression and happiness, optimism and pessimism, intelligence and stupidity, selfishness and altruism, responsibility and irresponsibility, infidelity and faithfulness, adaptive and maladaptive, functional and dysfunctional.

As these examples illustrate, to contrast a phenomenon with its polar opposite is to give definition to both terms. Just as thesis and antithesis can't be understood in isolation from each other, all polar opposites are dependent upon each other for their very conceptual existence. What, for instance, is the meaning of feminine without masculine? Unconscious without conscious?

*1875–1961, *Aion: Researches into the Phenomenology of the Self,* 1951/1959
**1885–1962, physicist and creator of quantum theory
***Hamlet,* Act III, Scene 2

Exciting without dull? Pain without pleasure? Dark without light? Order without chaos? Simple without complex? Empty without full? Strong without weak? Active without passive? Good without bad? Without one, conceptually speaking, its opposite ceases to exist.

The concept of polar opposites in the human condition is a theme that runs throughout the writings of the Swiss psychiatrist Carl G. Jung. According to Jung, within every personality there is a multiplicity of conflicting, sometimes complementary, but usually opposing forces. Jung (1921/1971) utilized the term *enantiodromia* (taken from the fifth century Greek philosopher, Heraclitus) to refer to these polar opposites. Jung (1943/1953; 1951/1959) believed that the failure to recognize the opposite tendencies within ourselves leads inevitably to the feeling of being torn apart; thus to live a whole and healthy life, we must learn to accept and integrate our inherent enantiodromia.

The historical development of psychological theory and research on attitude change provides a very interesting illustration of this Metathought. Beginning in the 1940s, and subsequently for many years, the predominant theme in social psychology was, "How can we cause attitude change?" In the late 1950s, William McGuire shed a different light on this problem and inspired a new direction in thinking simply by posing the opposite question: "How can we *resist* attitude change?" This led McGuire to develop his *inoculation theory* of attitude change, which essentially proposed that people are more resistant to the effects of persuasive communications after having been exposed to weak counterarguments (see McGuire & Papageorgis, 1961). Had McGuire not bothered to "consider the opposite," his innovative insights and important contributions might never have been realized.

Sigmund Freud most certainly considered the opposite when he conceptualized the ego defense mechanism of *reaction formation,* which involves the unconscious transformation of unacceptable impulses into their opposite, and thus more acceptable, forms (A. Freud, 1936). For instance, a mother who unconsciously harbors aggressive feelings toward her son may become excessively concerned for his welfare and safety. Or, a man who appears to be vehemently anti-pornography may be unconsciously motivated by the very sexual desires against which he is publicly crusading. In like manner, a person who fervently professes an ardent aversion to homosexuality may be using this attitude as a barrier against his or her own unconscious homosexual desires.

Considering the opposite also has a number of useful applications in the clinical setting. In particular, many techniques in Gestalt therapy (Perls, 1969) are designed to help clients confront (and thereby integrate) their inner opposites or polarities. For instance, if a psychotherapy client feels torn between his desire for change versus his fear of change, the Gestalt therapist might ask him to role play a dialogue between these opposing sets of feelings. When faced with a client who protests ("...too much, methinks") that she has no need whatsoever for an intimate relationship, the therapist may gently ask her to explore the part of herself that might, in fact, have such a need. Similarly, a client who adamantly professes nothing but disdain for his mother may be encouraged to examine what he likes about his mother. In these cases (and countless more), taking a few moments to consider the opposite frequently leads to very important therapeutic discoveries.

A fascinating illustration of this Metathought is the clinical technique of *prescribing the symptom* or *paradoxical intention* (see Frankl, 1959; Haley, 1976), in which a therapist gives the client a directive that he or she actually wants *resisted;* the resulting change takes place as a consequence of the client defying the therapist. This technique is utilized to undermine clients' resistance to change by, paradoxically, instructing them *not* to change, or even to deliberately engage in the unwanted or undesirable behaviors. In effect, the therapist's directives are precisely the opposite of the desired goal. For instance, a paranoid patient might be urged to become even *more* suspicious. Or, a married couple entering therapy with the complaint that they fight too much may be directed to go home and argue for three hours, twice daily, for one week. Similarly, a client who is afraid of being alone may be instructed for the next two weeks not to spend *any* time alone.

To take another example, how might we caution a person of things to *avoid* as a patient in psychotherapy? Utilizing this technique, we might prescribe the exact opposite behavior by imparting the following (paradoxical) instructions:

BOX 6-1

<u>How to Be a Good Psychotherapy Patient</u>[1]

There is a multitude of books and articles devoted to teaching people how to become effective psychotherapists. However, there is a dearth of literature on how to become good psychotherapy patients. The purpose of this essay is to offer you some practical guidelines, suggestions, and techniques that can help you to make the most out of your psychotherapy experience.

<u>Conducting Yourself in the Psychotherapy Session:</u>
<u>Twenty Easy "Dos" and "Don'ts"</u>

By far, the most challenging (and yet potentially the most entertaining) aspect of being a psychotherapy patient concerns your relationship with your psychotherapist. It is crucial, from the opening moments of that first phone call, that you get your therapist to like you, to become dependent on you, and to become convinced that only he has the power to cure you. While your therapist is busy delving deep into the inner recesses of your psyche, just follow these twenty easy-to-learn techniques and in virtually no time at all, you'll have him or her eating out of the palm of your hand.

continued

BOX 6-1   *Continued*

1. *Do* attribute all of your successes to your therapist, and all failures to yourself.
2. *Do* gaze reverently into your therapist's eyes as he pontificates about the nature of the human condition.
3. *Do* occasionally confuse something that your therapist said with something that Freud said.
4. *Do* complain about insensitive and judgmental parents, teachers, and, especially, prior psychotherapists.
5. *Do* apologize profusely to your therapist for not showing faster improvement.
6. *Do* casually inform your therapist that you're due to come into large sums of money in the near future.
7. *Do,* at random moments, say to your therapist, "You *really care* about me, don't you?"
8. *Do* tell your therapist that you passed up a week in Tahiti, just so you wouldn't have to miss your therapy session.
9. *Do* tell your therapist that when you win the Nobel Prize, you will announce to the world that you owe it all to him.
10. *Do* tell your therapist that you're totally committed to sticking with therapy—even if it takes fifty years.
11. *Don't* point out that your therapist constantly contradicts himself.
12. *Don't* embarrass your therapist by waking him up when he dozes off in the middle of your session.
13. *Don't* tell your therapist that his mind is obviously on everything else in the world, other than what you're saying.
14. *Don't* tell your therapist that his interpretations of your dreams are about as helpful as last year's horoscope.
15. *Don't* say to your therapist, "So, tell me something I *didn't* know."
16. *Don't* say to your therapist, "For *this,* I'm paying you money?"
17. *Don't* say to your therapist, "At least a plumber guarantees *his* work!"
18. *Don't* say to your therapist, "What's the matter? Not smart enough to get into law school?"
19. *Don't* say to your therapist, "Is doing therapy the *only way* you can get your intimacy needs met?"
20. *Don't ever* say to your therapist, "But what should I *do* about my problem?"

<u>Secondary Gains and Fringe Benefits:</u>
<u>Getting the Maximum Mileage from Being a Psychotherapy Patient</u>

Irrespective of what actually happens (or doesn't happen) in the course of psychotherapy, the very fact of being a psychotherapy patient can proffer you powerful leverage in all of your interpersonal relationships. Here are four easy pointers:

1. <u>Hide Behind Diagnostic Labels.</u>
   You can deftly absolve yourself of all personal responsibility for your annoying habits and obnoxious behavior by cloaking yourself in psychological diagnoses. For example, if someone is, in any way, critical of something you've done, just retort: "Hey, what do you *expect* from me? I'm a passive-dependent personality type with low-grade, uncrystallized borderline personality features!"

2. <u>Use Therapy against Your Mate</u>.
   Having an argument with your mate? No problem! Regardless of the content of the argument, you're sure to render your opponent powerless by smugly delivering the line: "Well, at least *I'm* in therapy. What are *you* doing to help this relationship?"

3. <u>Get Back at Your Parents</u>.
   When your parents ask you why you're in therapy, you have your choice of two very powerful strategies, either of which is guaranteed to leave them speechless and riddled with feelings of guilt and self-doubt.

   a) <u>The Passive–Aggressive Maneuver</u>:
   To execute this maneuver, simply follow this prescribed sequence: (1) Look confused and disappointed; (2) Emit a mildly exasperated, "some-people-never-learn" sigh; (3) Walk away, slowly shaking your head and muttering under your breath.

   b) <u>The Direct Frontal Attack</u>:
   For this tactic, just look them both straight in the eyes and shout with great vehemence, "*I'll give you two guesses!*"

4. <u>Impress Your Friends</u>.
   When in the company of your friends, make a habit of using psychological terms that you've picked up in your psychotherapy sessions and from watching television shows. Show them how deep you are by talking glibly about faulty introjects, repressed libido, inflated personas, irrational belief systems, incomplete gestalts, maladaptive learning patterns, ontological insecurity, dysfunctional family systems, your critical "inner-parent," your battered "inner-child," and your obnoxious "inner-aunt." Occasionally, squint your eyes, tilt your head, and ask people, "Don't you think you're projecting?"

<u>A Final Word</u>

Remember that it's *not easy* to become a good psychotherapy patient. Millions of people never learn. But, *don't get discouraged!* Trust that *you can do it!* Make these strategies a part of your life, and you're well on the way to complete recovery and true mental health.

Exercise: Toward the Resolution of Interpersonal Conflict

In the broader social context, the principle of considering the opposite can be utilized to increase one's understanding of—and empathy for—other people's point of view. As an exercise, select three specific issues (whether political, ethical, moral, legal, cultural, professional, familial, or intimate) about which you feel particularly strong. Now, for each issue, take the perspective of someone with the *opposite* attitude or opinion, and write out, as persuasively as you can *from their vantage point,* the reasons, arguments, and feelings pertaining to their position.

Issue #1:_____

Your attitude: _____

Opposite perspective: _____

_____

_____

_____

_____

_____

Issue #2: _____

Your attitude: _____

Opposite perspective: _____

_____

_____

_____

_____

_____

_____

Issue #3: _____

Your attitude: _____

Opposite perspective: _____

_____

_____

_____

_____

_____

_____

In reflecting on your responses to this exercise, briefly enumerate the potential value(s) of viewing these issues from opposing perspectives.

_____

_____

_____

_____

_____

Last, identify some particular instances or situations in which utilizing this method of considering the opposite may contribute to the successful resolution of interpersonal conflict.

_____

_____

_____

_____

_____

_____

Glossary Terms

The following terms (or variations) are defined in the Glossary:

attitude	opinion
attribution	paradox
behavior	paradoxical intention
belief	personality
cause	phenomenon
clinical	prescription
concept	projection
conscious	psyche
consequence	psychological
diagnosis	psychology
dysfunction	psychotherapy
effect	reaction formation
ego defense mechanism	repression
ethics	resistance
existence	social
experience	subsequent
extraversion	symptom
Gestalt therapy	theoretical
insight	theory
interpersonal	thinking
interpretation	truth
introversion	unconscious
mental	value
ontological	

Notes

[1] This essay originally appeared in the *Journal of Polymorphous Perversity* (Levy, 1991). (Yes, this journal actually *does* exist.)

Chapter *7*

VII. The Similarity-Uniqueness Paradox: All Phenomena Are Both Similar and Different

> *The more things change, the more they remain the same.*
> —*ALPHONSE KARR**

> *There is no new thing under the sun.*
> —*[THE] BIBLE***

> *You can't step twice into the same river.*
> —*HERACLITUS****

By way of introducing this Metathought, let's examine the following problem: Which of the following four words does not belong with the other three?

A. knee
B. eye
C. mind
D. rock

The correct answer to this question is *C*, because *mind* is the only term that represents a theoretical construct, rather than a physical object.

---

*1808–1890, *Les Guepes;* cited in *The New International Dictionary of Quotations,* Miner & Rawson, 1994
**Ecclesiastes* 1:9
***c.540–c.480 B. C., *On the Universe;* cited in *The New International Dictionary of Quotations,* Miner & Rawson, 1994

But, wait...the correct answer is *D,* because *rock* is the only term not related to a living organism.

Then again, the correct answer is *B,* because *eye* is the only word that isn't comprised of four letters.

Is that it? Not quite. The correct answer is *A,* because *knee* is the only word that contains a silent letter.

So, which is it? Can it be that all four answers are correct? If so, how can every term be both similar to and different from the others?

The solution to this apparent paradox lies in the cognitive schema or perceptual set with which one initially approaches the problem (see Metathought XXIII, the Assimilation Bias). More specifically, it is a function of the particular dimensions or variables on which one has elected to evaluate the response options.

For example, if you were "on the lookout" for grammatical phenomena, you would process the information in a manner that leads you to notice things like spelling, parts of speech, verb tense, abbreviations, the number and arrangement of letters, and even the presence of silent letters. By contrast, if you were to examine the same question with a mindset for semantical phenomena, you would be paying attention to definitions, synonyms, antonyms, and homonyms; you may attempt to group the terms into conceptually useful categories; and you might recognize and distinguish metaphorical versus literal word meanings.

Thus, as you can see, determining the similarities and differences between any set of events depends almost entirely on the perspectives from which you choose to view them. In this way, phenomena can be seen as both unique from and, at the same time, similar to other phenomena.

Keeping these principles in mind, let's try another problem:

A. heroin
B. cocaine
C. amphetamines
D. caffeine

Now, if you were to approach this question with an interest in identifying chemical substances that are likely to boost your energy level, the correct answer would be *A.* This is because heroin, in contrast to the other three drugs, is not a central nervous system stimulant.

If, on the other hand, you were to look at the same four choices but this time with legal issues foremost in your mind, the correct answer would be *D* (caffeine), because the other three drugs are either completely illegal, or are illegal as to their purchase, distribution, and usage without proper authorization.

Third, suppose that you are attempting to categorize substances in terms of their currently sanctioned, legitimate medical usage. Here, the correct answer would be *C*, because, of the four drugs, only amphetamines are commonly prescribed by doctors (typically for Attention–Deficit/Hyperactivity Disorder, weight reduction, and occasionally for depression).

Finally, let's say that you are conducting research into the derivation of product names given to popular soft drinks. From this vantage point, the correct answer is *B*, because cocaine ("coke") was originally an ingredient in one of the world's most famous sodas, Coca-Cola ("Coke"). (And no other term appearing on this list can boast of such a claim!)

Let's take a step back now and examine in greater detail the interlocking processes of comparing and contrasting phenomena. First, how do we determine the degree to which phenomena are similar? To begin with, any two phenomena in the cosmos share at least one fundamental commonality: namely, they are both phenomena. With this as a starting point, they may subsequently be compared along a virtually infinite array of dimensions or "sorting variables," ranging from the broadest of universal properties to the minutest of mundane details.

For instance, are the phenomena in question observable ("physical") or theoretical ("conceptual")? If theoretical, in which conceptual domain? If observable, of what chemical or molecular composition? Are the phenomena living or nonliving? Terrestrial or extraterrestrial? If living on earth, which phylum? Genus? Species? Sex? If human, what are the physical features (height, weight, hair and eye color, health, strength, attractiveness)? Demographic characteristics (age, race, nationality, culture, religion, income, occupation)? Social context (competitive, cooperative, structured, restrictive, supportive)? Personality attributes (intelligence, behavioral patterns, maturity, psychological problems, coping skills, cognitive and attributional style, creativity, motivation, insight, awareness, values, beliefs, attitudes, goals, interests, preferences in art, music, food, and wallpaper)?

When comparing any two phenomena on these (and a multitude of other) dimensions, initially they will "match" with respect to their mutual similarities. But no matter how many features they might share in common, there is no escaping the inevitable fact that at some point there will be a conceptual fork (or *bifurcation*) in the road, where the phenomena will differ. We may refer to this juncture as the *point of critical distinction* (PCD), before which the phenomena are similar, and after which they are different.

Clearly, then, when we are attempting to define, compare, and contrast any two phenomena, it is imperative that we identify and examine the PCDs which are relevant to the particular events under scrutiny. If, for instance, we are interested in exploring the *similarities* between the events, we should examine the variables that appear *before* the PCD; if, by contrast, we wish to analyze the *differences* between the same two events, we should focus on the variables that appear *at and after* the PCD. (Of course, to gain a full and comprehensive understanding of their relationship, we should examine the variables that appear *both before and after* the PCD, with particular attention to the PCD itself.)

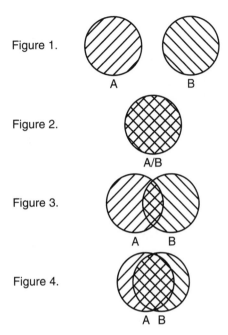

Figure 1.

Figure 2.

Figure 3.

Figure 4.

FIGURE 7-1   Four Relationships between Phenomena A and B

*Figure 1) Two different phenomena with absolutely nothing in common.

*Figure 2) Two different phenomena that are completely identical.

Figure 3) Two different phenomena with very little in common (that is, a low similarity-to-difference ratio).

Figure 4) Two different phenomena with a great deal in common (that is, a high similarity-to-difference ratio).

(*Note that Examples 1 and 2 cannot, by definition, actually occur.)

Some examples of these relationships are depicted in the Venn diagrams above. In interpreting these figures, note that overlapping areas indicate commonality between the two phenomena. Thus, a relatively large area of overlap indicates a high similarity-to-difference ratio (that is, more similarities than differences), whereas a relatively small area of overlap indicates a low similarity-to-difference ratio (more differences than similarities).

The following exercise will give you some practice at comparing, contrasting, and identifying points of critical distinction from a diverse array of phenomena. First, browse through the list below and select several word pairs that, for whatever reason, capture your interest. Then, utilizing any dimensions or sorting variables that might be useful, for each pair, answer the questions: (1) "How are they similar?" and (2) "How are they different?"

-God and Satan

-heaven and hell

-predestination and free will

-religion and art

-religion and science

-religion and slavery

-religion and freedom

-religious conversion and cult indoctrination

-Catholicism and Protestantism

-Judaism and Christianity

-religious leaders and political leaders

-television evangelists and television salesmen

-philosophy and science

-astronomy and astrology

-chemistry and alchemy

-neurology and phrenology

-cause and effect

-correlation and causation

-Event Theory and Construct Theory (see Metathought II)

-deductive reasoning and inductive reasoning (see Metathought XX)

-good and bad

-hot and cold

-dark and light

-pain and pleasure

-life and death

-any phenomenon and its opposite (see Metathought VI)

-fire and water

-earthquakes and hurricanes

-volcanic eruptions and anger

-rain and sadness

-brain and mind

-physical illness and mental illness

-physical abuse and emotional abuse

-depression and anxiety

-depression and death

-psychosis and creativity

-hypnosis and prayer

-psychotherapy and science

-psychotherapy and art

-psychotherapy and medicine

-psychotherapy and religion

-psychotherapy and friendship

-psychotherapy and prostitution

-men and women

-platonic love and romantic love

-love and psychosis

-sadism and masochism

-rape and consensual sex

-date rape and stranger rape

-rape and robbery

-sex and power

-sex and intimacy

-sex and aggression

-sex and dancing

-sex and pizza

-Spanish culture and Mexican culture

-Japanese art and Chinese art

-Israeli music and Arabic music

-Italian food and French food

-poverty and racism

-ignorance-based racism and hostility-based racism

-prejudice against blacks and prejudice against Jews

-affirmative action and discrimination

-discrimination and reverse discrimination

-racial inequality in 1955 and racial inequality in 1995

-Democrats and Republicans

-Communism and Naziism

-cult indoctrination and psychoanalysis

-apples and oranges

-apples and existentialism

-dogs and people

-wolves and gangs

-infancy and old age

-bullies and cowards

-actors and athletes

-sports and war

-Beethoven and Einstein

-ant colonies and human societies

-emotions and the stock market

-school and prison

-parents and jail wardens

-physician-prescribed medication and illicit street drugs

-your mate/spouse and your opposite-sexed parent

-yourself and any other person

-yourself now and yourself five years ago

-yourself now and yourself ten years ago

-yourself now and yourself when you were a young child

Word pair: _____
Similarities: _____

_____

_____

_____

_____

Differences: _____

_____

_____

_____

_____

Word pair: _____
Similarities: _____

_____

_____

_____

Differences: _____

_____

_____

_____

_____

Word pair:_____
Similarities:_____

_____

_____

_____

Differences: _____

_____

_____

_____

_____

Word pair:_____
Similarities:_____

_____

_____

_____

Differences: _____

_____

_____

_____

_____

What is the purpose of this exercise? First, it illustrates that any two phenomena in the universe, no matter how seemingly disparate at first glance, always share at least some similarities. Second, phenomena invariably are differentiated by various points of critical distinction, which, in essence, define the boundaries delineating one phenomenon from another. Third, by utilizing this method of comparing and contrasting phenomena, you probably gained new insights and discovered some fresh perspectives into these relationships that you heretofore might not have considered. Fourth, given the fact that any two events are similar *and* different, it is crucial to take them *both* into account in your assessment of the phenomena.

This same method (of comparing and contrasting phenomena by analyzing relevant PCDs) also may be utilized to evaluate the relative appropriateness, usefulness, or merit of analogies and metaphors. Remember that, by definition, an analogy never can be "perfect"; there always exists *some* difference between the original phenomenon (e.g., addiction to a drug) and its analogue (e.g., addiction to a job, game, or person). However, by focusing on what they *do* share in common, specifically, their similarities prior to the PCD (such as feeling overwhelmed by irresistible urges to perform certain behaviors), the analogy's applicability or value may be judged in terms of how well, on the whole, it seems to "fit." Thus, whether we are drawing a metaphoric parallel between physical illness and mental illness, between a broken machine and a broken family, or between repairing a damaged computer and repairing a damaged psyche, we must be alert not only to avoid committing errors of reification (see Metathought II), but also to identify and scrutinize all relevant PCDs, thereby acknowledging the limits inherent in our metaphoric representations.

Similarly, we should bear in mind that all conceptual divisions (such as categories, classifications, diagnoses, and taxonomies) are human-made simplifications that, by their very nature, are fundamentally flawed. Thus, although we need to accept such simplifications as "necessary evils" in science, we also should never forget that they are artificial, contrived, and to varying degrees distorted, inaccurate, and erroneous. Here again, a systematic examination of similarities and differences provides us with a useful method of understanding and coming to terms with this dilemma. As noted by social psychologists Susan Fiske and Shelley Taylor (1984), "Life is not a series of boxes connected by arrows. Although the boxes are a convenient fiction, . . . you would not want to live in them" (p. 306).

Sources of Error

In the course of evaluating similarities and differences between any phenomena, we are subject to committing errors in two directions: first, by allowing genuine differences to be obscured by similarities, and second, by allowing genuine similarities to be obscured by differences.

Differences Obscured by Similarities

In these situations, the person makes the mistake of permitting similarities between phenomena to eclipse their differences. For instance, someone who routinely engages in stereotyping members of particular groups (based on, for example, their sex, race, ethnicity, religion, profession, political affiliation, and so on) is prone to habitually, systematically, and automatically overestimate within-group similarities, while minimizing (or even ignoring) within-group variability (Fiske & Taylor, 1984). In other words, the individual perceives group members to be more alike than they really are and, at the same time, does not recognize many of the ways in which they are different from one another. As you can readily discern, in its most extreme form, this process is a fundamental component underlying prejudice, bigotry, chauvinism, racism, classism, sexism, ageism, and so on, wherein all members of the "outgroup" are seen as essentially the same, while their individuality goes virtually unnoticed.

In the context of psychotherapy, some therapists make this error when they fail to respect (or even recognize) the uniqueness indigenous to each individual client. Unfortunately, these therapists tend to perceive one client as basically the same as every other client. In this way, clients are viewed *not* as distinct and varied individuals, each possessing a separate and unique constellation of life experiences, memories, thoughts, feelings, perceptions, values, beliefs, goals, hopes, fears, and dreams. Instead, they are spontaneously filtered through the therapist's own cognitive "client role schema" (see Metathought XXIII, the Assimilation Bias), from which they emerge as a relatively undifferentiated, homogeneous, amorphous, two-dimensional "client-type." In this less-than-therapeutic environment, then, irrespective of individual clients' unique situations, problems, or needs, they all receive essentially the same procrustean, "cookie-cutter" approach to clinical assessment and treatment.

As a final example, let's examine the act of killing a human being. Here, regardless of any other factors, the outcome is invariant, unambiguous, and unequivocal: death. Thus, when viewed solely in terms of its consequences, all forms of killing are equivalent. What if, however, we were to consider other dimensions on which to compare and contrast various acts of killing? Suppose, for instance, that we could take into account such variables as social context, motivation, intentionality, and the target of the act. Without a doubt, substantial and meaningful differences (based on a wide range of PCDs) would immediately ensue. Specifically, we would now be confronted with relatively clear differentiations between: premeditated murder, self-defense, manslaughter, legal execution (capital punishment), symbolic acts of retribution, wartime combat, killing for food, killing for sport, killing out of jealousy, gang initiation rites, political assassination, physician-assisted or self-induced suicide, and even euthanasia ("mercy killing").

Similarities Obscured by Differences

How many times have you heard someone make the following pronouncement (or any derivation thereof): "You can't compare these two things because they're totally and completely different from each other!" Here we have a vivid illustration of a person who is making the converse mistake of allowing similarities between phenomena to be overshadowed by their differences. Thus, the individual who staunchly and adamantly maintains that, "One should *never* stereotype," is effectively blinding him or herself to authentic commonalities that actually do exist within specific subgroups. However, by obstinately clinging to this position, such individuals practically ensure that they will remain oblivious to true similarities within (as well as between) groups of people.

Similarly, psychotherapists who tenaciously cling to their belief that, "Every client should be viewed and treated as totally unique and without regard to other clients," run the risk of allowing true (and potentially helpful) similarities between persons to be overlooked, neglected, or omitted. Unfortunately, the therapist's overemphasis on individual differences typically is realized at the expense of minimizing interpersonal commonalities (see Metathought XXX, Every Decision Is a Trade-Off). As a consequence, deeply powerful and universal life experiences that appear to be intrinsic to the human condition—themes, for example, related to needs for love, acceptance, empathy, esteem, or success—are prone to be minimized, disregarded, or even rejected outright.

How might this Metathought be constructively applied in the clinical setting? The following brief vignette provides one such example.

Client: "There's no way that you can understand how I feel. After all, you're white, and I'm black. And you've never been discriminated against because of your race."

Therapist: "You're right. I can never know exactly what that feels like. We are truly different in that respect. But at the same time, I know what it's like to be discriminated against because of my gender. And I have had the experience of being persecuted out of ignorance and hatred. To that extent, we do share a common experience. We are indeed both similar and different."

To briefly summarize this Metathought, all phenomena are both *similar to* and *different from* each other, depending on the dimensions or variables that have been selected for purposes of evaluation, comparison, and contrast. Further, no phenomenon is *totally identical* or *totally unique* in relation to other phenomena. Finally, the degree of similarity or uniqueness revealed between any two events is a function of the relevant *points of critical distinction* (PCD).

What are some antidotes to this Metathought? First, when comparing and contrasting any two phenomena be sure to ask yourself, "In what ways are they similar?" *and* "In what ways are they different?" Even before you ask these questions, however, make certain that you are clear as to the specific *purpose* of your analysis. Next, carefully select the most relevant dimensions and variables on which you will base your evaluation. Despite what may be an overwhelming number of similarities between two phenomena, don't neglect to search for and take into account their differences; conversely, regardless of what may appear to be a virtual absence of commonality between the phenomena, be sure to identify and scrutinize their similarities. (For one application, see Levy & Nail, 1993.)

Keep these principles in mind whenever you are faced with the task of comparing and contrasting any phenomena. You are likely to be more than just a little surprised each time you realize that the dimensions or variables you select for purposes of evaluation ultimately will determine just how "similar" or "unique" the phenomena turn out to be!

Glossary Terms

The following terms (or variations) are defined in the Glossary:

ambiguous	intentionality
analogy	interpersonal
antidote	judgment
attitude	mental illness
attribution	metaphor
behavior	mind
belief	motivation
bifurcation	paradox
category	perception
causation	personality
cause	phenomenon
clinical	physical
cognitive	point of critical distinction (PCD)
concept	procrustean
consequence	psyche
construct	psychoanalysis
Construct (Type C) Theory	psychological
correlation	psychosis
deductive reasoning	psychotherapy
diagnosis	reification
dilemma	schema
dimension	science
disorder	semantic
effect	social
e.g.	stereotype
emotion	subsequent
erroneous	taxonomy
evaluation	theoretical
event	treatment
Event (Type E) Theory	universal
existentialism	value
experience	variable
fact	vignette
inductive reasoning	vivid
insight	

VIII. *The Naturalistic Fallacy: Blurring the Line between "Is" and "Should"*

We can, and must, distinguish clearly between facts and rules.
—*THOMAS SZASZ**

It is of fundamental importance not to make the positivist mistake of assuming that, because a group are "in formation," this means they are necessarily "on course."
—*R. D. LAING***

One very important way in which our personal values can bias our thinking is when we equate our description of what *is* with our prescription of what *ought* to be. This occurs, for instance, whenever we define what is good in terms of what is observable. This error in thinking is called the *Naturalistic Fallacy*.

Let's examine the following statements: "What's typical is normal; what's normal is good. What's not typical is abnormal; what's abnormal is bad." Notice how, in each case, a *description* of what exists becomes converted into a *prescription* of what we like or dislike.

As the Scottish philosopher David Hume pointed out over 200 years ago, values, ethics, and morality are based not on logic or reason, but on the sentiments and public opinions of a particular society. Thus, no description of human behavior, however accurate, can ever ordain what is "right" or "wrong" behavior. It makes no difference whether we are studying people's

*The Therapeutic State, 1984
**The Politics of Experience, 1967

political beliefs, religious customs, work performance, recreational activities, family upbringing, sexual practices, or table manners. If most people do something, that does not make it right; if most people do not, that does not make it wrong.

Of course, the converse also is true: If most people do something, that does not make it wrong; if most people do not, that does not make it right. In other words, there is no need to idealize someone just because he or she is different from the crowd. Likewise, we need not condemn someone solely for doing what others do. The point is that, in any case, we must be careful not to confuse *objective description* with *subjective value judgment*.

As an exercise, try to think of examples from everyday life that people may place into each of the following four categories:

Common, therefore good: _____
Uncommon, therefore bad: _____
Common, therefore bad:_____
Uncommon, therefore good: _____

Application 1: Maslow's Theory of Self-Actualization

No one is immune to making this error, not even social scientists. A case in point is Abraham Maslow's (1970) theory of motivation. Maslow, a pioneer of Humanistic psychology, proposed that humans have a number of innate needs, which are arranged in a hierarchy in terms of their potency. Malsow grouped these needs into five categorical levels: physiological, safety, love, esteem, and self-actualization. Once an individual has satisfied the cluster of needs at a particular level, he or she is able to progress to the next hierarchical level. Thus, for example, people typically are not prompted to seek acceptance and esteem until they have met their needs for food, water, and shelter.

TABLE 8-1   Abraham Maslow's Hierarchy of Needs

Level 5:	*Self-Actualization Needs*
Level 4:	*Esteem Needs*
Level 3:	*Belonging and Love Needs*
Level 2:	*Safety Needs*
Level 1:	*Physiological Needs*

Maslow noted that as one ascends the hierarchy of needs, one becomes less animal-like and more human. If the person has been able to satisfy adequately the needs in the first four levels, he or she is in a position to fulfill the highest-order needs, namely, to actualize one's fullest and unique potential. According to Maslow, once a person enters the realm of self-actualization, he or she becomes qualitatively different from those who are still attempting to meet their more basic needs. The self-actualizing person's life is governed by the search of "being-values" (B-values), such as Truth, Goodness, Beauty, Wholeness, Justice, and Meaningfulness.

In contrast to most personality theorists who preceded him, Maslow created his theory by studying healthy and successful people, rather than clinical cases of psychopathology. His interest in self-actualizing people began with his great admiration for Max Wertheimer (one of the founders of Gestalt psychology) and Ruth Benedict (the renowned cultural anthropologist). After discovering that these two individuals had many characteristics in common, Maslow began to search for others with the same qualities. The group that he finally isolated for more detailed study included Abraham Lincoln, Thomas Jefferson, Albert Einstein, Eleanor Roosevelt, Albert Schweitzer, Benedict Spinoza, Adlai Stevenson, and Martin Buber.

Based on his informal research, Maslow developed a composite, impressionistic profile of the optimally functioning, mature, and healthy human being. Maslow concluded that self-actualizing persons exhibit a number of similar characteristics, including: an accurate perception of reality, a continued freshness of appreciation and openness to experience, spontaneity and simplicity, a strong ethical awareness, a philosophical (rather than hostile) sense of humor, needs for privacy, periodic mystical ("peak") experiences, a democratic leader structure, deep interpersonal relations, autonomy and independence, creativeness, a problem-centered (rather than self-centered) orientation, a resistance of enculturation, and an acceptance of self, others, and nature.

Critics of Maslow's theory question whether such characteristics truly are a valid depiction of the fully-functioning person, or, instead, are a reflection of Maslow's own subjective value system. In other words, Maslow has been criticized for mixing ethical and moral considerations with his logic. Consider, for example, his portrayal of self-actualizing people as open, realistic, spontaneous, possessing a democratic leader structure, and accepting of self, others, and nature. Is this an objective description of human fulfillment? Or is it a *pre*scription, masked as a *de*scription, of Maslow's own subjective ideals? As noted by M. Brewster Smith (1978), perhaps Maslow simply selected his personal heroes and offered his impressions of them.

Let's explore this notion by conducting a little thought experiment. Imagine that some other theorist, with a distinctly different set of values, were to utilize Maslow's method of delineating the characteristics of self-actualization by studying *his* own heroes, who, for the sake of argument, happen to be Napolean Bonaparte, Alexander the Great, and General George S. Patton. In this alternative scenario, *now* what are some of the qualities that define the "self-actualized, optimally-functioning, healthy human being?" How about *totalitarian leader structure? Egocentric orientation? Obsessed with power? Need to conquer? Love of war?*

In defense of Maslow, he acknowledged that his theorizing and research on self-actualization lacked the rigor of strict empirical science. He fervently believed, however, that it was imperative to begin the process of rounding out the field of psychology by attending to "the highest capacities of the healthy and strong man as well as with the defensive maneuvers of crippled spirits" (1970, p. 33). Further, Maslow maintained that it would be misleading to believe that science is value free, since its methods and procedures are developed and utilized for human purposes.

Application 2: Erikson's Theory of Healthy Ego Functioning

As another illustration, let us consider Erik H. Erikson's theory of psychosocial development. Erikson (1950) theorized that all humans pass through a series of eight developmental stages, which stretch from birth to death. Each stage is characterized by a developmental conflict, problem, or *crisis*. If the crisis has a positive resolution, the person's ego is strengthened by gaining a *virtue,* which results in greater adaptation and a healthier personality. But, if the crisis has a negative resolution, the ego loses strength, resulting in inhibited adaptation and an unhealthier personality. For instance, if a young child's conflict between initiative and guilt has a positive resolution, he will emerge with the virtue of purpose; a negative outcome, however, would result in a sense of unworthiness.

TABLE 8-2   Erik H. Erikson's Stages of Psychosocial Development

Stage	Ego Crisis	Age	Positive Outcome
1	Basic Trust versus Mistrust	0–1	Hope
2	Autonomy versus Shame and Doubt	1–3	Will
3	Initiative versus Guilt	3–5	Purpose
4	Industry versus Inferiority	5–12	Competence
5	Ego Identity versus Role Confusion	adolescence	Fidelity
6	Intimacy versus Isolation	young adult	Love
7	Generativity versus Stagnation	adulthood	Care
8	Ego Integrity versus Despair	maturity	Wisdom

Erikson thus defined the healthy or mature personality as one that possesses the eight virtues (namely: hope, will, purpose, competence, fidelity, love, care, and wisdom) that emerge from a positive resolution at each stage of development. It was Erikson's belief that the outcome of every crisis resolution is reversible. The goal in his approach to psychotherapy, therefore, was to encourage the growth of whatever virtues the client happened to be missing.

As was the case with Maslow, Erikson has been criticized for mixing objective description with subjective prescription. Specifically, the virtues he uses to define the healthy individual are clearly in accordance with Western, Judeo-Christian ethics, values, and social institutions. In other words, Erikson, like many social theorists, may have been describing what he believes *should* be, rather than what *is*.

Caveat and Conclusion

I wish to emphasize that it is not my intention to impugn the value judgments implicit in the theories of Maslow and Erikson; in fact, I find myself closely aligned with many of their beliefs. However, *values and veracity are not synonymous.* Further, we must remember that our perceptions of the world are inescapably colored by our personal beliefs, and that the distinction between description and prescription frequently is a jumbled one indeed.

Glossary Terms

The following terms (or variations) are defined in the Glossary:

behavior	normal
belief	objective
bias	opinion
category	perception
clinical	personality
description	prescription
empirical	psychology
ethics	psychopathology
experience	psychotherapy
fact	resistance
fallacy	science
Gestalt psychology	social
Humanistic psychology	subjective
interpersonal	theory
judgment	thinking
logic	value
motivation	veracity
Naturalistic Fallacy	

IX. *The Barnum Effect: "One-Size-Fits-All" Personality Interpretations*

A good circus should have a little something for everybody.
—*ATTRIBUTED TO P. T. BARNUM**

There's a sucker born every minute.
—*P. T. BARNUM***

A *Barnum statement* is a personality interpretation about a particular individual that is true of practically all human beings; in other words, it is a general statement that has "a little something for everybody." The *Barnum Effect* refers to people's willingness to accept the validity of such overly inclusive and generic interpretations.

Barnum statements pervade the popular media (from television and radio shows to books, newspapers, and magazines) in the form of self-help primers, astrological forecasts, psychic hotlines, biorhythm and numerology readings, and interpretations of your dreams, palms, or favorite colors. To find Barnum statements, you need look no further than the contents of *Dianetics,* the *I Ching,* or your most recent fortune cookie. Unfortunately, however, they are also commonly proffered to an eager (and frequently gullible) public by media psychologists. Worse yet, Barnum statements sometimes parade in the guise of psychological assessments or clinical diagnoses at professional psychotherapy treatment planning meetings and case conferences. For instance, a therapist

*1810–1891
**Cited in Bartlett, Familiar Quotations, 1968

may confidently announce to his colleagues, "My patient's problem is that he has self-esteem issues." (*Who doesn't?*) Or, "My patient is sensitive to criticism." (*Who isn't?*) Or, "My patient doesn't want to be rejected." (*Who does?*)

The variations on this theme are virtually infinite. To list but a few:

>"He has ambivalent feelings about his parents."
>"Deep down, she craves love and approval."
>"He has control issues."
>"She has boundary issues."
>"He has trust issues."
>"She has issues around intimacy and commitment."
>"He has intrapsychic conflict."
>"She's afraid of being hurt."
>"He struggles with feelings of insecurity."
>"She doesn't like being overly dependent."
>"He's trying to find a balance between autonomy and closeness."
>"She just wants to be understood."
>"He's his own worst enemy."
>"She is holding a grudge that she really ought to let go."

In a number of experiments, researchers have presented subjects with Barnum-like personality descriptions, such as those in Box 9-1 (which was constructed from a horoscope book).

BOX 9-1

<u>Are any of these statements untrue?</u>

"You have a strong need for other people to like and admire you. You have a tendency to be critical of yourself... At times you have serious doubts as to whether you have made the right decision or done the right thing. You prefer a certain amount of change and variety and become dissatisfied when hemmed in by restrictions and limitations. You pride yourself on being an independent thinker and do not accept other opinions without satisfactory proof. You have found it unwise to be too frank in revealing yourself to others. At times you are extraverted, affable, sociable; at other times you are introverted, wary, and reserved. Some of your aspirations tend to be pretty unrealistic" (Forer, 1949).

When subjects in the experiments were led to believe that the bogus feedback was prepared especially for them, and when it was generally favorable, they nearly always rated the description as either "good" or "excellent" (Dickson & Kelly, 1985). In fact, when given a choice between a fake Barnum description and a *real* personality description based on an established test, people tended to choose the *phony* description as being more accurate![1]

The moral? *Be careful* about making—and accepting—such Barnum statements. Though they might (and in fact often do) have *prima facie* validity, they are not particularly helpful in telling us anything *distinctive* about a specific person, such as when we are attempting to arrive at a differential clinical diagnosis.

In fact, to stretch the point just a bit, I have constructed what I believe to be the ultimate Barnum description: "The One-Size-Fits-All Psychological Profile."[2]

BOX 9-2

The One-Size-Fits-All Psychological Profile

Developmental History
You are the kind of person who was biologically conceived by two, opposite-sexed parents. However, no one, including your parents, ever asked you if you wanted to be born. For a period of time, you were totally dependent on others for providing food, shelter, and safety. Your vocabulary was extremely limited, you found it impossible to stand up without assistance, and you were incapable of accomplishing even minor tasks, such as brushing your teeth. In fact, for a while there, you didn't even *have* any. On more than one occasion, your cries went unheeded.

Things are different for you now than they used to be. You are not as young as you were. You've had numerous experiences in your life. You've had some problems and suffered some disappointments in your past. When things didn't work out the way you wanted them to, you wished that they had. You are more likely to remember those things that you don't forget.

Physiological Processes
You're the type of person who has a variety of bodily needs. For example, when deprived of oxygen, you are likely to experience feelings of suffocation. Sometimes you are thirsty; at other times, you just aren't. When you are thirsty, you crave something to drink. When you are hungry, you crave something to eat. During periods of intense hunger, you are likely to seek, procure, and ingest food. When you've eaten too much food, you usually don't feel hungry for a while. You are prone to have very little appetite when you are in the act of vomiting.

If you were to go without sleep for several days in a row, you would be prone to experience feelings of fatigue, weariness, or even exhaustion. The longer you go without sleep, the more tired you are likely to become. When you are asleep, you don't know it. In fact, it's only after you've woken up that you know that you were.

You're the kind of person who derives pleasure from scratching an itch. Pain hurts you. In fact, you typically attempt to avoid pain. When you are too cold, you have a strong tendency to seek heat. When you are too hot, you try to cool down. When you feel sick, you experience a desire to get well. When having sex, you're the type of person who prefers to have an orgasm, rather than not have one. You experience a sense of relief, or even pleasure, after relieving your bladder or bowels. You prefer the smell of your own excreta to that of other people's (see Levy & Erhardt, 1988).

Many of your bodily processes have an "automatic" quality to them. For example, when you are engaging in strenuous physical activity, your heartbeat, blood pressure, and respiration increase, whether you like it or not. When your skin is cut, you are very likely to bleed. You're the type of person who experiences a "gagging" sensation whenever a foreign object (such as a stick, screwdriver, or cooking utensil) is shoved down your throat.

Personality Characteristics

You're a person who has many different sides to your personality. There are parts of your personality that you like more than others. Deep down, you have some pretty deep feelings. These feelings are likely to be much deeper than those feelings that are closer to the surface. When your feelings are hurt, you're the kind of person who doesn't like it. Given the choice, you'd rather feel good than bad. Sometimes you are happy; sometimes you aren't. You like feeling happy, but you don't like feeling lonely, depressed, or anxious. In fact, the more miserable you are, the more you dislike it.

Interpersonal Functioning

You are similar to other people in some ways, but not in other ways. There are many people whom you just do not know. You enjoy having the respect of others. You like some people more than others. When you lose someone dear to you, you are likely to feel sad. You are the kind of person who prefers not being ridiculed, mocked, or tortured by others.

Goals and Expectations

You wish that you could be more the kind of person who you really want to be. You wish that you had more control over your life. You want to accomplish more. You would prefer to be successful rather than unsuccessful.

Diagnostic Impressions (Check as many as desired, depending on the clinician's theoretical orientation.)

_____You have maladaptive learning patterns.
_____You have inner-child issues.
_____You have codependency issues.
_____You have repressed introjects.
_____You have unfinished business.
_____You are searching for meaning in life.
_____You come from a dysfunctional family.
_____You have a biochemical imbalance.

Future Prognosis

If you continue to live, you will grow older. The longer you live, the more experiences you are likely to have. You will always be older than your younger siblings. At some point in your future, you will be completely unable to talk, walk, or even breathe. And this condition will last for a very, *very* long time.

As an historical note, Donald G. Paterson once warned clinicians about a "personality description after the manner of P. T. Barnum" (cited in Meehl, 1956), who remarked that "a good circus should have a little something for everybody." Paul Meehl (1956, 1973) subsequently coined the term "Barnum effect," in honor of the renowned circus-master.

Barnum was also famous for declaring that, "There's a sucker born every minute." This observation may have been more prophetic than Barnum ever intended, both of clients who accept uncritically the validity of Barnum statements about themselves, and of clinicians who delude themselves into believing the veracity of their own pseudo-incisive personality interpretations.

Exercise: De-Barnumizing Barnum Interpretations

Begin this exercise by selecting a few Barnum interpretations from this chapter, or come up with some of your own. Then, "de-Barnumize" each statement by incorporating any potentially useful qualifiers, modifiers, or adverbs. To get you started, here are two examples:

Barnum statement: <u>My patient is sensitive to criticism.</u>
De-Barnumized statement: <u>My patient is moderately sensitive to criticism.</u>

Barnum statement: <u>She's afraid of being hurt.</u>
De-Barnumized statement: <u>She's profoundly afraid of being hurt.</u>

Barnum statement: _____
De-Barnumized statement: _____

Barnum statement: _____
De-Barnumized statement: _____

Barnum statement: _____
De-Barnumized statement: _____

Barnum statement: _____
De-Barnumized statement: _____

Barnum statement: _____
De-Barnumized statement: _____

Glossary Terms

The following terms (or variations) are defined in the Glossary:

Barnum Effect	description
Barnum statement	diagnosis
belief	differential diagnosis
clinical	dysfunction
decision	effect

expectation
experience
experiment
extraversion
generic
interpersonal
interpretation
intrapsychic
introversion
opinion

personality
prima facie
psychological
psychotherapy
repression
subsequent
theoretical
treatment
validity
veracity

Notes

[1] See Snyder, Shenkel, and Lowery (1977) for an excellent review of research in this area.

[2] The complete version of "The One-Size-Fits-All Psychological Profile" originally appeared in the *Journal of Polymorphous Perversity* (Levy, 1993).

Part Two

Explaining Phenomena

Chapter *10*

X. Correlation Does Not Prove Causation: Confusing "What" with "Why"

ROGERS'S LAW:
As soon as the stewardess serves the coffee,
the airliner encounters turbulence.
DAVIS'S EXPLANATION OF ROGERS'S LAW:
Serving coffee on aircraft causes turbulence.
—ARTHUR BLOCH*

President Bush taking credit for the collapse of Communism
is like a rooster taking credit for the arrival of the dawn.
—SOURCE UNKNOWN**

A *correlation* is a statement about the relationship or association between two (or more) variables. Correlations thus enable us to make predictions from one variable to another. For example, if two events are correlated, then the presence of one event provides us with information about the other event. A correlation does not, however, necessarily establish a *causal* relationship between the variables.[1] In other words, cause-and-effect can't be proven simply by virtue of a correlation.

As an example, let us consider the empirically validated correlation between creativity and mood disorders (see Andreason & Canter, 1974; Andreason & Powers, 1975; Jamison, 1993). Based on this correlation, what

*Murphy's Law, Book Two, 1980
**1992 Presidential campaign

may we conclude? That mood disorders cause creativity? Perhaps. But maybe creativity causes mood disorders. Then again, is it possible that creativity and mood disorders form a bi-directional causal loop? To complicate matters further, what about the possibility that some other variables, such as a genetic predisposition, cause both creativity and mood disorders?

Put another way, given a correlation between *A* and *B*, does *A* cause *B?* Does *B* cause *A?* Do *A* and *B* cause each other? Does *C* cause *A* and *B?* (See Figure 10-1.) Could there be some combination of these causal relationships? Unfortunately, a correlation alone does not (in fact, *cannot*) provide us with the answers to these questions.

Now, in some cases it is relatively safe to infer the direction of causation from a correlation. For example, there is a known positive correlation between rainfall and traffic accidents—the more it rains, the greater the number of traffic accidents. Clearly, rainfall causes accidents. (It is improbable that accidents cause rainfall!) To take another example, there appears to be a correlation between gender and aggressive behavior, in that boys typically are more aggressive than girls. Obviously, aggressiveness cannot cause gender; gender must, in some way, be causing aggressiveness.

Unfortunately, however, in most areas of life in general, and psychology in particular, there are very few circumstances in which causal explanations can be clearly determined from a correlation. The following are some examples of correlated variables about which people frequently (but erroneously) infer causality.

Example 1: Research indicates that watching violent television programs appears to be mildly but positively correlated with aggressive behavior (see Huesmann, 1982). This correlation does not prove, however, that TV violence causes aggressiveness. Perhaps aggressive people prefer to watch violent TV programs. Maybe aggressiveness and TV violence feed off each other in a "vicious cycle" (see Metathought XI, Bi-Directional Causation). Or, consider the possibility that family conflict causes both aggressive behavior and the watching of TV violence.

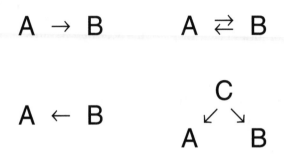

FIGURE 10-1   A Correlation between Event A and Event B with Four Possible Causal Relationships

Example 2: People who are depressed tend to have low self-esteem. In other words, depression and self-esteem are negatively (or inversely) correlated. But this doesn't prove the causal link (or links) between these two variables. Depression might cause low self-esteem. Conversely, low self-esteem might cause depression. Further, depression and low self-esteem may cause each other. Or, some other variables, such as chronic failure, distressing events, and learned helplessness might cause both depression and low self-esteem (see Metathought XII, Multiple Causation).

Example 3: Studies show that there is a positive relationship between "authoritative" (as opposed to "authoritarian" or "permissive") parents and socially competent children (Baumrind, 1983; Buri, Louiselle, Misukanis, & Mueller, 1988; Coopersmith, 1967). This evidence, however, is primarily correlational in nature. Thus, we must be very tentative regarding the conclusions we attempt to draw. We should take into account, for example, the possibility that other variables, such as high socio-economic status, a happy marriage, and/or common genes, also might be responsible for producing social competence.

Example 4: Most heroin addicts started on marijuana; thus, there is a positive correlation between heroin use and the previous marijuana use. But this correlation does not prove that marijuana use causes subsequent heroin use. Why not? Consider the fact that virtually all heroin addicts *originally* started on *milk*! Now, what does this correlation "prove"? That drinking milk in infancy eventually leads to hard drugs?

Consider also the correlations between homelessness and mental illness; obesity and the number of hours spent watching television; receiving poor grades in school and being in trouble with the law; dopamine and schizophrenia; kissing and pregnancy. In all of these instances (and countless more), *beware* of concluding causation based solely on correlation. Further, when a correlation is observed, be sure to consider all plausible pathways and directions of causation.

To give you some practice at applying these principles, try to identify some of the possible causal relationships, pathways, and explanations that could account for each of the correlations presented below.

Exercise 1. "Eveningness" and optimism appear to be negatively (inversely) correlated (Levy, 1985); that is, people who are "evening types" tend to be more pessimistic than "morning types." Why might this be true?

1. _Optimism may cause "morningness."_
2. _"Morningness" may cause optimism._
3. _Optimism and "morningness" may affect each other._
4. _Satisfying job may cause both optimism and "morningness."_

Exercise 2. Riots tend to occur with greater frequency during the hot, summer months than during other seasons of the year; thus there is a positive correlation between riots and summertime. Why? (*Hint:* Be sure to consider variables such as unemployment and vacation from school.)

1. _____
2. _____
3. _____
4. _____

Exercise 3. There appears to be a negative correlation between the neurotransmission of serotonin and depression. Why?

1. _____
2. _____
3. _____
4. _____

Exercise 4.a. A psychotherapist reports that, "Before the patient started seeing me for therapy, his life was a total mess. Since he's been in treatment with me, however, his life has completely turned around." Why?

1. _____
2. _____
3. _____
4. _____

Exercise 4.b. A psychotherapist reports that, "When the patient was seeing me for therapy, he was doing great. But since he terminated treatment, he's really gone downhill." Why?

1. _____
2. _____
3. _____
4. _____

Superstitions, Magical Thinking, and the Contiguity–Causation Error

Let us conclude with an interesting application of this Metathought to a particular type of faulty reasoning, the *Contiguity–Causation Error.* This mistake involves arriving at the erroneous conclusion that a cause and effect relationship exists between two events simply because the events occurred next to each other in time (that is, based on their *temporal contiguity*).[2]

For example, in the middle of a group therapy session, a member of the group starts to sob uncontrollably and then bursts out of the room. In attempting to explain his behavior, the other group members very likely would be tempted to rely on temporal contiguity by asking themselves, "What happened in the group just before he got upset?" In point of fact, however, the man's behavior could have been due to any number of causes, none of which necessarily occurred within the group immediately before he became upset.

Harry Stack Sullivan (1954) referred to this form of thinking as the *parataxic mode of experience.* Parataxic reasoning also may be seen as a kind of "magical thinking," because events that occur close together in time are construed as causally linked. As it turns out, most superstitions are based on parataxic reasoning. For example, if a football coach doesn't shave before a game, and his team then wins, he might assume that not shaving somehow caused the success. As a result, he may adopt this superstitious behavior for future games. Similarly, a gambler may be on a losing streak at the roulette table. If, however, she suddenly strikes it lucky, the Contiguity–Causation Error may lead her to conclude that the gentleman who just sat down nearby was the cause of her change in luck.

As these examples clearly illustrate, although correlations may provide us with accurate—and frequently very useful—information regarding *"what"* relationships exist, they cannot be counted on to answer the question, *"why?"* Even in those circumstances when a correlation strongly *implies* causation, remember that it does not *prove* causation.

Glossary Terms

The following terms (or variations) are defined in the Glossary:

behavior	experience
belief	explanation
bi-directional causation	fact
causal	infer
causal loop	mental illness
causality	mood
causation	parataxic reasoning
cause	*post hoc*
chronic	prediction
Contiguity–Causation Error	psychology
correlate	psychotherapy
correlation	reasoning
disorder	social
disposition	subsequent
effect	temporal contiguity
empirical	thinking
erroneous	treatment
event	variable

Notes

¹ For a definition and discussion of causal relationships, see Metathought III, Multiple Levels of Description. More comprehensive definitions and examples may be found in *Dictionary of Philosophy* (Angeles, 1981).

² This error in logic also is known as *post hoc, ergo propter hoc:* that is, the belief that because Event *B* follows Event *A*, then *B* must have been caused by *A*.

XI. Bi-Directional Causation: Causal Loops, Healthy Spirals, and Vicious Cycles

The ancestor of every action is a thought.
—RALPH WALDO EMERSON*

Thought is the child of Action.
—BENJAMIN DISRAELI**

See this egg. It is with this that the schools of theology and all the temples of the earth are to be overturned.
—DENIS DIDEROT***

Although we typically tend to think of causal relationships as being *uni-directional* (Event *A* causes Event *B*), frequently they are *bi-directional* (Event *A* causes Event *B*, *and* Event *B* causes Event *A*). In other words, variables may, and frequently do, affect each other. This relationship also may be referred to as a causal loop or, depending on our subjective evaluation of the particular situation, either a "healthy spiral" (if we happen to like it) or a "vicious cycle" (if we don't). (In this regard, see Metathought I, the Evaluative Bias of Language.)

*1803–1882, *Essays*, First Series
**1804–1881, *Vivian Grey*
***1713–1784, *Le Rêve d'Alembert*, pt. 1

$$A \rightleftarrows B$$

FIGURE 11-1 Bi-Directional Causation

As a prominent illustration of this Metathought, let's look at the endlessly debated question in psychology, "Does thought cause emotion, or does emotion cause thought? Which comes first? Which is the cause and which is the effect?" (see Berscheid, 1982; Mandler, 1975; Weiner, 1980; Zajonc, 1980). When viewed as a bi-directional relationship, however, the argument may be moot: clearly, thoughts and feelings affect each other.

To take another example, research indicates that the relationship between aggressive behavior and watching television violence is bi-directional (Huesmann, Lagerspetz, & Eron, 1983). That is, aggressive children are prone to watch violent TV programs, and television violence, in turn, results in aggressive behavior.

Consider also the bi-directional relationship between mental illness and one's social environment. Specifically, it is quite probable that cold, rejecting, and hostile parents can cause emotional and behavioral problems in their children. At the same time, don't ignore the possibility (and frequently the likelihood) that children with emotional and behavioral problems also might cause their parents to become cold, rejecting, and hostile!

Bi-directional relationships are as interesting as they are plentiful: hostility and rejection; weight gain and physical immobility; drug use and depression; optimism and success; pessimism and failure; self-esteem and popularity; thinking and language.

As an exercise, consider the bi-directional relationship between anxiety (Event *A*) and sexual dysfunction (Event *B*). First, describe some ways that anxiety (*A*) might impair sexual performance, thereby leading to sexual dysfunction (*B*). _____

_____

_____

_____

_____

Next, describe some ways that sexual dysfunction (*B*) can lead to anxiety (*A*). _____

_____

_____

_____

_____

Is it possible to determine which is (or was) the "initial" cause? If so, how?_____

_____

_____

_____

_____

_____

Under what circumstances might it be important to identify which was the initial cause? _____

_____

_____

_____

_____

_____

Under what circumstances might it be *unimportant* to identify which was the initial cause? _____

_____

_____

_____

_____

_____

For some more practice, select another bi-directional relationship (either from the list above or an original example from your own experience). First, describe the ways that Event *A* affects Event *B*.

_____

_____

_____

_____

_____

Then describe the ways that Event *B* affects Event *A*. _____

_____

_____

_____

_____

_____

Is it possible to determine which is (or was) the initial cause? If so, how?

_____

_____

_____

_____

_____

Under what circumstances might it be important to identify which was the initial cause? _____

_____

_____

_____

_____

Under what circumstances might it be unimportant to identify which was the initial cause? _____

_____

_____

_____

_____

As you can see, "cause" and "effect" are relative terms: a cause in one instance becomes an effect in another. From this perspective, asking the question, "Which comes first?" although interesting, may be unnecessary, irrelevant, even unanswerable. Thus, when faced with such chicken-and-egg questions, remember that your answer may depend entirely on where you happen to enter the causal loop!

Glossary Terms

The following terms (or variations) are defined in the Glossary:

affect	emotion
behavior	evaluation
bi-directional causation	event
causal	psychology
causal loop	social
causation	subjective
cause	thinking
dysfunction	uni-directional causation
effect	variable

Chapter **12**

XII. Multiple Causation: Not "Either/Or," but "Both/And"

It is very remarkable how often a symptom is determined in several ways, is "overdetermined."
—JOSEF BREUER & SIGMUND FREUD*

An effect may be, and usually is, the result of *several* causes, which are operating concurrently. Virtually every significant behavior has *many* determinants, and any single explanation is almost inevitably an oversimplification.

To take an example, what causes depression? Is it caused by early childhood trauma? Or a vital loss? Or a faulty belief system? Or a perception of failure? Or unresolved mourning? Or internalized anger? Or learned helplessness? Or a biochemical predisposition?

Now try replacing each *or* with *and*. Depression thus may be seen as caused by a *combination* of factors, including early childhood trauma, *and* a vital loss, *and* a faulty belief system, *and* a perception of failure, *and* unresolved mourning, *and* internalized anger, *and* learned helplessness, *and* a biochemical predisposition.

As another example, what causes aggression? Taking into account the principle of multiple causation, aggression appears to be due to some *combination* of profound frustration, and suppressed rage, and low self-esteem, and the reinforcement of aggressive behaviors, and the use of extreme punishment, and faulty role modeling, and social rejection (Feshbach & Weiner, 1986).

**Studies on Hysteria,* 1895

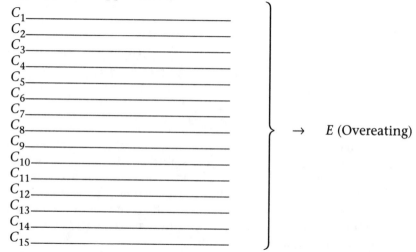

FIGURE 12-1   Multiple Causation

(*Note: C* = cause; *E* = effect.)

As an exercise, consider the multiple determinants of overeating. In the spaces below, list as many possible causes as you can think of. (Suggested answers appear in Appendix 2.)

$$C_1 \underline{\hspace{4cm}}$$
$$C_2 \underline{\hspace{4cm}}$$
$$C_3 \underline{\hspace{4cm}}$$
$$C_4 \underline{\hspace{4cm}}$$
$$C_5 \underline{\hspace{4cm}}$$
$$C_6 \underline{\hspace{4cm}}$$
$$C_7 \underline{\hspace{4cm}}$$
$$C_8 \underline{\hspace{4cm}} \rightarrow E \text{ (Overeating)}$$
$$C_9 \underline{\hspace{4cm}}$$
$$C_{10} \underline{\hspace{4cm}}$$
$$C_{11} \underline{\hspace{4cm}}$$
$$C_{12} \underline{\hspace{4cm}}$$
$$C_{13} \underline{\hspace{4cm}}$$
$$C_{14} \underline{\hspace{4cm}}$$
$$C_{15} \underline{\hspace{4cm}}$$

How might you put this Metathought into direct practice? First, in attempting to explain why an event occurred, don't limit your search to *one* cause. Instead, explore *multiple* plausible causes, *all* of which may be responsible for producing the effect. Second, every time you are faced with a question, issue, or problem that is presented in terms of *"either/or,"* stop for a moment. Now, try replacing *either/or,* with *both/and*. For example, the statement, "Prejudice is caused by either ignorance or hatred," becomes "Prejudice is caused by both ignorance and hatred." Then ask yourself, "Is this new formulation *useful*?" In a great number of situations, you are very likely to find that it is.

Gestalt therapists (see Perls, 1969) also would agree with this approach. In fact, it is common for the Gestalt psychotherapist to ask his or her client to replace the word *but* with *and*. For instance, "I like myself but I want to change" is replaced with "I like myself *and* I want to change." "I enjoy being alone but I need to be with people" is replaced with "I enjoy being alone *and* I need to be with people." "I love my mother but she drives me crazy," is replaced with "I love my mother *and* she drives me crazy." What is the rationale for this therapeutic technique? *But* is seen as divisive and thereby leads to fragmenting, splintering, and "disowning" parts of oneself. The result is psychological maladjustment. In contrast, *and* is integrative, thus fostering synthesis, unity, and a sense of wholeness—in short, psychological health.

Advanced Applications of Multiple Causation: Linear and Non-Linear Combinations

In a *linear* (or "additive") combination, even though an effect is due to several causes, the effect can theoretically be explained in terms of just one of the causes. In other words, each cause is, in itself, *sufficient* to produce the effect. Thus, a linear combination requires making a statement about only two variables—one cause and its effect. Consider, as an illustration, the causes of depression described above. Although depression involves multiple determinants, each cause alone may be sufficient to produce the same effect. Thus, depression appears to be due to a linear combination of causes.[1] To represent this concept algebraically (where C_1 and C_2 are causes and E is the effect): When $C_1 + C_2 \rightarrow E$, either C_1 or C_2 alone is sufficient to produce E. The same principle holds true, irrespective of the number of causes. Thus, when $C_1 + C_2 + C_3 + C_4 \rightarrow E$, the effect can be due to C_1 or C_2 or C_3 or C_4 independently.

In a *non-linear* (or "multiplicative") combination, by contrast, the effect *cannot* be explained without necessarily taking into account *at least two* causes. In other words, a non-linear combination *requires* making a statement about a third variable. Thus, where $C_1 \times C_2 \rightarrow E$, neither C_1 nor C_2 alone can produce the effect. In a non-linear combination, each causal factor is *necessary but not sufficient* to produce the effect. The statistical concept of an *interaction* (so named because the causes affect each other, or "interact") is, by definition, a non-linear combination.

Multiple Causation:
Linear Combination

$$C_1 + C_2 + C_3 = E$$

Multiple Causation:
Non-Linear Combination

$$C_1 \times C_2 \times C_3 = E$$

FIGURE 12-2

Note: C = cause; E = effect.

Examples of non-linear combinations include:

Heat × Oxygen = Fire
Blue × Yellow = Green
Ability × Motivation = Performance

In each of these non-linear examples, neither cause *alone* is capable of producing the effect; instead, they *must interact* with each other, or the effect cannot be achieved.

Glossary Terms

The following terms (or variations) are defined in the Glossary:

affect	event
antecedent	explanation
behavior	Gestalt therapy
belief	linear
causal	perception
causation	psychological
cause	reinforcement
concept	social
determinant	symptom
effect	variable

Notes

[1] As an historical note, Freud (1900/1953) used the term *overdetermination* to refer to a linear combination of causes, in which a number of different antecedent events (such as trauma, loss, and failure) combine to produce a psychological symptom (such as depression or anxiety).

XIII. Degrees of Causation: Not All Causes Are Created Equal

*Genius is one percent inspiration and
ninety-nine percent perspiration.*
—THOMAS ALVA EDISON*

'Tis the last straw that breaks the camel's back.
—ANONYMOUS**

In many situations, it may be overly simplistic to ask the question, "Is this a causal factor or not?" As discussed in Metathought XII, an effect may be (and usually is) the result of multiple causes. And these causes are likely to *vary in the degree to which they are responsible* for producing the effect. In other words, one cause may be more influential than another. This doesn't mean, however, that a cause with less weight is not responsible for the effect. In other words, it would be erroneous to conclude that a cause which contributes only a nominal proportion to the effect is therefore a "non-cause."

As an example, let's say a man wakes up early one morning, stumbles into the bathroom, and, while brushing his teeth, runs out of toothpaste. He becomes mildly annoyed. Before he leaves for work that morning, his wife scolds him for not earning enough money. His anger mounts. On the way to work his car breaks down, so he has to catch the bus. Now, he's furious. He finally arrives late for work, dashes into his office, and begins his assignments for the day. Then, his boss casually walks over to his desk and fires him. The guy is stunned. He tries to keep working, but he is in a daze. Then, when he inadvertently breaks a pencil lead, he suddenly loses all control, grabs his boss by the lapels, and launches him out of the sixteenth-story window.

*1847–1931, newspaper interview, quoted in *The Golden Book of Quotations*, 1964
**Quoted in Barber, *The Book of 1000 Proverbs*, 1876/1971

Now, why did the man kill his boss? What caused his behavior? To varying degrees, probably *all* of these events (and certainly more). Without a doubt, getting fired was one of the most important causes. And the pencil lead may have been tantamount to the proverbial straw that broke the camel's back. But can we completely rule out *any* of these events—including running out of toothpaste—as a "non-cause"? Certainly not.

This Metathought relates directly to the concept of personal—as well as legal—responsibility. For instance, a man may be seen as "more responsible" for deliberately throwing a glass against a wall, causing it to shatter, than he might be for lending his damaged bicycle to a friend, who subsequently has an accident on it. But that's not to say that the man has *no responsibility* for the bicycle accident. Rather, it is a matter of *degree*, however small.

Similarly, let's say that you choose to drive late at night through a section of the city which you know full well to be exceedingly dangerous. And, sure enough, no sooner do you enter the area than you are attacked by a gang of thugs. Now, where does the responsibility lie? Who should be held accountable? Without question, your assailants. But what about *you*? Based on the same line of reasoning, it would be both illogical and naive to maintain that you bear absolutely no responsibility, as small a proportion as it might be, for your ordeal.

To give you some practice at applying this Metathought, try the following exercise. First, select a situation involving multiple causation, either from examples in this book or, better yet, from your own personal experiences. You may wish to examine, for example, the factors that account for your decision to break off a romantic relationship, or for your choice of which college to attend, or even for your current mood. Second, list all plausible causal factors that could be contributing to the effect. Third, rank order the factors in terms of their relative impact on the final outcome. Fourth, assuming (for the sake of this exercise) that together they total 100% of the effect, assign relative weights, in the form of percentages, to each factor.

$$\left.\begin{array}{l} C_1\ (x\%) \\ C_2\ (y\%) \\ C_3\ (z\%) \end{array}\right\} \rightarrow \quad E$$

$$C_1(x\%) + C_2(y\%) + C_3(z\%) = E \text{ (linear combination)}$$
$$C_1(x\%) \times C_2(y\%) \times C_3(z\%) = E \text{ (non-linear combination)}$$

FIGURE 13-1   Degrees of Causation

(*Note: C* = cause; *E* = effect.)

As an illustration, let's say that you are interested in analyzing the factors that are causing your irritable mood. After completing the four steps outlined above, your responses might look something like this:

C_1 (50%) financial worries
C_2 (20%) pressure of final exams
C_3 (15%) tense relationship with roommate $\Big\} \rightarrow E$ (Irritable Mood)
C_4 (10%) an annoying baby pimple inside your lip
C_5 (5%) life in general

Do you have the idea? Now, try a couple on your own.

C_1 (%) _____
C_2 (%) _____
C_3 (%) _____ $\Big\} \rightarrow E$ ( )
C_4 (%) _____
C_5 (%) _____

C_1 (%) _____
C_2 (%) _____
C_3 (%) _____ $\Big\} \rightarrow E$ ( )
C_4 (%) _____
C_5 (%) _____

What are the primary lessons to be learned from this Metathought? First, remember that causation is not necessarily a dichotomous variable (that is, "causal" versus "non-causal"). Instead, causation can lie on a continuum with regard to its degree, magnitude, or weight (see Metathought V, Differentiating Dichotomous Variables and Continuous Variables). Next, attempt to assess the approximate proportion that each cause contributes to the outcome, keeping in mind that not all causes are equal. Finally, don't automatically disregard, ignore, or rule out causes solely because they possess less relative weight. In short, before reaching your conclusions, consider the contribution of *all* possible causes.

Glossary

The following terms (or variations) are defined in the glossary:

behavior	effect
causal	erroneous
causation	event
cause	linear
concept	mood
continuous variable	reasoning
decision	subsequent
dichotomous variable	variable

XIV. *Multiple Pathways of Causation: Different Causes, Same Effects*

Whether we force the man's property from him by pinching his stomach, or pinching his fingers, makes some difference anatomically; morally, none whatsoever.
—*JOHN RUSKIN**

All roads lead to Rome.
—*JEAN DE LA FONTAINE***

Any road leads to the end of the world.
—*EDWARD FITZGERALD****

A number of different antecedent conditions may lead to the same outcome. Put another way, the same observed result may spring from different causes. To take an example, the factors that cause a mother to become an alcoholic in one family may be completely different from the factors that cause a mother to become an alcoholic in another family, or from those factors that cause a mother to become an alcoholic in a third family. In other words, there are multiple routes or pathways[1] to alcoholism.

*1819–1900, *The Two Paths, V,* quoted in *The Pocket Book of Quotations,* Davidoff, 1952
**1621–1695, *Fables, XII,* quoted in *The Pocket Book of Quotations,* Davidoff, 1952
***1809–1883, *Polonius,* quoted in *The Pocket Book of Quotations,* Davidoff, 1952

$$C_1 \rightarrow E_1$$
$$C_2 \rightarrow E_1$$
$$C_3 \rightarrow E_1$$

FIGURE 14-1   Multiple Pathways of Causation

(*Note:* C = cause; E = effect.)

Here are some further illustrations of this Metathought:

LAUGHTER may be produced by a number of independent pathways, such as humor, nervousness, happiness, embarrassment, or physical tickling;

TEARS may be caused independently by sadness, joy, pain, frustration, anger, allergies, or direct ocular irritation (such as exposure to onions, soap, or smog);

MALE GENITAL ERECTION may be brought about by direct physical stimulation, by visual exposure to erotic photographs, by sexual fantasies, as a correlate of the REM sleep cycle, as a side effect of some antidepressant medications, or by being hanged by a rope from the neck until dead.

An extremely useful application of this Metathought involves identifying and examining the etiology of various types of psychopathology. Depression, for example, may be produced by numerous independent pathways, including:

>the ingestion of certain drugs (such as reserpine, methyldopa, oral contraceptives, or barbiturates);

>withdrawal from drugs (such as amphetamines or cocaine);

>vitamin deficiencies (such as pellagra, pernicious anemia, or thiamine deficiency);

>starvation;

>physical illness (such as hypothyroidism, Cushing's syndrome, or mononucleosis).

Depression also may be the result of "psychological" phenomena,[2] such as:

>faulty belief systems (unachievable expectations or goals);
>loneliness;

>helplessness;
>loss;
>failure;
>trauma;
>a sense of existential futility and meaninglessness.[3]

As an exercise, identify independent causal pathways that can produce anxiety (suggested responses appear in Appendix 2):

>_____ ;
>_____ ;
>_____ ;
>_____ ;
>_____ ;
>_____ ;
>_____ ;
>_____ ;
>_____ ;
>_____ ;
>_____ .

The notion of multiple causal pathways applies not only to the etiology of problems, but to their potential *resolution* as well. Specifically, in terms of psychopathology, there are *multiple pathways of treatment*. For example, depression may be successfully alleviated by psychopharmacology (such as heterocyclic antidepressants or Monoamine oxidase inhibitors), electroconvulsive therapy (ECT), cognitive psychotherapy, insight-oriented psychotherapy, emotional catharsis (such as the ventilation of anger), success experiences, supportive interpersonal relationships, or finding meaning and purpose in life.

Anxiety, too, may be reduced by a number of pathways, including psychopharmacology (such as benzodiazepines), cognitive therapy, insight-oriented psychotherapy, behavioral therapy (such as relaxation training, systematic desensitization, implosion, or flooding), exercise, a vacation, hypnosis, meditation, biofeedback, a change in jobs, supportive and comforting interpersonal relationships, or spiritual faith.

The moral of this Metathought? First, never assume *a priori* that similar outcomes must be the product of similar causes. Second, when exploring avenues of causation, always be on the lookout for alternate routes.

Glossary Terms

The following terms (or variations) are defined in the Glossary:

antecedent
a priori
belief
causal
causation
cause
cognitive
cognitive therapy
cognitive–behavioral therapy
concept
correlate
effect
etiology
event

existentialism
expectation
experience
insight
interpersonal
phenomena
physical
psychological
psychopathology
psychotherapy
syndrome
theory
treatment

Notes

[1] The concept of multiple pathways of causation is synonymous with the philosophical *principle of the plurality of causes* (see Angeles, 1981) and also is similar to the general systems theory term, *equifinality* (see Bertalanffy, 1968).

[2] In using the term *psychological,* I do not mean to suggest that these events are, in any way, "non-physical." I am, of course, assuming that *all* psychological phenomena necessarily have physical (biological, physiological, neurochemical, neuroanatomical, and other) components or correlates. (See Metathought III, Multiple Levels of Description.)

[3] This Metathought does not imply that pathways of causation are mutually exclusive.

Causal pathways can (and typically do) exist simultaneously; that is, *multiple pathways may involve multiple causation.* The point here is that each causal pathway alone is *sufficient,* and does not depend on the presence of another pathway, to produce the effect. This, in fact, is the distinction between the two Metathought principles, Multiple Causation (Metathought XII) and Multiple Pathways of Causation. Multiple Causation, by definition, always involves at least two causes that together produce a given effect. In Multiple Pathways, by contrast, there may be a single cause that is sufficient to produce the effect

Common
Misattributions

Chapter *15*

XV. The Fundamental Attribution Error: Underestimating the Impact of External Influences

> *Don't call a man honest just because he*
> *never had the chance to steal.*
> *—YIDDISH PROVERB*

> *One unable to dance blames the unevenness of the floor.*
> *—MALAY PROVERB*

How do we explain the causes of people's behavior? We typically attribute their actions either to their personality or to their circumstances. Put another way, we ascribe dispositional attributions or situational attributions. Dispositional attributions involve assigning the causes of behavior to people's personality traits, characteristics, or attitudes, that is, to "internal" influences. Situational attributions, in contrast, involve assigning the causes of behavior to people's circumstances, surroundings, or environment, that is, to "external" influences.

In reality, of course, behavior is due to a combination of many factors (see Metathought XII, Multiple Causation), both internal and external, that vary in the degree to which they are responsible for causing a person's actions (see Metathought XIII, Degrees of Causation). However, in arriving at causal attributions, we have a tendency to overestimate people's dispositions and to underestimate their situations. In other words, we are prone to weigh internal determinants too heavily, and external determinants too lightly. We are thus likely to explain others' behavior as resulting predominantly from their personality, while we often minimize (or even ignore) the importance of the particular situations in which they find themselves. This mistake is so prevalent, in fact, that the social psychologist Lee Ross (1977) termed it the Fundamental Attribution Error (see also Heider, 1958).[1]

What are some illustrations of this attributional bias? If people don't tip a waiter, we may conclude that they are stingy. If they don't go to work, they are lazy. If they say nice things, they are friendly. If they don't return phone calls, they are rude. If they cry, they are sensitive. If they don't smile, they are aloof. If they help you, they are caring. If they hurt you, they are cruel.

Notice how these attributions essentially disregard any external or situational factors that might be responsible for producing these behaviors. Consider, for instance, that people may not tip a waiter because the service was atrocious; they may not go to work because of a family emergency; they may say nice things because their behavior is being monitored; they may not return phone calls because they haven't received any messages; they may cry because they are in the midst of a tragedy; they may not smile because it's been "one of those days"; they may help you because their paycheck depends on it; and they may hurt you because you have hurt them. Remember that at any given time, how people behave depends *both* on what they bring to the situation ("who" they are), *as well as* the situation itself ("where" they are). Thus, we must guard against our tendency to minimize or discount the impact of external influences.

To take another example, imagine that a patient sits in your office for a clinical intake interview. During the interview, you observe that she is extremely quiet, she speaks in hushed tones, she squirms and fidgets in her chair, her hands tremble, and she avoids making direct eye contact with you. What is causing her to behave this way? If you are like most people, your first inclination probably would be to explain her behavior in terms of her personality characteristics. You might conclude, for instance, that she is an introverted, high-strung, insecure, or emotionally unstable person. You are liable, moreover, to overlook any number of situational factors that also could account for her behavior. For example, the patient's demeanor may be a consequence of the formality of the interview, an argument that she just had with her boyfriend, her just having received distressing news, the demands of her time schedule, or possibly even your own behavior. In short, the *circumstances themselves* may be stressful.

As another illustration, consider the dilemma of the homeless. An observer is likely to explain homeless people's condition as being due to characterological or personality factors, such as laziness, moral weakness, alcoholism, or mental illness. These attributions, however, fail to take into account the situational factors that can (and do) perpetuate homelessness, such as a lack of affordable housing, job scarcity, discrimination, and a depressed economy.

The following exercise serves to underscore the enormous, yet typically unnoticed, power of the social situation in influencing our feelings, attitudes, and behavior. Imagine yourself in the following scenarios and how you might respond to the simple question, "So, how are you doing?" For each situation, indicate not only what you might say, but also provide a brief description of your probable demeanor, body language, and the emotional tone of your response.

With your parents: _____
With your sibling:_____
With your grandparent: _____
With your child: _____
With your best friend: _____
With your current "significant other": _____
With your ex-"significant other":_____
With someone whom you know dislikes you: _____
With someone whom you dislike: _____
With an eight-year-old child: _____
With an eighty-year-old adult: _____
With your teacher: _____
With your therapist:_____
With your minister/priest/rabbi:_____
With your boss: _____
With your physician:_____
With a police officer: _____
With a used car salesman: _____
With a friendly waitress: _____
With a crabby receptionist: _____
With a beggar on the street:_____
While exercising: _____
While cramming for a test:_____
While doing the laundry: _____
At a party: _____
At a funeral: _____
At a job interview: _____
At a singles bar: _____
On a first date:_____
While having sex: _____

In looking over your answers, observe that *all* the variability in your responses is attributable to the situations themselves, because both you and the initial question were fixed and held constant. Before we move on, one final point deserves mention. Can you determine which of these responses reflects the "real" you? Notice that this question is, in itself, virtually unanswerable without also taking into account the *context* of the situation.

One of the most intriguing aspects of the Fundamental Attribution Error is that it frequently becomes *reversed* when people attempt to explain *their own* behavior. In other words, persons perceiving their own actions tend to overemphasize the impact of situational factors, while underestimating the impact of their own dispositional characteristics. The term *Actor–Observer Bias* (Jones & Nisbett, 1972) refers to the tendency for observers to overestimate the importance of another person's dispositions, but for that person (the "actor") to overestimate the importance of the situation in explaining his or her own behavior.

To take an example, let us return to the scenario of the clinical intake interview described above. An observer (in this case, the clinician) would be inclined to explain the patient's behavior primarily in terms of her dispositional characteristics ("This patient has an Anxiety Disorder with Avoidant Personality Features"). The patient, in contrast, is likely to explain her own behavior principally in terms of the circumstances that she is experiencing ("This therapist is so pushy, intrusive, and obnoxious that he's making me nervous"). In other words, the observer (clinician) overemphasizes dispositional causes, while the actor (patient) overemphasizes situational causes.

What is responsible for these attributional errors? Social psychologists have identified two principal sources: *cognitive biases* and *motivational biases*.

Cognitive biases refer to systematic mistakes that derive from limits that are inherent in our capacity to process information. Because of our intrinsic cognitive limitations, we attempt to simplify our thinking by utilizing various mental "shortcuts" that permit us to process information more rapidly and efficiently (albeit less accurately). For instance, because we are not capable of perceiving everything in our environment, our focus is automatically drawn to the most prominent, conspicuous or "eye-catching"—that is, *perceptually salient*—stimuli. Further, we rely heavily on salient information to help us explain the world around us. Unfortunately, however, perceptual salience leads us to formulate biased and inaccurate causal attributions (Taylor & Fiske, 1975). Specifically, we are prone to equate the most *perceptually salient* stimuli with the most *causally influential* stimuli.

How does this relate to the Fundamental Attribution Error? When somebody behaves, our attention is focused, almost instinctively, on the *person,* not on his or her *environment.* As noted by the eminent social psychologist Fritz Heider (1958), "Behavior...has such salient properties that it tends to engulf the field." In other words, the person's behavior so dominates our perceptions that the situation itself fades into relative obscurity. Thus, the salience of the person's behavior leads us to ascribe dispositional attributions of causality.

The Actor–Observer Bias also can be explained as a function of perceptual salience. That is, when *we* behave, our attention is focused not on ourselves, but on our *situation.* Because our environment is most salient to us, we are apt to perceive it as more causally influential. Thus, in explaining our own behavior, we are prone to arrive at situational, rather than dispositional, attributions.[2]

In sum, the observer focuses on the actor, which leads to dispositional attributions; by contrast, the actor focuses on the environment, which leads to situational attributions.

Motivational biases refer to systematic mistakes that derive from our efforts to satisfy our own personal needs, such as our desire for self-esteem, power, or prestige. Simply put, motivational biases serve the function of making us *feel better* (usually about ourselves), even if they do so at the expense of distorting, obscuring, or falsifying reality.

One of our most powerful psychological drives is our need for control. Without a sense of personal control over our lives, the world would seem unsafe, threatening, and dangerous. How do we attempt to achieve control? One very important way is by seeking to explain events around us—that is, by assigning causal attributions (Kelley, 1967). We thus strive to understand our world so that it will become more predictable and, therefore, controllable.

Are we motivated to prefer one type of causal attribution over another? It would appear so. From early childhood, we are socialized (particularly in Western cultures) to believe that people can control their destiny and are the masters of their fate. Society, then, generally condones dispositional attributions, while it discourages situational attributions.

Why? It is extremely unsettling to believe that people are at the mercy of unpredictable, haphazard, or random events that lie beyond their control. We would prefer, instead, to believe that people must have power over their fate. After all, if we assume that other people have control over *their* outcomes, it reassures us that we, too, can control *our* outcomes. Thus, it makes us feel better to assign dispositional, rather than situational, attributions.

So strong, in fact, is our need to believe in a dispositional (internal) locus of control, that we frequently fool ourselves into overestimating the degree of control that we actually do have, while underestimating the impact of external factors that lie beyond our control. Put another way, we simply don't have as much control over people and events as we'd like to believe that we do. Nevertheless, making dispositional attributions provides us with an *illusion* of control. We are prone, therefore, to exaggerate our perceptions of controllability.

One very unfortunate consequence of this motivational bias is that people who are harmed by forces that are truly out of their control may be held more responsible for their circumstances than they should be. In other words, our illusion of control may lead us to blame people for the bad things that happen to them.

Why does this occur? Melvin Lerner (1970) theorized that we have great difficulty accepting the unfairness and injustices of life. Further, we have a strong need to believe that we live in a "just world," a world in which good is rewarded and bad is punished. This belief leads us to conclude that people get what they deserve, and deserve what they get. In a just world those who succeed must merit their success; likewise, those who suffer must deserve their suffering.

Instances of "just world" attributions abound:

>*"Rape victims must have behaved seductively."*
>*"Battered spouses must have had it coming to them."*
>*"People who get cancer must have brought it on themselves."*
>*"Victims of persecution must be guilty of something, or they wouldn't be persecuted."*
>*"What goes around, comes around."*
>*"Sooner or later, your karma will catch up with you."*

Or, taken to its illogical extreme, in the vernacular of so-called "New Age" metaphysics, every human being is completely responsible for everything that happens to them, because "we all create and manifest our own reality." From this point of view, even a baby born with AIDS is seen as fully responsible for choosing that reality.

What compels people to make such attributions? Once again, in all likelihood, to preserve their illusion of control. Simply put, it is psychologically more comforting to blame others for the disasters that befall them, rather than face the cold reality that we live in an unjust world, a world in which such events can happen at random. After all, if negative events are uncontrollable, they could just as easily happen to *us*. By contrast, if the world is just, then presumably we can avoid catastrophe by behaving properly. In other words, by assigning dispositional attributions, we hope to experience a greater sense of control over our destiny.

Research shows that blaming people for accidents, for example, makes the events seem more predictable and hence avoidable by the self. Further, the more severe the consequences of the accident, the greater the blame we are likely to assign. In an experiment conducted by Elaine Walster (1966), subjects listened to one of several versions of a story, all of which began with a car that had been parked on a hill, and then accidentally rolled down. In one version, the car struck a tree, resulting in minimal damage. In another version, the car missed the tree, but struck another vehicle, damaging its bumper. In a third version, the car rolled into a shop, seriously injuring the shopkeeper and a small child. Subjects were then asked to ascribe blame based on the facts provided.

Walster found that greater blame was assigned according to the seriousness of the accidents. Thus, when the damage was minimal, subjects did not find the car's owner to be particularly blameworthy; however, when people were seriously injured, subjects believed that the owner was more responsible (for example, for not having had his brakes checked recently) and therefore ought to be punished. Walster concluded that subjects appeared to judge guilt not just on the act itself, but on the severity of the consequences of the act.[3] Here again, it appears that, in an effort to satisfy our needs for feeling less threatened by the world around us, we have a motivational bias to assign dispositional attributions.

What can we conclude about the Fundamental Attribution Error? This simple but powerful principle probably is the single most important lesson of twentieth-century social psychology. Keep this in mind whenever you attempt to explain someone's behavior: *Never underestimate the power of the situation.*

Glossary Terms

The following terms (or variations) are defined in the Glossary:

Actor–Observer Bias
ascribe
attitude
attribution
behavior
belief
bias
causal
causality
cause
clinical
cognitive
cognitive bias
consequence
determinant
dilemma
disorder
disposition
event
experience
explanation

external
external attribution
fact
Fundamental Attribution Error
internal
internal attribution
introvert
judgment
mental
mental illness
motivational bias
perception
personality
personality trait
prediction
psychological
psychology
random
social
stimulus
thinking

Notes

[1] For a series of research studies that empirically demonstrate the Fundamental Attribution Error, see Jones and Harris (1967), Napolitan and Goethals (1979), and Ross, Amabile, and Steinmetz (1977).

[2] See Storms (1973) for experimental evidence supporting the perceptual salience explanation of the Actor–Observer Bias.

[3] Similarly, the Swiss psychologist Jean Piaget (1948) found that children assign blame primarily on the severity of an event's consequences.

Chapter *16*

XVI. The Intervention–Causation Fallacy: The Cure Doesn't Prove the Cause

Although traditional psychotherapy has insisted that therapeutic practices have to be based on findings of etiology, it is possible that certain factors might cause neuroses during early childhood and that entirely different factors might relieve neuroses during adulthood.
—EDITH WEISSKOPF-JOELSON*

Treatability [is] not a legitimate criterion of illness.
—THOMAS SZASZ**

Our ability to *modify* an event does not, *per se,* prove what originally *caused* the event. In other words, we cannot necessarily determine an event's cause solely on the basis of its response to a particular intervention. As such, the solution to a problem does not inherently point to its etiology. To believe otherwise would be to fall prey to the *Intervention–Causation Fallacy.* To take a very obvious example, we may be able to surgically remove a kidney stone, but our capacity to do so does not, in any way, explain what originally caused the creation and development of the kidney stone.

In the field of mental health, the most prominent incarnation of this error in thinking is the *Treatment–Etiology Fallacy.* This refers to arriving at the erroneous conclusion that a positive response to a medical treatment inherently proves that there was a medical cause. Counterintuitive as it may seem, a

*Quoted in Viktor E. Frankl's *Man's Search for Meaning,* 1959
***Insanity,* 1987

favorable response to medication is *not* proof of disease. Nevertheless, if a psychotropic drug, for instance, is successful in alleviating the symptoms of a diagnosed mental disorder, many people wrongly conclude that the disorder therefore must have been caused by—or in fact *is*—a biological illness.

Let's explore these notions more fully by means of the following hypothetical scenarios. In the first example, imagine that you are practically crawling out of your skin with anxiety about an upcoming exam. In a state of near panic, you bolt to your medicine cabinet where you store your prescription of "mother's little helper" (i.e., Valium) for just such occasions. Within minutes after ingesting the precious yellow pill, lo and behold, your anxiety has vanished. What caused your anxiety to cease? Obviously, the Valium. But what caused your anxiety to occur in the first place? Can we, solely on the basis of its positive response to a prescription medication, attribute the etiology of your anxiety as being due to a biological illness? Of course not.

As another example, let's say that by the end of an exceptionally stressful day, you've developed a splitting headache. Once you've downed a couple of aspirin, however, your headache is history. Now, what cured the headache? The aspirin. But as for determining the initial cause of your headache, what are we to conclude? That you were suffering from a medical condition due to a "lack of aspirin?" Preposterous, right?

Let's examine one more scenario. Suppose that we observe someone with a diagnosis of schizophrenia who displays signs of auditory hallucinations, paranoid delusions, and bizarre affect. After we give him several doses of a powerful antipsychotic drug, his hallucinations diminish, his delusions abate, and his affect stabilizes. Did the medication reduce his symptoms? Yes. But can we take this favorable response to medication as incontrovertible proof that schizophrenia is, therefore, a biological disease? Using the same line of logic as in the above two examples, the answer is *no*.

This is not to argue that emotional or mental disorders don't have biological *correlates*. It would be shocking if they didn't. In fact, I would argue that *all* thoughts, feelings, perceptions, and experiences—both "normal" and "abnormal"—are reflected or mapped, in some form, in some configuration, in the human body (see Metathought III, Multiple Levels of Description). But remember, a *correlate* is not the same thing as a *cause* (see Metathought X, Correlation Does Not Prove Causation), and biological *differences* are not, *per se,* equivalent to biological *pathology* (see Metathought III, Multiple Levels of Description). Further, even if we were to hypothesize that all mental disorders are, in fact, rooted in biological pathology, don't make the mistake of assuming that their favorable response to medication provides the evidence. Again, a positive response to medical treatment is not proof of medical disease.

To underscore this last point, imagine a scenario in which you receive regular injections of an extremely valuable medication that virtually eliminates all signs and symptoms of anxiety, depression, and emotional distress. Assume further that, immediately upon receiving your dosage, you invariably and instantaneously feel significantly better, irrespective of your psychological status prior to the treatment. Last, suppose you discover that the precious medication is, in fact, an opioid analgesic by the chemical name of diacetyl morphine (better known as *heroin*).

On the basis of this information, what conclusions can you draw? That you are suffering from some kind of medical problem because the prescribed treatment always "improves" your status? That you, in fact, must have a "disease," because after receiving your medicine you consistently experience less "dis-ease?" That your response to the treatment provides insight into the etiology of your pre-existing "condition?" That your medical condition is attributable to a "chemical imbalance"—namely, a deficiency of heroin in your bloodstream?

In closing, it is important to keep in mind that, although the solution to a problem does not *necessarily* provide proof of its cause, there certainly are instances where a successful intervention *can*, in itself, determine such cause. Take, for example, a situation where filling your empty tank with gasoline serves to answer the question of why your car wouldn't start. Here, the intervention clearly would establish the cause of the problem.

The following exercise is intended, therefore, to provide you with some practice at identifying the relationship—or lack thereof—between interventions (solutions) and etiology (causes).

First, briefly describe three instances in which the cause of a problem *can* be determined directly from its solution (in other words, when a successful intervention *does* inherently provide proof of etiology).

1. _____
_____
_____
_____

2. _____
_____
_____
_____

3. _____
_____
_____
_____

Next, describe three instances in which the cause of a problem *cannot* be determined directly from its solution (that is, when a successful intervention *does not* inherently provide proof of etiology).

1._____

_____

_____

_____

2._____

_____

_____

_____

3._____

_____

_____

_____

Glossary Terms

The following terms (or variations) are defined in the Glossary:

affect	hypothetical
attribution	i.e.
belief	insight
causation	Intervention–Causation Fallacy
cause	logic
correlate	mental disorder
counterintuitive	normal
criterion	pathological
delusion	*per se*
diagnosis	perception
disease	prescription
disorder	psychological
emotion	psychotic
erroneous	psychotropic
etiology	response
event	symptom
experience	thinking
explanation	treatment
fallacy	Treatment–Etiology Fallacy

Chapter **17**

XVII. The Consequence–Intentionality Fallacy: The Effect Doesn't Prove the Intent

Never attribute to malice that which is adequately explained by stupidity.
—ARTHUR BLOCH*

Nonintentionality is one of the criteria of mental illness.
—THOMAS SZASZ**

How do we go about determining the intent of someone's behavior? Quite commonly, we base our explanation solely on the *result* of the behavior. That is, we assume that the consequences of the behavior directly reflect the person's intent. And in many cases, this is likely to be an accurate assessment. However, the effect of someone's behavior does not, *per se, prove* the intent of the behavior. In other words, intentionality cannot be proven solely by consequences.

As a vivid illustration, let us examine one of the most puzzling and disturbing occurrences in the entire realm of human behavior: self-mutilation. The deliberate self-infliction of bloody wounds, typically by means of a razor, knife

*Murphy's Law, Book Two, 1980
**Insanity, 1987

or needle, is, unfortunately, not an infrequent event in psychiatric inpatient hospital settings. And as you might well imagine, the reactions of those who witness such behavior (staff and patients alike) range from shock, horror, disgust, and outrage to sympathy, compassion, and pity, to terror, panic, and frantic helplessness. In a word, self-mutilation invariably stirs up lots of *attention.*

Thus, the *consequences* of the behavior are crystal clear. But how do we explain why the behavior occurred in the first place? Can we rely on the effects of the patient's behavior on others to infer that gaining attention was, therefore, her primary goal? In other words, does the effect prove the intent? Although seeking the attention of others is one very tempting (and certainly plausible) explanation, before we jump to this conclusion let us consider some other possible reasons that might motivate self-mutilating behavior.[1]

1. *Self-punishment:* "I am so evil, I *deserve* to be hurt."
2. *Sensory stimulation:* "I'd rather feel *something*—even pain—than nothing, emptiness, or numbness."
3. *Confirmation of life:* "I feel dead inside. Seeing my own blood reassures me that I do have something inside of me."
4. *Reification of emotion:* "My emotional pain is confusing because it isn't tangible. By cutting myself and seeing my blood, it makes my pain somehow seem more *real.*"
5. *Catharsis:* "I just want to get the pain that's inside, outside. I'm trying to relieve this horrible pressure that's built up inside of me."
6. *Revenge against pain:* "It's like my way of getting back at the pain."
7. *Displacement of anger:* "It's safer to hurt myself than the person I *really* want to hurt."
8. *Psychological control:* "My emotional pain is totally out of my control. At least when I cut myself, I get some control over how much pain I feel, where I feel it, and when I feel it."
9. *Suicide:* "I just want to end this pain—once and for all."

Even granting the possibility of these explanations, an observer would not necessarily be wrong in asserting that the patient was mutilating herself simply so that others would pay attention to her. The patient's intent may indeed have been principally (or even exclusively) to gain the attention of others. But the flaw in thinking occurs when the observer draws this conclusion *solely* on the basis of the consequences of the patient's behavior. In other words, the observer should not assume that the effect, in and of itself, proves the intent.

To take another example, let's evaluate the most prevalent of all the male sexual dysfunctions—premature ejaculation—as viewed from the psychoanalytic perspective. One of the most common consequences of premature ejaculation is that the man's partner is left feeling unsatisfied, frustrated, and angry because she has been deprived of a pleasurable sexual experience. But do her reactions reflect the man's intent, conscious or otherwise? Psychoanalytic theory would have us believe so.

Psychoanalytic theorists maintain that premature ejaculation is a neurotic symptom of deeper psychopathology (see Kaplan, 1974). Specifically, Freudian theory contends that premature ejaculators harbor unconscious feelings of sadistic hatred toward women. Premature ejaculation thus serves the unconscious functions of degrading and defiling the man's partner (symbolically, his mother), while also depriving her of pleasure. On the basis of this theory, psychoanalytic treatment attempts to uncover and resolve the patient's unconscious Oedipal conflicts and sadistic orientation toward women, which supposedly then results in an automatic improvement in his sexual functioning. The treatment sessions are conducted two to five times a week, over a period of several years, and employ the standard psychoanalytic techniques of free association, dream interpretation, and analysis of transference.

How valid are these theoretical assumptions and therapeutic procedures? Simply put, not very. In point of fact, decades of research have failed to support the Freudian tenet that the primary cause of premature ejaculation is unconscious hostility toward women. Further, there is no empirical evidence of any systematic correlation between premature ejaculation and either specific sexual conflicts or other forms of psychopathology. Moreover, clinical outcome research shows that psychoanalysis, as a method of treatment, is virtually worthless for premature ejaculation.

On what basis, then, did psychoanalysts develop their theories and reach their conclusions? It would appear that they might have fallen prey to a misattribution of causation by confusing consequences with intentionality; that is, they seem to have erroneously concluded that the *effects* of premature ejaculation prove its *cause*.

I am not arguing that unconscious hostility never contributes to the occurrence of premature ejaculation. Rather, as with the case of self-mutilating behavior, I am pointing out that consequences do not *necessarily* prove intentionality. In other words, intent cannot be determined solely by the effect.

What, then, are some alternative explanations for premature ejaculation? First, it may be due to faulty learning patterns (for example, stressful conditions during the young man's initial sexual encounters). Second, it may be a consequence of the man's hypersensitivity to erotic sensation. Third, it may be the result of the man's excessive concern over his partner's response (i.e., "performance anxiety"). Fourth, according to systems theory it may be a manifestation of a couple's maladaptive interpersonal dynamics. Fifth, it may be due to the man's failure to perceive preorgastic sensations which are necessary to bring the reflex function under control. Sixth, although rarely the case, it may be caused by certain medical conditions (such as local disease of the posterior urethra, multiple sclerosis, or other degenerative neurological disorders). Clearly, premature ejaculation is a complex phenomenon that, in all likelihood, involves a combination of both multiple causation as well as multiple pathways of causation (see Metathoughts XII and XIV, respectively).

The case of suicide is yet another instance where people frequently are quick to explain the intent of someone's behavior on the basis of the effects of the behavior. What are the consequences when a person takes his or her own life? The impact on others is, almost invariably, profound. They usually are left to struggle with intense feelings of hurt, guilt, sorrow, shame, remorse, or even animosity and resentment.

What motivates people to kill themselves? It is a common belief (held by many therapists and the general population alike) that suicide is, in essence, an act of anger and hostility, directed not just toward oneself, but toward others as well. On what grounds do people base this assumption? Here again, probably on the *consequences* of the act. The feelings evoked in others by suicide are so striking that it may seem as though the person *must* have intended to cause them. However, consequences do not prove intentionality. If, for example, somebody's suicide were to leave others feeling hurt or guilty, it would be a mistake to conclude that this was, therefore, the person's primary motive. People commit suicide for many reasons, of which "getting back" at others is but one.

In fact, as preposterous as it may seem, even the suicidal act itself is not necessarily proof of suicidal intent. Consider the tragically ironic scenario of a person who may be attempting to communicate a "cry for help" to others by means of a dramatic suicidal gesture, but who miscalculates the lethality of her method. The hapless individual may inadvertently succeed in committing suicide by, for instance, underestimating a fatal dosage of sleeping pills. Thus, even a suicidal outcome does not, *per se,* prove suicidal intent.

As a final illustration of this Metathought, let us examine the consequences and possible motives of so-called passive-aggressive behavior. What does this term mean? In clinical psychology it refers to a person's indirect expression of anger or hostility through seemingly innocuous or innocent behavior. For instance, the individual may display passive and negativistic resistance to the demands of others in the form of procrastination, dawdling, lateness, stubbornness, inefficiency, or "forgetfulness."

In its extreme form, it temporarily achieved the status of a full-blown mental disorder, classified in the *Diagnostic and Statistical Manual of Mental Disorders* (American Psychiatric Association, 1987) as Passive Aggressive Personality Disorder.[2] According to the DSM, "The name of this disorder is *based on the assumption* [emphasis added] that such people are passively expressing covert aggression" (p. 356). How does an observer make this assumption? By inferring the person's intent. And on what grounds is this intent inferred? Of course, almost invariably by the *consequences* of the person's behavior. Thus, the attribution of passive-aggressiveness is gauged primarily by the reactions of others who feel upset, frustrated, or angered by the person's seemingly innocent (yet "covertly hostile") actions. Consider these scenarios:

The employee who frequently misplaces his work orders
The housewife who repeatedly forgets to hang up clean bath towels

The student who consistently comes late to class
The therapy patient who habitually reschedules his appointments
The supervisor who routinely mispronounces her employee's name
The husband who forgets his wife's birthday present at work
The teenager who loses the family's house keys
The young woman who yawns throughout a dinner date
The executive who is "too busy" to return phone calls
The person who asks for advice, but politely rejects all suggestions.

All of these situations (and countless more) are ripe for attributions (or, perhaps more accurately, *accusations*) of passive-aggressive intent, which frequently assume some variant of the following exchange:

Person A: "Your behavior upset me. Therefore, you must have *intended* to upset me."

Person B: "But I didn't do it deliberately!"

Person A: "Then you must have *unconsciously* intended to upset me!"

As you can see, this is "checkmate," leaving Person B in the unenviable position of being completely powerless to disprove Person A's virtually invincible indictment.

What is the lesson to be learned here? We cannot safely infer other people's intentions (conscious or unconscious) solely on the basis of the consequences of their behavior. How can we overcome the problem of the Consequence–Intentionality Fallacy? One antidote is to force yourself to think about other plausible causes of the behavior, in addition to the one suggested directly by its consequences. (This process may be seen as analogous to exploring multiple pathways of causation; see Metathought XIV.) In other words, when attempting to understand or explain why someone behaved in a particular way, *consider alternative intents.*

To give you some practice in applying this antidote, let's analyze the following scenarios. For each event, first state the likely consequence of the behavior in question. Then, identify as many alternative intents as you can that could also plausibly account for the behavior.

1. *A spouse who has an extramarital affair*
Primary Consequence:

_____

Alternative Intents:

_____

_____

_____

2. *Parents who decline to financially support their adult son*
Primary Consequence:

Alternative Intents:

3. *A teenager who runs away from home*
Primary Consequence:

Alternative Intents:

Glossary Terms

The following terms (or variations) are defined in the Glossary:

analogous
antidote
assumption
attribution
behavior
belief
category
causation
cause
clinical
conscious
consequence
Consequence–Intentionality Fallacy
correlation
criteria
Diagnostic and Statistical Manual
   of Mental Disorders (DSM)

disease
disorder
displacement
DSM
dynamics
dysfunction
effect
emotion
empirical
erroneous
evaluation
event
existence
experience
explanation
fallacy
i.e.

infer
intentionality
interpersonal
interpretation
mental illness
motive
neurotic
per se
personality disorder
phenomenon
psychoanalysis
psychological
psychology

psychopathology
reification
resistance
response
sensory
symptom
theoretical
theory
thinking
transference
treatment
unconscious
vivid

Notes

[1] I collected this set of explanations over a period of several years at an inpatient psychiatric treatment center where I worked as the clinical supervisor. These quotes were taken virtually verbatim from the patients themselves, as well as from the team of psychiatrists, psychologists, and counselors at the weekly treatment planning conferences.

[2] I say temporarily because, in the most recent edition of the DSM (American Psychiatric Association, 1994), Passive Aggressive Personality Disorder was voted out of existence as a formal diagnostic category.

XVIII. The "If I Feel It, It Must Be True" Fallacy: The Truth Hurts; But So Do Lies

My mother loves me.
I feel good.
I feel good because she loves me.

I am good because I feel good
I feel good because I am good
My mother loves me because I am good.

My mother does not love me.
I feel bad.
I feel bad because she does not love me
I am bad because I feel bad
I feel bad because I am bad
I am bad because she does not love me
She does not love me because I am bad.
—R. D. LAING*

An Englishman thinks he is moral
when he is only uncomfortable.
—GEORGE BERNARD SHAW**

I never give them hell. I just tell the
truth, and they think it's hell.
—HARRY S TRUMAN***

Knots, 1970
**1856–1950, *Man and Superman*
***1884–1972, cited in William Safire, *Safire's Political Dictionary,* from The *New International Dictionary of Quotations,* Miner & Rawson, 1994

We rely on our feelings for many purposes, the most fundamental of which involves determining whether we like something or not. Although specific emotions (such as anger, sadness, happiness, or fear) vary tremendously in terms of their individual and unique characteristics, they all, to some degree, reveal the extent to which something *pleases* or *displeases* us. Our feelings thereby serve as the basis on which we formulate our subjective evaluations of events around us.

How do we come to know what we are feeling? Put another way, by what means do we identify our emotions? Simply stated, primarily by an awareness of our *somatic* or *physiological sensations*. Remember that emotions, like all psychological phenomena, are rooted in biochemistry and are therefore "mapped" in various physiological configurations (see Metathought III, Multiple Levels of Description). We thus learn to link particular visceral sensations to specific emotional states.

In general, when our somatic condition is comprised of comfortable or pleasurable sensations, we experience "feeling good"; in contrast, when it involves uncomfortable or unpleasurable sensations, we experience "feeling bad." In this way, our physiological status along the comfort–discomfort continuum functions as a barometer to help us ascertain our overall feelings.

As noted above, our feelings tell us whether or not an event is pleasing. But how do we determine whether or not the event is *true*? In many cases, we rely principally on our subjective perceptions of the event. Do you see a problem here?

The fact is, our experience of emotional comfort or discomfort is not a valid gauge for differentiating what is true from what is false. In other words, how we *feel* about an event is not proof of its *veracity*. Hence, what feels good isn't necessarily correct, and what feels bad isn't necessarily incorrect. Conversely, what feels bad isn't necessarily correct, and what feels good isn't necessarily incorrect.

TABLE 18-1 Interactions of Feelings and Events

Subjective Feelings	Veracity of Event	Descriptive Summary of Condition
Comfort +	**True +**	
Discomfort–	**False –**	
1. +	+	congruence between comfort and truth; receiving accurate and pleasing evaluations
2. +	–	living in a fantasy world, "in denial" of distressing facts; incongruent feelings
3. –	+	facing a painful truth; "unjustifiable defensiveness"
4. –	–	stung by a false accusation; "justifiable defensiveness"

Stated in a different way, feelings and truth are not intrinsically correlated; in fact, they are conceptually independent of (that is, *orthogonal* to) each other. As such, subjective feelings of comfort may be prompted by a pleasing truth as well as by a pleasing falsehood. Similarly, feelings of emotional discomfort may be due to a displeasing truth as well as a displeasing falsehood.

By treating subjective feelings (comfort versus discomfort) and the veracity of an event (true versus false) as two independent variables, I have summarized in Table 18-1 the four combinations to which they give rise, namely: comfortable truths, comfortable falsehoods, uncomfortable truths, and uncomfortable falsehoods.[1]

Comfortable Truths

This condition, represented in Row 1 of Table 18-1, involves pleasurable feelings that are a consequence of factual events, truthful assertions, or accurate observations. You may, for instance, experience pride, satisfaction, self-esteem, or self-respect when you solve a difficult problem, achieve a desired goal, or fulfill your own personal standards and expectations.

These situations also include feeling good about accurate evaluations, assessments, or appraisals from others. This may take the form of recognition, praise, or even constructive criticism from your teacher, coach, employer, or therapist. Similarly, it may entail receiving honest and valid feedback from a trusted family member, friend, or colleague. In sum, these are conditions in which there exists a state of congruence between the veracity of an event and one's experience of emotional comfort.

Comfortable Falsehoods

This condition, represented in Row 2, involves feeling emotionally comfortable in regard to statements, events, or beliefs that are *not* true. In other words, in these situations the acceptance of false or invalid information results in pleasurable feelings.

As an example, your best friend may succeed at alleviating your emotional distress by reassuring you of something that you *wish* were true, but *know* to be false (for instance, that your doomed romantic relationship still has a chance of working out). Thus, even in the face of irrefutable evidence to the contrary, convincing yourself that your friend is right permits you to experience a sense of comfort. The problem, of course, is that just because your friend's prediction makes you *feel better* doesn't make it any more *accurate*. In other words, a falsehood—even a pleasing falsehood—is still a falsehood.

Similarly, your psychotherapist may provide you with feedback, observations, or interpretations that make you feel good, but are entirely *inaccurate*. He might, for instance, persuade you to take credit for events over which you, in reality, have absolutely no control. The fact that his erroneous attributions leave you feeling emotionally contented demonstrates, once again, that what feels good isn't necessarily true.

In order to experience pleasurable feelings in the face of potentially unpleasurable facts, these situations typically require a certain degree of distortion, falsification, or invalidation of reality. Specifically, they frequently entail the concomitant use of two Freudian ego defense mechanisms: *denial* and *fantasy* (A. Freud, 1936). In utilizing denial, the individual reduces his or her emotional discomfort by refusing to accept—or even perceive—a psychologically painful reality. Fantasy, by contrast, involves the creation of an imaginary and less threatening reality in which the individual seeks gratification in fictitious events, activities, or achievements.

Like the proverbial ostrich whose response to danger is to bury its head in the sand, people too may cope with emotionally threatening situations by burying their perceptions in the sands of denial, thereby blocking out any reminders of their actual circumstances. They may then *imagine* a reality that provides them with the illusion of safety, control, and comfort. As an illustration of how denial and fantasy can operate in tandem, a person who is faced with the calamity of having just been diagnosed with a terminal disease may cope with this information first by denying its presence and then escaping into a fantasy world in which the disease ceases to exist. We may resort to this same coping strategy in response to a wide range of disturbing events: denying the fact that you've been dumped by someone you love while fantasizing that they desperately beg you to take them back; denying your chronic problems with alcohol while fantasizing about being able to control its use; denying the reality of your dire financial straits while fantasizing about how you're going to spend your imminent lottery jackpot.

When taken to its most extreme form, this condition reaches psychotic proportions in which the individual exhibits gross impairments in reality testing. Here, people are virtually severed from the real world, living instead in a fantasy world of their own creation. Further, in an ironic twist, their expressed state of "emotional comfort" is likely to be interpreted by others as a manifestation of their *disease,* to which a host of psychopathological descriptors can be readily attached: mood-incongruent delusions, manic denial, hysterical denial, and pathological reaction formation, to name but a few. In these cases, their belief system permits them to feel emotionally comfortable, but at an enormous cost: loss of touch with reality.

Uncomfortable Truths

This condition, represented in Row 3, involves feelings of emotional discomfort that are a function of upsetting but true or factual events. Although these situations differ tremendously in terms of their specific manifestations, the common thread that links them together is the process of recognizing, acknowledging, trying to reconcile, or otherwise coming to terms with various forms of "painful reality," "painful truth," or "painful fact."

For example, you may be facing the painful realization that you have been betrayed by a trusted friend. Or that certain people in your life are never going to change. Or that your marriage is all but over. Or that you really do have a drug problem. Or that someone dear to you has a terminal illness. Or that your career is doomed. Or that you have no financial security in your old age. Or that you will never accomplish what you always wanted to. Or that your hopes, plans, and dreams have amounted to naught. Or that you just aren't as [fill in the blank] as you thought you were.

In the context of psychotherapy, this condition manifests itself when clients are confronted with potentially painful truths about themselves, to which they commonly respond with resistance or defensiveness (see discussion of "defensiveness" below). This occurs, for instance, when the therapist provides clinical observations, feedback, or interpretations which reveal particularly upsetting or disturbing aspects of the client's personality. For example, the therapist may be entirely correct in interpreting her client's dreams as revealing an unconscious hatred toward his parents. Despite the fact that this interpretation is valid (or, more accurately, *because* it is valid), the client is therefore prone to feel threatened, defensive, and to respond by denying, rejecting, or "resisting" the interpretation, all in the effort to avoid accepting this painful truth. In these cases, "the truth hurts."

Uncomfortable Falsehoods

This condition, represented in Row 4, involves feeling uncomfortable in the face of untrue assertions or false accusations. Here, one's state of emotional discomfort is a consequence of having been *wrongfully* accused, for instance, of committing unethical behaviors or of harboring immoral desires. Some specific examples would include a student being wrongfully accused of cheating on an exam; an employer of sexual harassment against an employee; a landlord of racial discrimination against a tenant; a son of intentionally harming his sister; a spouse of being unfaithful to his or her mate; a father of having molested his daughter; or a psychotherapy patient of being resistant to treatment.

One very common outcome of this process may be conceptualized as *justifiable defensiveness*, in which a person's "defensive" response is, in fact, an act of self-protection against a false charge or untrue accusation. This phenomenon can be differentiated from its theoretical polar opposite (see Metathought VI), namely *unjustifiable defensiveness*, which involves a defensive response to a *true* accusation (Row 3 above); in other words, the person is reacting defensively because "the truth hurts." By contrast, in the case of justifiable defensiveness the person is reacting defensively because "the lie hurts." Clearly, then, when it comes to understanding or interpreting displays of defensiveness, we should exercise great caution. Specifically, for example, if someone's comments provoke you to respond defensively, don't assume—based solely on your feelings of discomfort—that their observations must therefore be true.[2] Stated more generally, emotional discomfort is not, in itself, proof of veracity.

As an illustration of this phenomenon, try the following simple exercise. First, think of a person in your life whom you especially dislike, despise, or who, for whatever reason, just "rubs you the wrong way." More precisely, select someone around whom you feel particularly uneasy, anxious, offended, or in some way threatened.

Now take out a piece of paper and write down all of that person's personality traits, characteristics, and mannerisms that cause you to feel the way you do. In other words, make a list of all the adjectives you find to be loathsome, odious, abhorrent, repugnant, or otherwise aversive. Be completely candid and honest, and try to identify as many specific descriptors as you can.

[Note: In order for this exercise to achieve maximum impact, please complete the instructions above before you continue reading this section!]

Let's briefly examine the purpose and rationale underlying this exercise, which I routinely utilize in my graduate psychology classes to demonstrate Carl G. Jung's personality theory. According to Jung (1943/1953), each of us has parts of our own personality that are so repulsive, threatening, or frightening to us that we refuse to acknowledge their very existence. Because they are denied expression in our conscious self-identity, they coalesce into an unconscious and relatively autonomous "splinter personality," which Jung termed the *shadow* archetype.

Thus, the shadow is the "dark side" of our personality and is comprised of everything we hate or fear about ourselves. Moreover, instead of recognizing the shadow as being a part of us, we unconsciously project these "disowned" characteristics onto other people. Thus, Jung theorized, when we feel extreme aversion toward another person, we probably are responding to those very attributes that we despise and reject in ourselves.

The purpose of this exercise now should be apparent: from a Jungian perspective, it is intended to introduce you to your own shadow.

Okay, once you've completed your list, let's proceed to the next step. To the left of each descriptor, write out any one of the following phrases:

"I'm afraid that I am ...";
"I'm afraid of the part of me that is ...";
"I despise the part of my personality that is ..."; or
"I hate the fact that, deep down, I am so ..."

For example, if your list were to include the adjectives *stupid, aggressive, dependent,* and *insecure,* you would modify it as follows:

"I'm afraid that I am *stupid.*"
"I'm afraid of the part of me that is *aggressive.*"
"I despise the part of my personality that is *dependent.*"
"I hate the fact that, deep down, I am so *insecure.*"

Now, slowly and deliberately read the sentences *aloud*. Pay attention to your feelings as you hear yourself recite each statement. Although your reactions probably will vary from one "confession" to the next, on the whole you are very likely to experience a distinct and pervading sense of *discomfort*.

But what does this *mean*? And what does it *prove*? From one perspective, your feelings of discomfort could be interpreted as providing evidence which confirms the validity of Jung's shadow theory. After all (a Jungian might argue), these statements wouldn't be making you squirm unless they were "triggering" aspects of yourself that already exist and that, deep down, you know to be true. Further, the more discomfort you experience, the more likely it is that you have hit upon a series of "painful truths." Right?

Not necessarily. Recognizing a painful truth, by definition, involves feelings of discomfort. *But so does experiencing the sting of a false accusation!* In essence, painful truths *and* false accusations *both* produce uncomfortable feelings (see Metathought XIV, Multiple Pathways of Causation). Obviously, then, we cannot reliably differentiate true versus false statements solely on the basis of the feelings that ensue.

In a broader clinical context, this conundrum rears its ambiguous head whenever psychotherapists attempt to gauge the accuracy of their interpretations by their clients' concomitant emotional reactions (or lack thereof). In all such cases, therapists must remain cognizant of the fact that while an interpretation may be disturbing to the client because it is true, it also may be disturbing because it is *false*.

The task is especially problematic for traditional psychoanalysts, who routinely interpret the meaning of their patients' cognitions and behaviors (with particular emphasis on free associations, transferences, dreams, fantasies, defense mechanisms, resistances, and parapraxes or "Freudian slips"). Let's say, for instance, that an analyst interprets his female patient's career choice of a business executive as evidence of her repressed "penis envy." This interpretation, naturally, prompts her to feel extremely uncomfortable, if not outright hostile. Of course, the analyst is then likely to view her "defensiveness" and "resistance" to his interpretation as further evidence of its veracity. And the more vehemently she protests, the more convinced he may become that he has, in fact, exhumed a painful truth. But how can he be certain that she is not responding, instead, to a false (and rather demeaning) accusation? The fact of the matter is, in the absence of any corroborating evidence, *he cannot*.

To take another example, an analyst may interpret his patient's dream of plowing a field as symbolic of an unconscious wish to engage in sexual intercourse with his mother. On the one hand, the analyst's interpretation may be entirely accurate, which would (understandably) produce feelings of discomfort in the patient. Conversely, however, the interpretation may be completely *false*, which *also* could give rise to essentially the same emotional response.

To summarize, feelings of discomfort may be the result of a painful truth *as well as* a false accusation. Thus, hearing an interpretation which makes you feel uncomfortable does not, in itself, prove that the interpretation is *correct* or *incorrect;* in fact, the *only* thing it proves with any degree of certainty is that it makes you feel *uncomfortable!*

As a final illustration, let's briefly touch on what has been, and continues to be, one of the most controversial, protracted, and impassioned debates in the field of psychology, namely, the validity of repressed traumatic memories of childhood sexual abuse.[3] One area of particular contention concerns the degree to which human memory can be counted on as an accurate and trustworthy record or representation of our life experiences. Specifically, can we unconsciously forget (i.e., "repress") the occurrence of certain traumatic events, and then, at a later time, accurately recover these buried memories? By contrast, can we "remember" events that did not, in fact, ever actually occur? And if so, how can we distinguish between such "true memories" (actual events that have been *retrieved* or *recovered*) and "false memories" (illusory events that have been *constructed* or *created*)?

These questions are especially critical for individuals who are seeking to discover the truth about their past by attempting to "unearth" repressed memories. Unfortunately, their hunt is impeded (and their goal is all the more elusive) by virtue of the fact that both types of memory (authentic and manufactured) can seem equally "real."[4] Nevertheless, in the hopes of retrieving buried memories, people have turned to a diverse array of methods, techniques, and procedures, including individual psychotherapy; self-help workbooks, workshops, and seminars; participation in incest survivor support groups; traveling to childhood homes; hypnosis; guided imaging and visualization; age regression; and even sodium amytal (so-called truth serum) interviews.

How trustworthy are these methods? In two words, *not very.* Despite all the rhetoric and theorizing, pronouncements and declarations, claims and counterclaims, the stark reality is that *we do not yet have the tools to reliably distinguish true memories from false ones* (Loftus, 1993). Further, although the techniques we currently have at our disposal may indeed "lift the lid" of repression by unlocking authentic distant memories, they also might induce the manufacture of illusory memories. It is, therefore, most unfortunate that these methods not only may fail to accurately recover true memories, but, ironically, also can actually foster the creation of honestly believed but false traumatic memories!

These facts notwithstanding, many well-intentioned individuals continue to place their faith (not to mention their time, energy, and money) in such methods. On what basis do people gauge their veracity? As you probably have already anticipated, primarily (and sometimes exclusively) by the *feelings* they arouse. Specifically, in attempting to determine whether or not they were victims of childhood sexual abuse, the mere fact that a particular technique (such as hypnotically induced age regression) leaves them feeling uneasy or uncomfortable may lead them to conclude that the traumatic event, therefore, must *actually* have occurred. In other words, a state of emotional discomfort is seen as sufficient "proof" of abuse, even in the total absence of any specific memories or other corroborating evidence.

Regrettably, this fallacious line of reasoning and subsequent conclusion is frequently and actively encouraged by suggestions from popular writings, and, even worse, from some psychotherapists. For instance, in *The Courage to Heal* (Bass & Davis, 1988), which is often referred to as "the bible of incest survivors," the authors state, "If you are unable to remember any specific instances [of abuse]... but still have a *feeling* that something abusive happened to you, *it probably did*" (p. 21, italics added). Clearly, in light of the present discussion, this bit of advice stands out as being remarkably ill-informed, unsubstantiated, and potentially harmful.

The following exercise will serve to illustrate the danger in relying solely on one's feelings to make such a determination. Picture yourself as an infant, less than a year old, lying in a crib in your childhood bedroom. Now, try to imagine, as vividly and in as much detail as possible, one of your parents coming into your room late one night and sexually molesting you.

Invariably, just picturing this extremely disturbing scene is bound to arouse in you at least some feelings of discomfort, perhaps confusion, helplessness, fear, anger, nausea, pain, or other forms of distress. But obviously it would be a grave mistake to conclude that this traumatic event must *actually* have happened, based *solely* on your feelings of discomfort when imagining this unsettling scenario.[5] Clearly, the lesson to be learned here is not to misinterpret your emotional discomfort—no matter how distressed you might feel—with the likelihood that any given event is true.

To summarize this Metathought, feelings alone are neither an accurate nor trustworthy guide to the truth. Be careful, therefore, not to confuse your state of emotional comfort or discomfort with what is correct or incorrect. Further, do not rely on your emotions as the sole barometer for distinguishing what is true from what is false. Remember that how you feel is *one* source of data—and in many cases an *important* source of data—but it is not the *only* or *definitive* source of data. As a consequence, exercise caution in how you interpret the meaning of your emotional responses, keeping in mind that the only real certainty is *what* you are feeling, not necessarily what it *"proves."*

Glossary Terms

The following terms (or variations) are defined in the Glossary:

ambiguous	clinical
attribution	cognition
behavior	conscious
belief	consequence
cause	continuous variable
chronic	correlate

critical	personality
data	personality trait
delusion	phenomenon
denial	prediction
description	projection
diagnosis	psychoanalysis
dichotomous variable	psychological
disease	psychology
ego defense mechanism	psychopathology
emotion	psychotherapy
erroneous	psychotic
evaluation	reaction formation
event	reasoning
existence	reliability
expectation	repression
experience	resistance
fact	response
fallacious	shadow archetype
fallacy	somatic
fantasy	subjective
i.e.	subsequent
independent variable	theoretical
intentionality	theory
interpretation	transference
intuition	treatment
mood	truth
observation	unconscious
orthogonal	validity
parapraxis	variable
pathological	veracity
perception	vividness

Notes

[1] Note that although the two variables included in this table are, in fact, continuous phenomena, for the purpose of conceptual simplicity they are presented and discussed here as if they were dichotomous variables; see Metathought V, Differentiating Dichotomous and Continuous Variables.

[2] Put another way, when comparing these two types of defensiveness, be careful not to allow their similarities to obscure their differences (see Metathought VII, the Similarity–Uniqueness Paradox).

[3] For a sampling of the divergent points of view on this topic, I refer you to the following sources: Erdelyi & Goldberg, 1979; Holmes, 1990; Loftus & Ketcham, 1994.

[4] The same may be said of *intuition,* clinical or otherwise: When you have an intuitive hunch, remember that although the intuition is always *real,* it may or may not be *right.*

[5] I am, at the same time, not making an argument that such an event therefore definitely did *not* occur. Rather, to reiterate the primary theme of this Metathought, feelings *alone* are not sufficient proof of veracity.

XIX. The Spectacular Explanation Fallacy: Extraordinary Events Do Not Require Extraordinary Causes

There are more things in heaven and earth, Horatio,
Than are dreamt of in your philosophy.
—WILLIAM SHAKESPEARE*

Shit happens.
—ANONYMOUS

What happens when you experience an extraordinary event? If you are like most people, your first inclination probably is to search for some extraordinary cause to explain the event. Let's take an example. Imagine that you were to flip a coin 100 times and, to your utter astonishment, the coin turns up heads 100 times in a row. Assuming that the coin had not been tampered with, this would truly be an extraordinary event. But was there necessarily an extraordinary *cause*? Not unless you consider the ordinary laws of probability extraordinary.

Allow me to explain. When a coin is flipped, what is the probability that it will turn up heads? The answer, of course, is one out of two, or fifty-fifty. Now, what is the probability of getting heads the very *next* time you flip the coin? Exactly the same as it was the first time: fifty-fifty. Why? Coins don't have memories. Since a coin cannot remember the results of the previous flip, it starts from scratch every time. In other words, each coin flip is independent

*Hamlet, Act I, Scene 5

of (that is, completely and totally uninfluenced by) the preceding one. Thus, the fifty-fifty probability remains constant with every flip of the coin, whether it's the second, third, or hundredth time in a row that it turns up heads.

This same principle holds true for all games of pure chance, from slot machines and wheels of fortune to roulette and dice. Of course, streaks do occur, as any gambler would testify. But streaks are to be expected by chance alone, and do not require extraordinary causes (lucky rabbit's feet, superstitious chants, behavioral rituals, or the presence of an attractive stranger notwithstanding) to account for their occurrence. In other words, extraordinary events, such as unusual winning or losing streaks, can be due to very ordinary causes.

As an exercise, let's consider some less mundane examples. In the spaces provided below, give your best estimates as to the approximate frequency of each event in question.

1. Have you ever had the uncanny experience of listening to the radio, when you are startled to hear the very song that you had just been thinking of? _____
  If so, approximately how many times over the past month? _____
  The past year? _____
  In the course of your entire lifetime? _____

2. Have you ever received an unexpected telephone call from someone whose memory had just crossed your mind? _____
  If so, approximately how many times over the past month? _____
  The past year? _____
  Your entire lifetime? _____

3. Have you ever had a dream that coincided with, or even predicted, an event that actually occurred? _____
  If so, approximately how many times over the past month? _____
  The past year? _____
  Your entire lifetime? _____

Before you complete the second part of this exercise, let's examine some rather intriguing attempts to account for these unusual phenomena. One explanation was offered by the illustrious and controversial Swiss psychiatrist and personality theorist, Carl G. Jung. In essence, Jung's (1952/1969) extremely complex theory proposed that, in addition to direct causation, there exists another order in the universe, *synchronicity,* which involves an acausal yet meaningful relationship between two events, as mediated by the collective unconscious. Another explanation, set forth by parapsychologists (i.e., those who study events that are "beyond the normal"), postulates the existence of *extrasensory perception* (ESP) and various manifestations thereof, including telepathy, precognition, and clairvoyance.

But are extraordinary explanations of this kind necessary to account for such events? Could these unusual phenomena be due to nothing more than statistical coincidence, that is, pure chance? Ponder this alternative explanation while answering the following questions:

4.a. Have you ever been thinking of a song that *didn't* then appear on the radio? _____
    If so, approximately how many times over the past month? _____
    The past year? _____
    In the course of your entire lifetime? _____

4.b. Have you ever heard a song on the radio that you *hadn't* just been thinking of? _____
    If so, approximately how many times over the past month? _____
    The past year? _____
    Your entire lifetime? _____

5.a. Have you ever been thinking of someone who *didn't* subsequently call you on the telephone? _____
    If so, approximately how many times over the past month? _____
    The past year? _____
    Your entire lifetime? _____

5.b. Has someone ever called you on the phone whom you *hadn't* just been thinking about? _____
    If so, approximately how many times over the past month? _____
    The past year? _____
    Your entire lifetime? _____

6.a. Have you ever dreamt about an event that *didn't* actually occur? _____
    If so, approximately how many times over the past month? _____
    The past year? _____
    Your entire lifetime? _____

6.b. Have any events ever occurred that you *hadn't* previously dreamt about? _____
    If so, approximately how many over the past month? _____
    The past year? _____
    Your entire lifetime? _____

Now, in comparing your responses to the second part of this exercise with those of the first part, do you notice a not-so-subtle trend? What conclusions might you draw? Clearly, the occasions in questions (4), (5), and (6) are so commonplace that actually attempting to count them would prove to be a nearly impossible task. This stands in stark contrast to the relatively rare instances of "synchronistic" and "parapsychological" phenomena suggested in questions (1) through (3).

In fact, when we stop to consider the fact that literally billions of events occur in our lives every day, it would be shocking if there *weren't* any "uncanny coincidences"! Once again, we see that, by pure chance, exceptional events must occasionally be expected. Put another way, it is normal for some events to appear abnormal.

The age-old debate on the genetic transmission of psychological and behavioral phenomena provides fertile ground for yet another illustration of this Metathought. Have you ever wondered if one's personality traits, behavior patterns, or even specific attitudes and preferences can be inherited? Many publicized reports of identical twins seem to support this notion.

Consider the extraordinary case of "the Jim twins" (see Holden, 1980a, 1980b; Tellegen et al., 1988). Jim Springer and Jim Lewis were identical (monozygotic) twins who, after being separated at infancy, were reunited thirty-nine years later. Despite the fact that they had been raised in completely different environments, the similarities between the two brothers were truly startling. After having married and divorced women named Linda, both men married women named Betty. One had a son named James Allan; the other, James Alan. Both named their dogs "Troy." Both had worked as sheriff's deputies. Both chain-smoked Salem cigarettes and chewed their fingernails to the nub. Both drove Chevrolets and liked to race stock cars. Both had carpentry workshops in their basements and constructed white circular benches around trees in their yard.

Now, what is responsible for these remarkable similarities? Can such specific personality and behavioral characteristics be inherited? Are deeply-embedded genetic codes capable of exerting such astonishing outcomes?

Perhaps. But before we jump to this rather tempting conclusion, consider the similarities of the following two women (reported by the Associated Press on May 2, 1983): Both were named Patricia Ann Campbell. Both were born on March 13, 1941. Both had fathers named Robert. Both worked as bookkeepers. Both studied cosmetology and enjoyed oil painting as a hobby. Both had two children of the same age. Both married military men, within 11 days of each other. And these two women had *no genetic relationship* to each other.

How is this possible? Let us turn, once again, to the not-so-extraordinary laws of probability. Take any two strangers of the same sex and age, drawn at random from the telephone book. Ask them to spend hours and hours comparing their lives, from the broadest of descriptors to the most minute of details: their personality characteristics; their personal attitudes, beliefs, values, and goals; their vocational, educational, relationship, and sexual experiences; their behavioral habits and mannerisms; their family lineage; their interests, hobbies, and travels; their childhood heroes, tastes in food, and preferences in books, movies, and music.

If you ask enough questions, what are you likely to find? No doubt, an impressive array of "remarkable coincidences"![1]

In the realm of clinical psychology, consider any extraordinary (that is, "out of the ordinary") cases of human behavior, from delusions, hallucinations, catatonia, multiple personality, bestiality, or necrophilia to stunning acts of courage, bravery, and altruism, or remarkable instances of raw talent, artistic creativity, or intellectual genius. In these examples, and many more, we are prone to assume that aberrant behavior must be the product of aberrant causes. In fact, the more bizarre the behavior (such as cannibalistic serial murders), the more likely we are to search for bizarre causes (such as ritualistic Satanic cult abuse) or even to create bizarre theories (such as demonic possession) to account for it.

Yet, as Sigmund Freud pointed out many years ago (1900/1953), there is no need to assume that the principles underlying abnormal behavior are qualitatively different than those that govern normal, common, or "healthy" behavior. This Metathought would well be worth keeping in mind whenever you are confronted with instances of human behavior that are unusual, rare, or spectacular. Remember: *extraordinary events do not require extraordinary causes*. With all due respect to Hamlet's sage advise to Horatio, there are more things dreamt of in our philosophy than actually exist in heaven and earth.

Glossary Terms

The following terms (or variations) are defined in the Glossary:

acausal	fallacy
assumption	i.e.
attitude	normal
behavior	parapsychology
belief	personality
causation	personality trait
cause	phenomena
chance	probability
clinical	psychological
delusion	psychology
et al.	random
event	Spectacular Explanation Fallacy
existence	subsequent
expectation	synchronicity
experience	theory
explanation	thinking
fact	unconscious

Notes

[1] Along these lines, I refer you to the compelling research conducted by Robert Plomin and Denise Daniels (1987), who concluded that, despite our commonly held assumptions to the contrary, two children in the same family are, on average, as different from each other as are pairs of children selected randomly from the population.

P a r t *Four*

Investigating
Phenomena

XX. *Deductive and Inductive Reasoning: Two Methods of Inference*

All men are mortal.
Socrates is a man.
Therefore Socrates is mortal.
—ARISTOTLE*

Assuming that persons lie and that mental
patients and psychiatrists are persons, we
should expect them to lie also. Indeed they do.
—THOMAS SZASZ**

The temptation to form premature theories upon
insufficient data is the bane of our profession.
—SHERLOCK HOLMES***

Thinking tasks involve different forms of reasoning. Two of the most important methods are *deductive* and *inductive* reasoning. Whenever we draw an inference from a general premise to a specific conclusion, we are engaging in deductive thinking. In contrast, whenever we draw an inference from specific instances to a general conclusion, we are utilizing inductive thinking.[1]

*384–322 B.C.
**Insanity, 1987
***In Arthur Conan Doyle's *The Valley of Fear*, 1914

Deductive Reasoning

In deductive reasoning (also known as *theory-driven* or *top-down* cognitive processing), we begin with general or universal assumptions that we know (or believe) to be true. We then use these assumptions to arrive at particular conclusions. If the assumptions we begin with are indeed true, and if our logic is valid, then our conclusions must be true. To take a rather mundane example, we know as a general rule that all dogs have four legs. We are therefore justified in concluding that Rex, a specific dog we do not know, has four legs.

Scientists use deductive thinking when testing theories. To describe this process (known more formally as the *hypothetico-deductive method of scientific investigation*) step-by-step: We begin with a proposed explanation for understanding observable phenomena (i.e., a theory), from which we derive specific predictions (i.e., hypotheses). We then collect and quantify the relevant observations (i.e., data). If the data match the predictions, we conclude that our theory has empirical support.

Let us take, as an interesting illustration of the deductive process, the earliest empirical research on Leon Festinger's (1957) theory of cognitive dissonance. The theory maintains that whenever we hold two inconsistent or contradictory attitudes (cognitions), we experience an aversive drive state (dissonance) which impels us to reduce our discomfort by altering our behavior or our attitudes. Given this theory, we might make the specific prediction that when people perform an unpleasant behavior for minimal external rewards, they will experience a high degree of cognitive dissonance; as a consequence, they will alter their attitudes toward their behavior in a more favorable direction.

This hypothesis was, in fact, tested experimentally in 1959 by social psychologists Festinger and J. Merrill Carlsmith. The investigators asked research subjects to perform a series of dull, boring, and tedious tasks (that consisted of packing spools and turning pegs for about an hour). The subjects then were coaxed to convince other students (who were really a part of the experiment) that the tasks actually were fun, interesting, exciting, and enjoyable. For their assistance, some of the subjects were paid $20 (remember, this was 1959!); other subjects received only $1. All subjects were subsequently asked about their *true* attitudes toward performing the tasks.

Based on cognitive dissonance theory, which subjects do you think reported *enjoying* the experiment more, those who were paid $20 or those paid $1? As was originally hypothesized, those subjects who received *less money* ($1) rated the tasks *more favorably*. Why? They experienced more dissonance than did the $20 subjects; as a result, they felt compelled to *justify* their behavior by altering their attitudes toward the tasks. Festinger's theory of cognitive dissonance thereby received its first noteworthy empirical support. In this example, it is clear how deductive thinking guided the researchers from general assumptions to specific conclusions.

What are some common mistakes that we are prone to commit in our use of deductive reasoning? The first type of error involves utilizing valid logic, but beginning with an erroneous premise. For the sake of debate, let's consider the belief that mental illness is equivalent to physical illness. Under the assumption that this premise is true, it would logically follow that an individual with a mental illness should be diagnosed and receive medical treatment as a patient under the direction of a physician. However, if this premise is invalid (as has been argued by Thomas Szasz, 1960, 1987), the conclusion is suspect and surely must be reconsidered.

In the second type of error, one's initial assumptions are valid, but the subsequent logic is flawed. Such is the case in instances of tautologous or circular reasoning (see Metathought IV). For example, "People who are pessimistic expect the worst; therefore, people who expect the worst are pessimistic." Another variety of faulty logic is illustrated in the following parody of Aristotle's now famous syllogism:

> *All men are mortal.*
> *Socrates is a man.*
> *Therefore all men are Socrates.*

Inductive Reasoning

In inductive reasoning (also known as *data-driven* or *bottom-up* cognitive processing), we begin with particular observations and then generalize to broader principles. As a simple exercise, consider the following series of numbers: "2,4,6,...." Now, which number do you believe should be next? Why? What is the principle that underlies this series? Our use of inductive reasoning would lead us to conclude that the next number is 8, based on a pattern consisting of a sequence of even numbers.

To take another example, suppose you notice that whenever you think about taking classroom exams, you experience heart palpitations, difficulty breathing, dizziness, sweaty palms, dry mouth, nausea, hot flashes, diarrhea, a sensation of choking, and a fear of dying. You thus might conclude, by induction, that you have some test anxiety.

Scientists use inductive thinking when creating or building theories. Initially, the scientist collects enough data that a pattern begins to emerge. From this pattern, he or she induces the underlying principle that appears to account for the pattern. In this way, the scientist formulates an explanation (that is, a theory) on the basis of specific observations. For example, physicists, in their attempt to identify and understand a large number of physical phenomena in the universe, have inductively created theoretical constructs such as "force," "gravitation," and "energy."

In like fashion, we use induction when we create psychological constructs (such as the mind, personality, motivation, and intelligence). Consider, as an illustration, the following scenario: You observe that certain people in the world tend to evaluate their attributes and abilities in very positive terms; they describe themselves as worthy and competent, and they report feeling confidence in and respect for themselves. They also seem not to worry excessively about things that might go wrong for them; they easily "bounce back" from failure and frustration, and they aren't easily threatened by criticism. You might then think to yourself, "This constellation of characteristics appears to set these people apart from other people. How shall we refer to this common theme? What shall we call it? How about *self-esteem*?" Note that self-esteem was not "discovered" as an observable or concrete entity (see Metathought II, the Reification Error). Rather, it was a perceiver-created invention, arrived at inductively, to help us account for and better understand our observations.

What are some of the potential pitfalls associated with inductive reasoning? One of the most pervasive errors involves jumping hastily to a conclusion on the basis of an insufficient or unrepresentative sampling of data. For example, when a client is observed under the highly structured, artificial, and time-limited constraints of a first psychotherapy session, the therapist may erroneously *overgeneralize* from this behavior and thereby arrive at an incorrect clinical diagnosis.

How else might we go wrong? In a number of ways, many of which are presented and examined at length in other sections of this book. These include our tendencies:

>to draw upon data from our memory solely because it is vivid or salient (Metathought XXVIII, the Availability Bias);

>to ignore important statistical information, such as sample size and prior probability (Metathought XXVII, the Representativeness Bias);

>to selectively seek out observations that are consistent with our prior beliefs (Metathought XXIV, the Confirmation Bias);

>to ignore or reject observations that are inconsistent with our beliefs (Metathought XXV, the Belief Perseverance Effect);

>to oversimplify and artificially distort continuous phenomena by conceptualizing them as dichotomous (Metathought V, Dichotomous and Continuous Variables);

>to misinterpret correlation and causation (Metathought X, Correlation Does Not Prove Causation);

>to confuse deductive and inductive thinking, and the circumstances under which each is appropriate.[2]

As an exercise in recognizing errors in deductive and inductive reasoning, consider the potential pitfalls that have been identified and described thus far.

Then, select three specific errors and provide an original example of each. For instance:

> *Error:* Potential flaw in deductive reasoning due to an invalid premise.
> *Example:* Gaps in memories of childhood are always due to some kind of significant sexual, emotional, or physical trauma. My client can't remember much of his childhood. Therefore, he must have been traumatized as a child.

> *Error:* Potential flaw in inductive reasoning due to overgeneralizing from an unrepresentative sample.
> *Example:* Every designer I've ever met is homosexual. Therefore, my design instructor, whom I've not yet met, has got to be homosexual.

Ready to try some on your own?

> *Error:* _____
> *Example:* _____
> _____
> _____

> *Error:* _____
> *Example:* _____
> _____
> _____

> *Error:* _____
> *Example:* _____
> _____
> _____

Solutions and Applications

Let's briefly enumerate some solutions for these various problems. First, learn to differentiate between deduction and induction, recognizing that different types of problems call for different reasoning strategies. Second, make your selection based on the nature and goal of the particular question, task, or situation. Third, with respect to deductive reasoning, be sure that your initial assumptions are correct and that your logic is sound. Fourth, when utilizing inductive reasoning, in addition to the specific solutions discussed in each of the chapters cited above, be especially careful not to hastily overgeneralize from unrepresentative, inadequate, or otherwise biased observations.

Note that some situations call for *both* deductive and inductive strategies. In arriving at a differential clinical diagnosis, for example, the psychotherapist uses both types of reasoning. Suppose that a person comes to see you, a therapist, for a clinical intake interview. She complains that, for the past six months, she has been feeling sad, hopeless, and worthless. She reports further that she has no energy, poor appetite, difficulties in concentrating, and thoughts of death. Using your powers of inductive reasoning, you put these pieces together and conclude that she has some kind of mood disorder.

But what type? Could it be a bipolar (i.e., manic-depressive) disorder? You would use the process of deduction to test this hypothesis. So, you ask her, "Have you ever experienced any periods of time when you've had exceptionally high energy, very little need for sleep, racing thoughts, a euphoric mood, and been extremely talkative and easily distractible?" She replies, "No, I haven't." With this hypothesis disconfirmed, you then tentatively conclude that she probably is suffering from a unipolar depressive disorder.

Of course, this depiction of the clinical diagnostic process is, of necessity, overly simplistic. However, it does serve to illustrate how deductive and inductive strategies can, and do complement each other in the real-world setting of clinical psychology.

Glossary Terms

The following terms (or variations) are defined in the Glossary:

assumption	empirical
attitude	erroneous
attribution	evaluation
behavior	experience
belief	experiment
bias	explanation
causation	external
clinical	hypothesis
cognition	i.e.
concrete	induction
consequence	inductive reasoning
construct	inference
continuous variable	logic
correlation	mental illness
data	mind
deduction	mood
deductive reasoning	motivation
description	observation
diagnosis	personality
dichotomous variable	phenomena
differential diagnosis	physical
disorder	prediction

premise
probability
psychological
psychology
psychotherapy
quantify
reasoning
representativeness
scientific

social
subsequent
tautologous reasoning
theoretical
theory
thinking
treatment
universal
vivid

Notes

[1] For philosophical perspectives on deductive and inductive reasoning, I refer you to the writings of Aristotle, Francis Bacon, Galileo Galilei, John Stuart Mill, and David Hume.

[2] A comprehensive discussion of errors and biases in deductive and inductive reasoning may be found in *The Teaching of Thinking* (Nickerson, Perkins, & Smith, 1985).

XXI. Reactivity: To Observe Is to Disturb

Search not a wound too deep lest thou make a new one.
—*ANONYMOUS**

The scientific method is based on tampering with what would be happening if we were doing nothing to it.
—*R. D. LAING***

One could not find the location of any one subatomic particle because any measurement, necessarily with light, affected the result.
—*WERNER KARL HEISENBERG****

Reactivity is a phenomenon in which the conduct of research affects the very entity that is being studied. The problem of reactivity exists to some extent in practically all fields, but is particularly acute in the social sciences.[1] Specifically, whenever people are aware that they are being studied, they are likely to alter (either consciously or unconsciously) their responses. Thus, the investigation of normal human activity is impeded, ironically, by the investigator himself. The dilemma is profoundly consequential: How can we possibly know what people are "really" like if, by observing them, we cause them to change?

Whether utilizing survey or experimental research methods, and whether conducting research in the field or in the laboratory, social scientists find themselves constantly plagued by the effects of reactivity.[2] When we wish to study people's attitudes or opinions, for example, our most commonly used

*Quoted in Barber, *The Book of 1000 Proverbs,* 1876/1971
**The Facts of Life,* 1976
***1901–1967, German physicist

research method is to ask them questions about a particular topic. Unfortunately, however, such questions may be highly reactive by stimulating the respondents to think about the topic in a new way, or even by instigating them to formulate an opinion when they previously had none. Yet how can we know if an attitude or opinion exists at all until it has in some way been elicited?

Reactivity is especially problematic in the conduct of psychological laboratory research. Almost without exception, the moment that subjects enter the laboratory setting, they quickly and automatically develop expectations, hunches, or hypotheses about the purpose of the experiment and how they may be expected to behave. Suppose, for example, that a researcher is interested in studying whether self-disclosing statements by one person will elicit self-disclosures in another person. Because the subjects are aware of being observed, they may be prompted to behave in ways that they believe to be socially desirable (perhaps by being more self-disclosing). Thus, whether subjects are cooperative or uncooperative, trusting or suspicious, sociable or inhibited, submissive or defiant, the experimenter will be unable to measure their "natural" behavior, thereby compromising the validity of her observations.

As a consequence, reactivity limits the extent to which investigators can confidently generalize, apply, or relate their findings to other populations and settings. In the parlance of social scientists, reactivity is a threat to the study's *external validity* (see Campbell & Stanley, 1963). Two specific forms of this threat are the *reactive effect of testing* (when subjects' receptivity to the experimental treatment is altered by preceding observations or testing) and the *reactive effects of experimental arrangements* (when the artificiality of the research setting itself causes subjects in the experiment to respond differently to the treatment than would people in nonexperimental settings). Thus, whenever external validity or generalizability are issues of concern, problems related to reactivity always must be considered.

Reactivity is sometimes referred to as the *Hawthorne Effect,* deriving its name from a classic study conducted at the Hawthorne Plant of the Western Electric Company in Chicago (see Roethlisberger & Dickson, 1939). The researchers were interested in studying some of the factors, such as rest periods and quitting times, that might affect employees' work performance. Much to their surprise (and initial confusion), the researchers achieved positive results no matter what they did. Even when employees' rest periods were *eliminated* or when *later* quitting times were instituted, the result was still an increase in work output. The researchers concluded that a reactive effect had occurred; that is, the workers' morale (and therefore their productivity) had been boosted simply because somebody was paying attention to them. In effect, the researchers' very presence altered worker productivity.

The ubiquity of reactivity cannot be overemphasized. In the clinical context, it occurs, to some degree, whenever we attempt to diagnose a patient by conducting an intake interview, assess personality by asking people what they see in blots of ink, measure intelligence by administering standardized IQ tests, gauge someone's level of stress by taking their blood pressure, explore unconscious processes by instructing a person to "free associate," examine a family's communication patterns by observing them in therapy, evaluate a clinical trainee by observing how she conducts group therapy sessions, or study human sexual responses in the laboratory by attaching physiological measuring devices to research subjects' genitalia.

More broadly defined, reactivity is evident throughout our daily lives, influencing everything, from how we respond to public opinion polls to our behavior on job interviews and first dates. The impact of reactivity is particularly salient in the context of media broadcasting. Consider, for instance, news interviews with "people on the street"; the presence of television cameras in courtroom trials; media coverage of meetings, demonstrations, or riots; and various "reality programs," such as those that capture law enforcement activity on videotape. In all of these cases, and countless more, remember that simply measuring something can change it.

As an exercise, select three situations (either from the examples above or of your own choosing) in which you consider the issue of reactivity to be especially problematic. Then, for each situation, describe specifically how reactivity might influence the outcome. Last, offer your suggestions for reducing the problem (see below for some suggestions).

Situation 1: _____

Effects of Reactivity: _____

_____

_____

_____

Solution(s): _____

_____

_____

Situation 2: _____

Effects of Reactivity: _____

_____

_____

Solution(s): _____

_____

_____

Situation 3: _____
Effects of Reactivity: _____
_____
_____
_____
Solution(s): _____
_____
_____

Because one of the most common criticisms of the social sciences is that we frequently alter the behavior that we seek to study, it is crucial that we not only remain constantly vigilant as to the presence of reactivity, but that we also make every effort to minimize its impact. How can this be accomplished? For all practical purposes, if people are not aware of being studied, reactivity ceases to be a problem. This fact has prompted social scientists to devise a wide variety of innovative *unobtrusive* or *nonreactive* techniques: clandestine observation (using, for example, hidden cameras, tape recorders, or one-way mirrors), indirect measures (such as the erosion of carpeting to measure foot traffic), and document analysis (also known as "archival research," such as the inspection of academic or personnel files). Clearly, the decision to utilize such unobtrusive measures has its drawbacks, not the least of which involves complex ethical and legal issues, particularly the invasion of privacy. But, of course, as with all matters, every decision is a trade-off (see Metathought XXX).

Glossary Terms

The following terms (or variations) are defined in the Glossary:

acute	effect
affect	ethics
attitude	evaluation
behavior	expectation
belief	experiment
cause	external validity
clinical	fact
concept	generalizability
consequence	measure
continuous variable	normal
decision	observation
diagnosis	opinion
dichotomous variable	personality
dilemma	phenomenon

psychological
reactive effect of testing
reactive effects of experimental arrangements
reactivity
response
science

social
treatment
ubiquitous
unconscious
validity

Notes

[1] Of historical note, the concept of reactivity is related to the *uncertainty principle,* first stated mathematically by the German physicist, Werner Heisenberg. The uncertainty principle maintains that, in the domain of quantum mechanics, the mere act of observation affects what one is observing. Specifically, it is impossible to determine, with absolute certainty, the exact position and momentum of any one subatomic particle because the measuring device itself affects the particle's position and momentum.

[2] Bear in mind that reactivity typically is a continuous, rather than dichotomous, variable (see Metathought V). As such, it usually is more a question of its relative magnitude or degree, rather than its absolute presence or absence.

XXII. The Self-Fulfilling Prophecy: When Expectations Create Reality

Respect a man, and he will do the more.
—ANONYMOUS*

LIZA: *You see, really and truly, apart from the things anyone can pick up . . ., the difference between a lady and a flower girl is not how she behaves, but how she's treated. I shall always be a flower girl to Professor Higgins, because he always treats me as a flower girl, and always will; but I know I can be a lady to you, because you always treat me as a lady, and always will.*
—GEORGE BERNARD SHAW**

The attitudes and beliefs that we hold toward other people can, with or without our intent, actually produce the very behaviors that we expect to find. In other words, a perceiver's assumptions about another person may lead that person to adopt those expected attributes. This phenomenon is known as the *Self-Fulfilling Prophecy.*

In what is probably the most famous (and still very controversial) study of the self-fulfilling prophecy, Robert Rosenthal and Lenore Jacobson (1968) informed teachers at a San Francisco elementary school that, on the basis of a reliable psychological test, some of the pupils in their classroom would show dramatic spurts in academic performance during the upcoming school year. In

*Quoted in Barber, *The Book of 1000 Proverbs,* 1876/1971
**1856–1950, from *Pygmalion,* 1913

reality, there was no such test, and the children designated as "intellectual bloomers" were chosen *at random*. Nevertheless, when the children's performance was assessed several months later, those students who had been earmarked as "bloomers" did, indeed, show an improvement in their schoolwork; even more remarkably, their IQ scores had increased! The teachers thus unwittingly *created* the very behaviors that they *expected*.[1]

In another fascinating illustration of the self-fulfilling prophecy, student experimenters were told that some of their laboratory rats were "maze-bright," while others were "maze-dull" (Rosenthal & Fode, 1963). The experimenters subsequently found that the "bright" rats actually learned a standard maze faster than did the "dull" rats, this despite the fact that the rats had been *randomly* designated as "bright" or "dull" and did not differ initially with respect to their maze-learning ability. Apparently, the students' prior expectations must have caused them to handle the two groups of rats differently, which in turn affected the animals' behavior. Here again, we see that entirely false beliefs can generate their own reality.

The self-fulfilling prophecy has been demonstrated with a diverse array of both positive and negative perceiver expectancies,[2] including hostility (Snyder & Swann, 1978), extraversion (see Snyder, 1984), gender stereotypes (Skrypnek & Snyder, 1982), racial stereotypes (Word, Zanna, & Cooper, 1974), and even stereotypes concerning physical attractiveness (Snyder, Tanke, & Berscheid, 1977). These studies underscore how prejudice of any kind can set in motion a self-perpetuating and ever-escalating vicious cycle of adverse repercussions (see Metathought XI, Bi-Directional Causation), in which the self-fulfilling prophecy serves to influence not only how the prejudiced person behaves toward the victim, but also how the victim may then behave in a way that confirms the person's initial prejudices.

In the examples we have considered thus far, the perceivers were aware of their own expectations; that is, their expectations were conscious. Can self-fulfilling prophecies occur also as a consequence of expectations, attitudes, or beliefs that are, for the most part, out of awareness or *unconscious?*

Some theorists think so. Melanie Klein (1946), for example, introduced the term *projective identification* to describe the unconscious splitting of one's own unacceptable (that is, *ego-dystonic*) attributes, and the projection of these attributes onto another person. The perceiver then relates to the other person in terms of these disowned attributes—for example, with fear, dread, disgust, or rage—and, in so doing, elicits the other's behavior along these lines (see Horwitz, 1983).

Similarly, R. D. Laing (1969) used the term *induction* to denote unconscious components of the self-fulfilling prophecy. As an illustration, a husband may unconsciously "induce" his wife to embody his projection of his own mother. As noted by Laing, "It is not sufficient to say that my wife introjects my mother, if by projection, I have manoeuvred her into such a position that she actually begins to act, and even to feel, like her" (pp. 119–120).

It must be emphasized that not only are we seldom aware of the extent to which our expectations can influence others' behavior, but moreover we probably are even less aware of how others' expectations are capable of influencing *our* behavior. It is thus important to remember that our actions are shaped not only by our own attitudes, but also by the expectations of those with whom we interact. Put another way, we are continually cultivating the construction of each other's social realities.

Given the ubiquity of the self-fulfilling prophecy, we would do well to consider its potential impact in all of our social interactions. In the clinical setting, for instance, what do you suppose might occur if a therapist expects his or her new client to be cooperative? Resistant? Emotionally fragile? Seductive? Paranoid? Borderline?

In like manner, what if a client expects his or her therapist to be empathic? Critical? Accepting? Devious? Intimidating? Insincere? Gentle? Rejecting? The therapist and client can ultimately end up creating a reciprocally-reinforcing projection system that supports their respective initial expectations, much of which may be occurring entirely outside of their direct awareness.

As an exercise, select three scenarios—either hypothetical or factual—involving the self-fulfilling prophecy. In making your selections, consider a variety of

>topics (e.g., stereotyping, prejudice, clinical assessment and diagnosis, child rearing, impression management, creativity, athletic competition, sexual performance);

>settings (e.g., classroom, therapy, workplace, religious, military, laboratory, courtroom);

>relationships (e.g., professional, familial, romantic, platonic);

>units of analysis involving broad societal or governmental policies, programs, and laws (e.g., welfare, unemployment, affirmative action, desegregation, immigration, mandatory retirement, competency to stand trial, insanity defense).

Then, for each scenario, present your thoughts as to how Person A's expectations might influence his or her behavior toward Person B. (As a hint, you may wish to peruse Metathoughts XXIII and XXIV, the Assimilation Bias and the Confirmation Bias, respectively).

Last, discuss how Person A's actions could cause Person B to behave in accordance with Person A's prior expectations. In other words, identify some of the specific factors or events that you believe are capable of transforming Person A's initial expectations into the reality of Person B's subsequent attitudes and behavior.

Scenario 1: _____

Effects of Person A's expectations on his or her behavior toward Person B:

_____

_____

_____

_____

Effects of Person A's behavior on Person B's subsequent actions:

_____

_____

_____

_____

Scenario 2:_____

Effects of Person A's expectations on his or her behavior toward Person B:

_____

_____

_____

_____

Effects of Person A's behavior on Person B's subsequent actions:

_____

_____

_____

_____

Scenario 3:_____

Effects of Person A's expectations on his or her behavior toward Person B:

_____

_____

_____

_____

Effects of Person A's behavior on Person B's subsequent actions:

_____

_____

_____

_____

Glossary Terms

The following terms (or variations) are defined in the Glossary:

assumption   attribution
attitude   behavior

belief
cause
clinical
consequence
denote
e.g.
ego-dystonic
event
expectation
extraversion
fact
hypothetical
induction
intent
phenomenon

projection
projective identification
psychological
random
reciprocal
reinforcement
reliability
resistance
Self-Fulfilling Prophecy
social
stereotype
subsequent
ubiquitous
unconscious

Notes

[1] Interestingly, the self-fulfilling prophecy has also been demonstrated in *students'* expectations of their *teachers* (see Feldman & Prohaska, 1979; Feldman & Theiss, 1982; Jamieson, Lydon, Stewart, & Zanna, 1984).

[2] See Darley and Fazio (1980) for an excellent and comprehensive review of research on the self-fulfilling prophecy.

XXIII. The Assimilation Bias: Viewing the World through Schema-Colored Glasses

Two-thirds of what we see is behind our eyes.
—CHINESE PROVERB

To the man who wants to use a hammer badly, a lot of things look like nails that need hammering.
—MARK TWAIN*

Rules govern the whole social field. Unless we can "see through" the rules, we only see through them.
—R. D. LAING**

One of the most fundamental and pervasive of all human psychological activities is the propensity to categorize. People appear to possess an innate drive to classify, organize, systematize, group, subgroup, type, subtype, or otherwise structure the world around them.

We categorize everything from people, objects, places, and events to concepts, experiences, feelings, and memories. The phenomenon is omnipresent, the breadth is enormous, and almost nothing is immune: sex and race; plants and animals; words and numbers; books and records; occupations and hobbies; religious denominations and political affiliations; anatomical structures and geographic territories; subatomic particles and celestial constellations; time and space.

*1835–1910
***The Politics of the Family*, 1969

In the field of psychology we have created taxonomies of personality traits, types, and characteristics; intellectual, interpersonal, and emotional functioning; mental disorders; theoretical orientations; methods of research; approaches to psychotherapy; communication styles; ego defense mechanisms; and stages of psychosexual, psychosocial, cognitive, and moral development, to list but a few.

We can conceptualize all such categories (yet another category!) as mental representations, or *schemas*.[1] A schema is a cognitive structure that organizes our knowledge, beliefs, and past experiences, thereby providing a framework for understanding new events and future experiences (see Cantor & Mischel, 1979; Fiske & Taylor, 1984; Levy, Kaler, & Schall, 1988; Piaget, 1952; Sears, Peplau, & Taylor, 1991). Put another way, schemas (or *schemata*) are general expectations or preconceptions about a wide range of phenomena. In the social domain, these include perceptual sets about yourself, about particular people whom you know, and even about people whom you do not know, based on their sex, race, nationality, occupation, social role, or any other characteristic. In fact, we may view stereotypes as equivalent to group schemas (Hamilton, 1979, 1981).

What function do schemas serve? First and foremost, they enable us to process the plethora of stimuli we continually encounter in a relatively rapid, efficient, and effortless manner. In other words, schemata reduce our cognitive processing load. Whenever we are faced with new information, we quickly and automatically compare it to our preexisting schemas, which greatly simplifies the task of organizing and understanding our experiences.

What happens when we come across information that is discrepant from our preconceptions? Put another way, what do we do when there is a clash between the data and our schemas? The Swiss psychologist Jean Piaget (1954, 1970) identified two complementary processes that we utilize in such situations: *accommodation* and *assimilation*. According to Piaget, both of these responses are integral components of cognitive development and constitute the means by which we adapt to our environment and construct our reality.

Accommodation refers to the process wherein we modify our schema to fit the data. In other words, we change our preexisting beliefs so that they make room for (that is, "accommodate") new information. Assimilation, by contrast, means to modify the data to fit our schema. Here, we incorporate new information into our preexisting beliefs, even if it means changing or distorting the information itself.

The conduct of scientific investigation involves the processes of both assimilation and accommodation. Specifically, scientists use their preconceived theories to help them make sense out of an overwhelming array of seemingly disjointed, frequently bewildering, sometimes incoherent, and all-too-often ambiguous events. In other words, they assimilate observed phenomena into their conceptual schemas. And so long as the data and the theory "fit" each other, assimilation effectively and successfully serves its purpose. Suppose, however, that a particular observation disconfirms or contradicts the scientist's expectations; that is to say, the new datum does not fit the old theory. Now what? In the pursuit of knowledge, good scientists put aside their pride, their stubbornness, and their egos, and they alter their theory to accommodate the facts.[2]

But do people in general make appropriate use of assimilation and accommodation? The answer, by and large, is *no*. Considerable research shows us time and time again that discrepancies between data and schemas typically are resolved more in the direction of assimilation than accommodation. In other words, we are more likely to make the data fit the schema, rather than the other way around.

Before we explore some specific illustrations and applications of this Metathought, let's take a step back and evaluate the advantages and disadvantages inherent in schematic processing. How do schemas both help and hinder our thinking process?

On the plus side of the ledger, the advantages of schematic processing are significant and well-documented (see Fiske & Taylor, 1984). In addition to the benefits discussed above, schemas help us to perceive, recognize, and remember new information; to retrieve from memory old information; to fill in gaps in our knowledge; to draw inferences; to make interpretations; and to prepare for the future by providing us with experience-based expectations (Cantor & Mischel, 1977; Taylor & Crocker, 1981).

Of course, benefits are always accompanied by costs, and schematic processing is no exception to this principle (see Metathought XXX, Every Decision Is a Trade-Off). Our use of schemas entails a host of predictable and systematic mistakes and biases in thinking. First, schemas are, by their very nature, abstractions and simplifications of reality; as a consequence, they tend to foster incomplete, inaccurate, and sometimes naive generalizations that fail to take into account the complexity of real-world phenomena. Further, because schematic processing occurs automatically and relatively unconsciously, it is very resistant to change, even when it is fraught with errors.

With respect to this Metathought, schemas bias the perception, processing, and interpretation of information in the direction of confirming our expectations; conversely, we tend to overlook, misconstrue, or even reject valid information when it is not consistent with our schemas. In a word, a fundamental and pervasive liability of schematic processing can be seen as a problem of *assimilation*.

This bias manifests itself in a wide variety of forms and contexts, the most important of which are listed here (along with references to pertinent Metathoughts). Specifically, we are more likely

>to notice information that is consistent, rather than inconsistent, with our schemas (the Availability Bias);

>to rely excessively on vivid but not necessarily appropriate information (the Availability Bias);

>to interpret ambiguous, irrelevant, or even contradictory information as fitting our schemas (the Belief Perseverance Effect);

>to selectively search for information that corroborates our schemas (the Confirmation Bias);

>to recall or misinterpret information about past events so that it validates our schemas (the Hindsight Bias);

>to draw inaccurate inferences and erroneous conclusions (Correlation Does Not Prove Causation, errors in Deductive and Inductive Reasoning); and

>to unwittingly elicit the very events that we expect to find (the Self-Fulfilling Prophecy).

We also are prone

>to distort our perception, coding, and storage of new information;

>to fill in gaps in our knowledge with schema-consistent but erroneous information; and

>to engage in and perpetuate stereotyping (all of which directly involve the Assimilation Bias).

In sum, schemas bias our perceptions of reality to make them consistent with what we already believe. As such, the Assimilation Bias represents a significant obstacle to clear thinking and effective problem-solving. In viewing the world through "schema-colored glasses," we subject virtually all incoming information to varying degrees of distortion, misinterpretation, and invalidation.

Scores of research studies have concluded that schemas greatly influence what we perceive and the manner in which we perceive it (see, for example, Bruner & Potter, 1964; Reason & Mycielska, 1982; Vokey & Read, 1985). To take one example, the impact of the Assimilation Bias on schematic processing was demonstrated in a classic experiment by the eminent social psychologist Harold H. Kelley. The experiment (known as the "warm–cold" study) was conducted in 1950 at MIT and used undergraduate students as research subjects. All the students were informed that they would be attending the lecture of a guest speaker and were provided with some brief background information about him.

Half of the subjects were told that the speaker was twenty-nine years old, married, and that people considered him "a rather cold person, industrious, critical, practical, and determined." The rest of the subjects were given the same information, with one exception: They were told that he was considered to be "a rather warm person, industrious, critical, practical, and determined." Thus, the *only difference* between the two groups of subjects was that half were informed that the visitor was cold, and the other half were told that he was warm.

Kelley had selected the warm versus cold dimension based on prior research carried out by one of the pioneers of modern social psychology, Solomon Asch (1946). In his study, Asch found that *warm–cold* is a significant "central trait" in terms of its impact on the impressions we form of other people. Kelley hypothesized therefore that this one-word difference would create substantial expectancy and perceptual differences between the two groups.

Both groups of students subsequently saw the *same speaker* presenting the *same lecture,* and both groups spent the entire class period with him. Yet, their impressions of him were, as Kelley had predicted, powerfully affected by the one-word difference. Each group interpreted the speaker's behavior based on their "knowledge" of him as either warm or cold. Specifically, the subjects who were told that the speaker was warm had significantly more positive impressions of him than those who were told that he was cold. In essence, the subjects had filtered (i.e., assimilated) the speaker's behavior through their respective schemas, and, as a consequence, arrived at strikingly different impressions of him. As was elegantly demonstrated in this experiment, the impact of a single expectancy variable on our perceptions can be profound. The underlying principle here again becomes manifest: More than believing what we see, we tend to see what we believe.

As an illustration of the Assimilation Bias in the clinical setting, consider how a therapist's beliefs and expectations may predispose him to "see" psychopathology wherever he looks. Suppose you were to ask a therapist to explain the meaning of behaviors that clients might exhibit on arriving for their scheduled therapy session. Let's imagine further that this therapist happens to view the world through a densely filtered schema of psychopathology. He thus calmly, cooly, and confidently offers you the following interpretations:

> *If the patient arrives early for his appointment, then he's anxious. If he arrives late, then he's hostile. And if he's on time, then he's compulsive.*

This witticism about psychoanalysis dates back to the 1930s. Although originally intended as a joke, it may have been more prophetic than anyone at that time could have anticipated, for it is not just a humorous illustration of the Assimilation Bias, but is also a revealing and sobering parable that alerts us to the dangers inherent in maintaining schemas that allow—and even encourage—virtually any human behavior to be subsumed under one or another of pathological categories.

Let's examine another clinical application of schematic processing. Psychotherapists typically align themselves with, and work from a foundation of, some clinical frame of reference known as a "theoretical orientation." A theoretical orientation is, in essence, the clinician's schema for identifying, mapping, and understanding the behavior of his or her clients. As such, these schemata are, of course, subject to the same biases in assimilation discussed above. In this way, the therapist would be inclined to perceive, interpret, and explain clients' symptoms principally (or perhaps even exclusively) in terms of his or her own theoretical orientation, sometimes irrespective of its actual relevance or suitability.

We shall designate this phenomenon the *Clinical Orientation Assimilation Bias* (COAB), which, by definition, may predispose therapists to systematically overlook, discount, or reject alternative perspectives and ways of understanding their clients. We can further delineate specific subcategories of the COAB, several of which are identified below. Also indicated are the factors that, in extreme forms of the COAB, are held exclusively accountable for producing the problems of every client:

The *Biomedical Assimilation Bias*
–neurochemical imbalances and disease processes;
The *Psychodynamic Assimilation Bias*
–unconscious motivations and conflicts;
The *Psychosocial Assimilation Bias*
–situational and environmental stimuli;
The *Cognitive–Behavioral Assimilation Bias*
–faulty belief systems and maladaptive learning;
The *Humanistic–Existential Assimilation Bias*
–incongruent perceptions and loss of meaning in life;
The *Family Systems Assimilation Bias*
–dysfunctional family relationships;
The *Substance Abuse Assimilation Bias*
–an addictive personality;
The *New-Age Metaphysical Assimilation Bias*
–unlearned lessons from "past lives."

The following exercise will give you some practice at viewing the same event through the lenses of different clinical orientations. Suppose that you are a therapist and a client comes to see you with the complaint of feeling "very unhappy." Select one of the clinical orientations listed above (or from any other source) and write a few statements that, from that perspective, attempt to explain and to solve the client's presenting problem.

Here is an example:

Clinical Orientation: <u>Cognitive-Behavioral Therapy</u>
Explanation and Solution: <u>The client's unhappiness probably is due to his or her unreasonable expectations and self-defeating behaviors. Therefore, the appropriate</u>

treatment would consist of challenging these faulty beliefs and rewarding more adaptive behavioral responses.

Ready to try one on your own?

Clinical Orientation: _____

Explanation and Solution: _____

_____

_____

_____

_____

Now, "switch lenses" by approaching the same problem from a different orientation.

Clinical Orientation: _____

Explanation and Solution: _____

_____

_____

_____

_____

Do the same with another orientation.

Clinical Orientation: _____

Explanation and Solution: _____

_____

_____

_____

_____

Diagnostic Labels as Schematic Filters: The Assimilation of Psychopathology

Nowhere is this Metathought more vividly illustrated than in David L. Rosenhan's (1973) renowned study that dramatically demonstrated the biasing power of diagnostic labeling. In the study, eight researchers (including Rosenhan), posing as "pseudopatients," gained voluntary admission into psychiatric hospitals in six different states. The pseudopatients complained of "hearing voices" that said "empty," "hollow," and "thud." Other than presenting this complaint (and giving false names and occupations), the pseudopatients truthfully answered all questions asked of them. All eight pseudopatients were diagnosed as psychotic, seven of them as suffering from schizophrenia.

The pseudopatients entered the hospitals with the knowledge that it was up to them to get themselves discharged, essentially by convincing the staff they were "sane." On admission to the hospital ward, the pseudopatients immediately ceased simulating any signs of mental disturbance, and thereafter behaved on the ward as they "normally" behaved.

Rosenhan and his pseudopatient–colleagues found that their relatively healthy behavior in the ward did not serve to invalidate, nullify, or revoke their diagnoses; as a matter of fact, once they were designated as abnormal, all of their other behaviors and characteristics were profoundly colored by the diagnostic labels. Specifically, the hospital staff molded their observations of the pseudopatients into a portrait consistent with "mental illness." For example, many of the pseudopatients' quite normal life histories, when viewed in a psychopathological context, appeared somehow aberrant: "[The patient manifests]. . . ambivalence in close relationships, which begins in early childhood" (see Metathought IX, the Barnum Effect).

The diagnostic labels were so powerful, in fact, that ordinary human activity on the part of the pseudopatients was perceived as a manifestation of their psychopathology. For example, after observing a pseudopatient–researcher taking notes, one nurse commented in her daily report, "Patient engages in writing behavior," thereby pathologizing an ostensibly mundane human activity. In another instance, a psychiatrist observed some patients sitting outside the hospital cafeteria half an hour before lunchtime. The psychiatrist explained to a group of residents that such behavior on the part of the patients was "characteristic of the oral-acquisitive nature of the syndrome." (Rosenhan points out that it appeared not to occur to the psychiatrist that, in a psychiatric hospital, there are very few events to look forward to, with the exception of eating.)

In spite of their appearance of sanity, not one of the pseudopatients was ever detected.[3] None of the pseudopatients was discharged in less than a week. The average length of hospitalization was nineteen days; the longest stay was fifty-two days. When the pseudopatients were released, it was not because they were discovered to be sane fakers; rather, they typically were discharged with a diagnosis of "Schizophrenia, in remission." Clearly, as emphasized by Rosenhan, "a psychiatric label has a life and an influence of its own."

Are there any ways in which we can guard against the adverse effects of the Assimilation Bias? First, make it a point never to underestimate the extent to which your prior beliefs, knowledge, and expectancies (that is, your schemata) can affect your current experience, impressions, and perceptions. Second, try to become as conscious as possible of the schemata that are most important to you. Remember that awareness of schemata greatly increases your ability to modify them. Third, experiment with temporarily lowering (or even removing) your "perceptual filters" and "schema-colored glasses" by attempting to understand, as fully as possible, someone else's subjective (phenomenological) perceptions and experience. Fourth, learn to differentiate your use of assimilation versus accommodation, particularly when you are faced with a discrepancy between your beliefs (schemas) and the information (data). Further, attempt to identify those specific situations in which you are more likely to engage in assimilation. Last, prod yourself to accommodate when, out of habit, reflex, or just sheer laziness, you typically would be inclined automatically to assimilate. By striving to enhance your cognitive flexibility, you will decrease the likelihood of falling prey to "hardening of the categories."

Glossary Terms

The following terms (or variations) are defined in the Glossary:

abstract	experiment
accommodation	explanation
affect	fact
ambiguous	family therapy
assimilation	generalization
Assimilation Bias	humanistic therapy
Availability Bias	i.e.
behavior	inference
belief	interpersonal
bias	interpretation
category	knowledge
clinical	mental
Clinical Orientation Assimilation Bias (COAB)	mental illness
	motivation
cognition	normal
cognitive–behavioral therapy	observation
concept	pathological
conscious	perception
consequence	personality
construct	personality trait
critical	phenomenology
data	phenomenon
diagnosis	preconception
dimension	psychoanalysis
disease	psychodynamic therapy
disorder	psychological
dysfunction	psychology
effect	psychotherapy
ego defense mechanism	psychotic
emotion	reification
erroneous	response
evaluation	schema
event	scientific
existential therapy	social
expectation	stereotype
experience	stimulus

subjective
subsequent
symptom
syndrome
taxonomy
theoretical

theory
thinking
trait
unconscious
variable
vividness

Notes

[1] The word *schema* is derived from the Greek word for "form," thus referring to the overall form or outline of our knowledge about any given concept or stimulus. Bear in mind, of course, that the concept of a schema is just that, a theoretical construct. Thus, be careful not to reify schemas by treating them as if they were tangible objects (see Metathought II, the Reification Error).

[2] Keep in mind that the operative word here is *good* scientists, lest we fail to take heed of Hans Eysenck's not-so-subtle admonition that "Scientists...are just as ordinary, pig-headed, and unreasonable as anybody else, and their unusually high intelligence only makes their prejudices all the more dangerous because it enables them to cover these up with an unusually glib and smooth flow of high-sounding talk" (1957, p. 108).

[3] Interestingly, however, it was quite common for the *real* patients to recognize the pseudopatients' sanity. For example, one patient remarked, "You're not crazy. You're a journalist, or a professor. You're checking up on the hospital."

XXIV. The Confirmation Bias: Ye Shall Find Only What Ye Shall Seek

What the analyst shows interest in, the kinds of questions he asks, the kind of data he chooses to react to or ignore, and the interpretations he makes, all exert a subtle but significant suggestive impact upon the patient to bring forth certain kinds of data in preference to others.
—JUDD MARMOR*

If you look hard enough for what doesn't exist, eventually it may appear.
—ANONYMOUS

The psychiatrist's eagerness to find mental illness wherever he looks is matched only by his reluctance to define mental illness.
—THOMAS SZASZ**

Whether we are conducting formal scientific research investigations or simply attempting to solve everyday problems, we are faced with a host of obstacles and pitfalls that can impede our pursuit of valid and trustworthy results. One particularly problematic area involves the manner in which we go about gathering evidence to answer our questions.

In order to evaluate the veracity of our assumptions, expectations, and beliefs, we ultimately must subject them to some kind of empirical test by

*Quoted in Hans J. Eysenck's *Decline and Fall of the Freudian Empire*, 1985
**Insanity, 1987

weighing them against the evidence. If our beliefs are supported by the data, we become that much more confident of their accuracy. If, by contrast, the data are disconfirming, we need to revise (or perhaps even abandon) our original beliefs.

But before we are in a position to *weigh* the evidence, we first must *collect* the evidence. Ideally, our search should be conducted in a manner that is impartial, fair, and free of prejudices or biases. Unfortunately, however, the ways in which we actually procure such information frequently are far from unbiased. Specifically, we tend to selectively gather information that is consistent with our prior expectations. That is, we more eagerly search for evidence that will confirm our beliefs, while we are less likely to seek out evidence that might refute them. Our proclivity to gather information in this slanted fashion is called the *Confirmation Bias*. We may, for instance, unintentionally ask "leading questions" that serve to verify our initial beliefs. Because social information often is ambiguous and subject to numerous interpretations, it is not difficult to amass evidence that inevitably ends up supporting our expectations.

The Confirmation Bias has been examined in a diverse array of research settings (Klayman & Ha, 1987; Skov & Sherman, 1986; Wason, 1960), all of which demonstrate how people employ strategies for eliciting information from others that preferentially support their initial beliefs (see Higgins & Bargh, 1987, for a review). In one such study (Snyder & Swann, 1978), college students were instructed to conduct individual interviews with other students to ascertain the presence of certain personality traits. Half of the subjects were told that their goal was to determine if the interviewee was an extravert (i.e., outgoing, sociable, and gregarious); the goal for the other half was to determine if the interviewee was an introvert (i.e., shy, reserved, and timid). All subjects then were presented with a list of questions that assessed extraversion and introversion, from which they were instructed to select questions to ask the interviewee.

Results of the study showed that subjects who were asked to find out if the interviewee was an extravert preferentially chose extraversion questions (e.g., "What would you do if you wanted to liven things up at a party?"), whereas those who were told to determine if the interviewee was an introvert selected introversion questions (e.g., "What factors make it really hard for you to open up to people?"). As a consequence, simply by answering the questions asked of them, the interviewees revealed those aspects of themselves that corroborated the particular goal of the interviewer. Thus, those who were tested for extraversion actually appeared more extraverted; likewise, those who were tested for introversion appeared more introverted. In essence, interviewers "found" the very personality traits for which they had been probing, *solely on the basis of the questions they had chosen to ask.*[1]

In the context of psychotherapy, the Confirmation Bias can lead therapists to selectively elicit clinical information that affirms their initial diagnostic impressions or expectations. As an example, suppose you are informed by a colleague that your new therapy patient, whom you have not yet met, is an alcoholic. Based on your academic training, clinical experience, and knowledge of the research literature on alcohol abuse, you begin to form an image of him as a person who is likely to

>under-report how much he drinks;

>hide his drinking habit from others;

>sometimes drink secretly;

>socialize with people who also drink;

>have hangovers;

>experience memory blackouts;

>suffer periods of depression;

>have bouts of insomnia;

>display mood lability;

>experience family conflicts;

>manifest problems at his place of employment, such as lateness, absenteeism, or low productivity; and

>to be generally dishonest in admitting to the extent of his problems.

So, in your initial therapy session you ask him a wide range of questions about his drinking habits ("How much do you drink?" "How often do you drink?" "With whom do you drink?" "Do other people know how much you drink?" "Have you ever had occasion to drink alone?"); you explore his history of substance use ("Have you ever had hangovers?"); you query him about any lapses in his memory ("Have you ever forgotten events that happened to you the night before?"); you investigate his experiences with depression and disturbances in his sleeping habits ("Do you sometimes feel very sad?" "Do you ever have problems falling or staying asleep?"); you assess for the presence of mood lability ("Do you ever find that your moods sometimes change very quickly?"); you probe into his marital conflicts ("Do you have arguments with your wife?"); you inquire about any irresponsible behavior he might display at work ("Do you ever have problems getting to work on time?"); and you search for indications of dishonesty ("Do you sometimes not tell the truth to others?").

You are not surprised one iota, of course, to find that all of his responses confirm your beliefs about him as a closet drinker who is in denial about his chemical dependence problem, but who, nevertheless, fits the profile of an "alcoholic personality." After working with him for several weeks, however, you slowly come to the disconcerting realization that, in fact, he doesn't have a drinking problem at all!

Once you've gotten over the initial shock and have overcome your own inevitable resistance to accepting this new conclusion (see Metathought XXV, the Belief Perseverance Effect), you probably would attempt to ascertain what went wrong. Did your patient or your colleague deliberately deceive you by providing you with false information? Let's assume not. More likely, you deceived *yourself* by selectively seeking information that supported your prior expectation. In retrospect, (see Metathought XXVI, the Hindsight Bias), it now strikes you as glaringly obvious that *many* people who are *not* alcoholic

>are reluctant to disclose fully their alcohol usage to others;
>drink at parties or by themselves;
>have endured hangovers;
>experience occasional lapses in memory;
>suffer through periods of depression or insomnia;
>display mood swings;
>argue with their wives;
>are sometimes irresponsible at their place of employment;
>and are less than totally honest in their dealings with others.

But because of the context and manner in which you queried your patient about these events, he provided you with all the evidence you needed to corroborate your prior belief about him as an alcoholic. In other words, due to the Confirmation Bias, you unintentionally guided him down the path of affirming your preconceived conclusion.

In the same manner, a therapist may erroneously "verify" the presence of a multitude of other specific clinical problems, ranging from depression, anxiety, impulsivity, paranoia, and dependency to eating disorders, sexual disorders, personality disorders, or even repressed incidents of childhood sexual abuse.[2]

As an exercise in learning to identify and to remedy the Confirmation Bias, select a particular psychological problem, either from the list above, or one of your own choosing. Now, imagine that you, as a clinician, are assigned the task of conducting an initial intake interview with a client about whom you know nothing, except for his or her "admitting diagnosis" (which, for purposes of this exercise, is the problem you have just selected).

Next, construct a list of *leading questions* that, by their very nature, are virtually certain to confirm the diagnosis. For instance, if the admitting diagnosis happens to be paranoia, some of your questions might include: "Do you ever feel suspicious of other people's motives?" "Do you believe that other people talk about you when you are not present?" or "Have others sometimes behaved toward you in a way that is threatening or demeaning?" (Additional suggestions appear in Appendix 2.)

" _____ ?"
" _____ ?"
" _____ ?"
" _____ ?"
" _____ ?"
" _____ ?"
" _____ ?"
" _____ ?"
" _____ ?"
" _____ ?"

How, then, shall we address the problem of overcoming the Confirmation Bias? The antidote lies in adopting a strategy of eliciting information that is deliberately *not consistent* with our prior expectations. Specifically, your task is to generate a series of questions that could, in principle, refute, disconfirm, or invalidate the admitting diagnosis. To continue with the example of paranoia, sample questions could be: "What evidence or proof do you have that other people have intended to harm you?" "On a scale from one to ten, how sensitive to criticism are you?" or "How frequently do your suspicions about others usually turn out to be true?" (Other suggestions are presented in Appendix 2.)

" _____ ?"
" _____ ?"
" _____ ?"
" _____ ?"
" _____ ?"
" _____ ?"
" _____ ?"
" _____ ?"
" _____ ?"
" _____ ?"

The Confirmatory Bias of Theoretical Orientations

The impact of the Confirmation Bias can be both insidious and pervasive, guided in large measure by the therapist's own personal and professional convictions, values, and beliefs. Specifically, for instance, therapists tend to ask questions, probe for information, and direct the focus of treatment based on their respective theoretical orientation. As a consequence, clients are apt to provide evidence that supports their therapist's particular school of thought, thereby "confirming" the validity of their approach. In this way

>Freudians search for and therefore are more likely to "find" unconscious infantile sexual conflicts;

>Jungians find unreconciled psychological opposites and nonintegrated archetypes;

>Adlerians find strivings for superiority that compensate for perceived inferiority;

>Eriksonians find deficient ego strength arising from inadequate resolution of psychosocial crises;

>Rankians find separation anxiety;

>Kleinians find sadistic rage toward one's mother;

>Sullivanians find unhealthy interpersonal relationships;

>Kohutians find narcissistic injuries;

>Horneyites find alienation from one's real self;

>Humanists find incongruent self-perceptions and hindered actualization tendencies;

>Existentialists find struggles for meaning in life and ontological insecurity;

>Gestaltists find restricted awareness and incomplete gestalts;

>Behaviorists find maladaptive learning patterns;

>Classical Behaviorists find disruptive conditioned associations;

>Social Learning therapists find faulty role modeling;

>Cognitive therapists find irrational belief systems;

>Family therapists find dysfunctional family systems;

>Bowenian family therapists find low levels of differentiation;

>Communications family therapists find ineffective communication patterns;

>Strategic family therapists find interpersonal power struggles;

>Psychodynamic family therapists find unconsciously motivated repetition compulsions; and

>Structural family therapists find maladaptive boundaries, roles, and coalitions.

To summarize, the Confirmation Bias can profoundly influence the overall focus, direction, and course of psychotherapy. In particular, therapists are inclined to selectively probe for information and to ask leading questions that serve to verify their preconceived theoretical convictions; in short, they are likely to find only what they seek.

The Confirmatory Bias of Projective Psychological Testing

As a final illustration of the Confirmation Bias, let's examine one of the most controversial topics in psychology: projective personality testing. To provide a brief background, projective tests refer to a variety of psychological assessment techniques, all of which involve exposing the examinee to a relatively unstructured or ambiguous stimulus and then soliciting his or her perceptions. The rationale underlying the use of projective tests is known as the projective hypothesis (Frank, 1939), which in essence proposes that when people are presented with an ambiguous stimulus, they will respond by automatically assigning or imposing (that is, "projecting") structure, organization, or meaning onto the stimulus, thereby revealing their psychological dynamics (such as their attitudes, beliefs, fantasies, conflicts, needs, expectations, fears, and so on), both conscious and unconscious.

The most well-known projective tests are the Rorschach Inkblot Test, the Thematic Apperception Test (TAT), the House-Tree-Person (HTP) Projective Drawing Test, and various versions of sentence completion tests (for example, the Curtis Completion Form). Criticisms of projective tests are numerous and well documented (see Anastasi, 1988), but for our purposes we shall focus on just one, namely, the problem of Confirmation Bias.

In most settings, clinicians employ projective tests as one component of a full psychological assessment battery, which typically includes a diverse array of methods and techniques (such as a structured interview, behavioral observations, standardized personality questionnaires, and measures of cognitive functioning). The clinician then analyzes and integrates the data from these sources, usually with the goal of arriving at a diagnosis and treatment plan.

What role, then, do projective tests play in this process? Although they may serve several functions, one purpose in particular is to confirm the clinician's diagnostic impressions. (Do you see any potential problems here?)

Let's examine one hypothetical scenario. Suppose that, based on the results of other components of an assessment battery, a clinician tentatively concludes that the examinee (Mr. X) has "aggressive tendencies." To confirm this provisional diagnosis, she decides to utilize the Rorschach Inkblot Test. Following standard procedure, for each of the ten inkblots she asks Mr. X, "What might this be?" and then scrupulously jots down verbatim his responses, some of which include: "Two animals are fighting there... It looks like a bullet smashing through something... It looks like a piece of denim that's being torn... Two people arguing about something... Two insects are trying to knock down this post... Their mouths are open like they're gonna bite something... The part in the center is getting blown up."[3]

Now, what specific evidence does the clinician look for to support her diagnosis? According to John Exner (1993), the world's leading authority on the Rorschach, aggressive tendencies are manifested in responses which involve actions such as fighting, breaking, tearing, stalking, exploding, or looking angry. Thus, Mr. X's responses clearly confirm the clinician's initial diagnosis. She therefore concludes that, "Mr. X exhibits evidence of aggressive tendencies, which appear to constitute a significant component of his psychological dynamics."

But now let's suppose, by contrast, that Mr. X had *not* provided *any* responses of this kind. Would this disconfirm the clinician's diagnosis? Not necessarily. She could just as easily conclude that, "Mr. X appears to be resisting, denying, or covering up his aggressive tendencies, which are likely to be buried just beneath the surface of his nonaggressive veneer." Thus, even the complete *absence* of "aggressive" responses can confirm her "aggressive" diagnosis!

Finally, what if the examinee were to manifest a "typical" number of aggressive responses on the Rorschach? The clinician still may confidently conclude that, "Mr. X appears to be only partly successful in his attempts at controlling his aggressive tendencies." Once again, her diagnosis has been validated. In short, no matter what Mr. X does or does not actually perceive, his responses may be interpreted as confirming the clinician's diagnostic expectations.

How is this possible? Remember that projective tests involve stimuli that are ambiguous not only for the examinee, but for the clinician as well. As a consequence, they permit *both* persons to project their respective psychological perceptions. In other words, an ambiguous stimulus, just like the proverbial knife, "cuts both ways." Thus, irrespective of what the examinee happens to perceive in the stimuli, the Confirmation Bias can lead the clinician to selectively perceive evidence that corroborates her initial beliefs. (In this respect, keep in mind that projective tests can reveal as much about the examiner as they do about the examinee.)

Taken to its extreme, virtually any diagnosis can be "confirmed" with the use (or, more accurately, the *misuse*) of projective tests. Moreover, the intrinsic nature of these tests all but ensures that the clinician's diagnosis won't (and frequently *can't*) be directly disconfirmed. This is due to the fact that the results of projective tests can be open to a variety of interpretations. Thus, even if genuinely disconfirming evidence were to exist somewhere amongst the examinee's responses to inkblots, pictures, drawings, or incomplete sentences, we currently have no reliable way of identifying them and ruling out alternative or conflicting explanations. All told, it is ironic indeed that the very purpose for which these tests frequently are utilized (that is, to confirm a diagnosis) is the one that they are least capable of achieving and least likely of providing valid results.

How can we guard against the Confirmation Bias? First and foremost, by being aware that we are prone to be biased collectors of evidence. Specifically, never forget that the questions we ask may lead us selectively to arrive only at those answers that corroborate our initial beliefs. As a consequence, make it a point to actively seek out evidence that *could,* in principle, *refute* your preconceptions. In this way, you will help to ensure that a conclusion will not have been reached before the search has even begun.

Glossary Terms

The following terms (or variations) are defined in the Glossary:

ambiguous
antidote
assumption
attitude
behavior
behavior theory
belief
bias
clinical
cognitive
cognitive therapy
cognitive–behavioral therapy
Confirmation Bias
conscious
consequence
data
denial
diagnosis
disorder
dynamics
dysfunction
e.g.
empirical
erroneous
evaluation
event
existential therapy
expectation
experience
explanation
extraversion
family therapy
Gestalt therapy
humanistic therapy
hypothetical
i.e.

interpersonal
interpretation
intrapsychic
introversion
knowledge
measure
mental illness
mood
motive
observation
ontological
perception
personality
personality disorder
personality trait
preconception
projective hypothesis
projective test
psychodynamic therapy
psychological
psychology
psychotherapy
reliability
repression
resistance
response
scientific
social
stimulus
subsequent
theoretical
treatment
truth
unconscious
validity
veracity

Notes

[1] In a noteworthy replication of this study, Fazio, Effrein, and Fallender (1981) reported that interviewees who had been asked the extraversion questions subsequently even perceived *themselves* as more outgoing than those who had been asked the introversion questions (see Metathought XXII, the Self-Fulfilling Prophecy).

[2] On this last point, I highly recommend *The Myth of Repressed Memory* (Loftus & Ketcham, 1994), which presents a superb examination of the alleged recovery of repressed memories.

[3] These examples of "aggressive" (AG) responses were taken directly from Exner's (1990) *Rorschach Workbook*.

Chapter **25**

XXV. The Belief Perseverance Effect: The Rat Is Always Right

The great tragedy of Science—the slaying of a beautiful hypothesis by an ugly fact.
—T. H. HUXLEY*

If the facts don't fit the theory, so much the worse for the facts.
—GEORG WILHELM FRIEDRICH HEGEL**

We are least open to precise knowledge concerning the things we are most vehement about.
—ERIC HOFFER***

In our attempts to understand the world around us and to navigate our way through life, we adopt a wide variety of beliefs, the content of which ranges from the mundane (e.g., the best brand of detergent, the most flattering hairstyle) to the profound (e.g., the meaning of life, the existence of God). One of the most significant characteristics of our beliefs is the degree to which we become personally invested in them. The attachment may be so strong, in fact, that our beliefs feel as if they are a vital and indispensable component of our very identity.

What happens, then, when our beliefs are challenged? Particularly those beliefs that we happen to *like*? Or those that we regard as *important*? Or those that we have come to accept as *truths*?

*1825–1895, Collected Essays, 1959
**1770–1831
***1902–1983, The Passionate State of Mind, 1954

155

If we were to respond to such challenges in a purely rational manner, we would simply detach our personal feelings from the dispute, evaluate the substance of the challenge as objectively and dispassionately as possible, and then, if appropriate, modify our beliefs accordingly. We would, in other words, accommodate the new information by modifying our preexisting schemas (see Metathought XXIII, the Assimilation Bias).

But we are not always so rational. In fact, sometimes we are not rational at all. Specifically, when our beliefs are being challenged, we are prone to feel that *we personally* are being challenged. When our beliefs are criticized, we feel criticized. When our beliefs are attacked, we feel attacked. Our first impulse, therefore, typically is to *protect* our beliefs, as if to protect ourselves. As such, we tend to cling to our beliefs, sometimes even in the face of contrary evidence. This bias in thinking is called the *Belief Perseverance Effect* (sometimes also referred to as the Belief Perseverance Phenomenon; see Lord, Ross, & Lepper, 1979).

When we engage in belief perseverance, we usually respond to such challenges by discounting, denying, or simply ignoring any information that runs counter to our beliefs. That is, we treat potentially disconfirming evidence as if it didn't even exist. For instance, suppose a friend of yours believes that eating a meal late at night causes more weight gain than eating the same meal earlier in the day. So, you carefully explain to her the results of widely accepted scientific research demonstrating that weight gain is not related, *per se,* to the time of day at which food is ingested. She then pauses for a moment, apparently mulling it over, and replies, "Oh, I see what you mean. But, you know what? I *still* think that it causes more weight gain at night." Her position is, of course, tantamount to maintaining that, "If the facts don't support my theory, the facts must be wrong."

The Belief Perseverance Effect was demonstrated empirically in a study by Charles Lord and his associates (1979). The researchers began by selecting two groups of college students, one in favor of capital punishment and the other opposed to it. The subjects then were shown the results of two purportedly new research studies, one that supported the efficacy of capital punishment as a deterrent to crime, and one that refuted its efficacy. Thus, each group was presented with the identical body of mixed evidence. How did they respond? Subjects in *both* groups were favorably impressed with the study that supported their own prior beliefs, while they discounted the study that contradicted them. The researchers concluded that showing the two opposing groups an identical body of mixed evidence failed to narrow their disagreement; as a matter of fact, it actually *increased* it.

Our beliefs can be so intractable, in fact, that they stubbornly persevere even when we acknowledge that the evidence supporting them is erroneous. This phenomenon was evidenced in a research study in which subjects were administered a personality test that purportedly showed them to be especially "socially sensitive" (Ross, Lepper, & Hubbard, 1975). Subjects were subsequently informed that the test actually was *fake*, and therefore provided invalid results. Even with this knowledge, however, subjects *still persisted* in believing that they were socially sensitive. Other studies have corroborated the general conclusion that it requires much more compelling evidence to *change* our beliefs than it did to *create* them in the first place (Ross & Lepper, 1980).[1]

Can we engage in belief perseverance without rejecting contradictory information? What if we are not able, or even choose not, to discount, deny, or ignore potentially disconfirming evidence? Is there any way that we can continue to cling to our cherished beliefs and still emerge victorious?

The answer, as you probably have already anticipated, is yes. Like the martial arts expert who masterfully redirects and transforms his opponent's force to his own advantage, in a brilliant feat of logical contortionism, we simply find a way to bend, twist, or reframe the information so that it actually *supports* our original belief.

The following parable will illustrate how people can reinterpret contradictory and potentially disconfirming data to support their preexisting beliefs.

> *A woman walks into a psychiatrist's office, complaining that she's a zombie. The psychiatrist, trying his best to convince her otherwise, says, "You're walking and talking, aren't you?" "Zombies walk and talk," replies the patient. "Well, you're breathing, too." "Yes, but zombies breathe." "Okay, what don't zombies do? Do they bleed?" "No, of course not," says the patient, condescendingly. The doctor replies, "Good. Then I'm going to stick this needle into your arm and we'll see if your belief is right or wrong." So, he plunges the needle into the woman's arm, and, of course, blood starts to trickle out of the wound. The woman is stunned. In utter dismay, she slowly turns to the psychiatrist and says, "I guess I was wrong . . . Zombies do bleed."*

Another illustration of how the Belief Perseverance Effect can lead to the negation and gross distortion of disconfirming evidence to support one's original beliefs comes from the autobiography of Carl G. Jung, *Memories, Dreams, Reflections* (1961). In describing his early experiences as an apprentice in a psychiatric clinic, Jung recalled:

> . . . *I had to be most circumspect about treating my schizophrenic patients, or I would have been accused of woolgathering. Schizophrenia was considered incurable. If one did achieve some improvement with a case of schizophrenia, the answer was that* it had not been real schizophrenia *(p. 128; emphasis added).*

Let us now turn to a sampling of variations on this very robust theme. In particular, note how the participants in these brief scenarios are able to support their positions by employing a creative assortment of flaws in thinking, including tautologous logic (Metathought IV), misattributions of intentionality based on consequences (Metathought XVII), confusing feelings with truth (Metathought XVIII), and errors in deductive and inductive reasoning (Metathought XX).[2]

Wife People who love someone should just *know* what they need.

Husband I do love you—I just don't know what you need.

Wife Then, you must not *really* love me. Because if you *did,* then you'd know.

Confidant Man I'm telling you, she is really attracted to me.

Unconvinced Friend But she totally ignores you.

Confidant Man Well, that proves it! She wouldn't be making such an active effort to ignore me if she weren't, deep down, really attracted to me.

Student Trainee My patient possesses the deeply ingrained characterological traits of Dependent Personality Disorder.

Clinical Colleague But she conducts her life in a fashion that is self-reliant, independent, and autonomous.

Student Trainee Obviously, that's just her way of engaging in the ego defense mechanism of overcompensation, which she utilizes to deny the fact that she's really got Dependent Personality Disorder.

Freudian Psychoanalyst All women have unconsciously repressed penis envy.

Female Student I'm a woman, and I don't wish to have a penis.

Freudian Psychoanalyst See what I mean? That just shows how deeply repressed in the unconscious your penis envy is.[3]

Worried Person They're plotting against me! They're plotting against me!

Doubter Now, hold on. Do you have any *evidence* that they're plotting against you?

Worried Person No, but I *feel* that they are, therefore they *must* be.

Sociopolitical Theorist Jews control the media.

Skeptic But the vast majority of people who head the networks and newspapers aren't Jewish.

Sociopolitical Theorist Exactly my point. All that proves is how *clever* they are in creating the appearance that they don't have any power. They have *so much* control that they've been able to dupe you into believing that they don't have *any* control.

Crusader All atheists, deep down, are profoundly depressed due to a lack of faith in God.

Nonbeliever But I'm an atheist, and I'm not depressed.

Crusader Then you can't really be an atheist.

Female Group Therapy Member All men really want is sex.

Male Group Therapy Member I'm a man, and that's not all *I* want.

Female Group Therapy Member Well, then either you're lying to me, or you're lying to yourself, or you're not *really* a man.

As an exercise in further examining the various manifestations of belief perseverance, try completing a few more of these scenarios on your own.

Person A You're planning on betraying me. I just *know* it.

Person B But I've treated you with nothing but honesty, respect, loyalty, and unconditional love.

Person A _____

_____ .

Person A You can't love anybody else unless you first love yourself.

Person B Well, I don't really love myself all that much, but I do love my child.

Person A _____

_____ .

Person A People who are frightened of intimacy were abused as children.

Person B But my boyfriend, who is very frightened of intimacy, wasn't abused as a child.

Person A _____

_____ .

Person A You've got a real problem with your anger issues.

Person B But I don't feel particularly angry, I don't have violent thoughts, and I almost never lose my temper.

Person A _____

_____ .

Person A You're attracted to your wife because she unconsciously reminds you of your mother, toward whom you have an unresolved Oedipal conflict with highly repressed incestuous sexual desires.

Person B But my wife is nothing like my mother.

Person A _____

_____ .

Person A The defendant is insane.

Person B But he claims to be completely responsible for his actions.

Person A _____

_____ .

As for antidotes to the Belief Perseverance Effect, there appear to be two useful strategies. The first one involves becoming more aware of our own cognitive processes. Specifically, we should remind ourselves (and others as well) to think carefully about how we evaluate evidence and to closely monitor our biases as we formulate conclusions (Fiske & Taylor, 1984). For instance, if you are a strong adherent of a particular method of psychotherapy, you should caution yourself against the tendency to exaggerate the evidence in favor of your own point of view while discounting evidence that supports the efficacy of other types of therapy.

Another method for reducing the impact of belief perseverance is to actively *counterargue* your preexisting beliefs (Anderson, 1982). In other words, ask yourself in what ways your beliefs might be wrong. Similarly, you can encourage others to explain why their beliefs might be wrong. One specific technique of doing so is to *consider the opposite* (see Metathought VI). Research shows that when people are instructed to consider the possibility that the opposite of their beliefs might be true, they are less likely to fall victim to belief perseverance (Lord, Lepper, & Preston, 1984).

For instance, if you are of the belief that the only effective way to ameliorate emotional distress is by exploring one's unconscious dynamics (such as unresolved early childhood trauma), consider the opposite: Namely, ask yourself in what ways one might be able to reduce emotional distress by focusing on one's *conscious* processes (for example, current goals or choices in life). Similarly, if it is your belief that significant changes in behavior can occur only by modifying one's *internal attitudes,* ask yourself how behavior might also be changed by modifying one's *external situations.*

To conclude, make an effort to keep an open mind to different, alternative, and (especially) challenging points of view. Unless you actively guard against the tendency to cling stubbornly to your beliefs in the face of disconfirming evidence, you may find that you will have unknowingly painted yourself into a corner where your only recourse and last line of defense will be to whimper woefully, "*Please* don't confuse me with the facts!"

Never forget that, in the final analysis, "the rat is always right." What is the meaning of this Metathought's cryptic subtitle and admonition? As a thought experiment, imagine that you have developed a magnificent theory concerning the behavior of rats in your laboratory maze. From your theory, you derive a specific hypothesis (that is, a prediction) that rats will always turn right in the maze. Now, let's say that you run thousands, even millions, of trials of rats in your maze. And, time after time, you are delighted to observe that, *without exception,* the rats do, in fact, turn right. Then late one night, to your astonishment (not to mention horror), one rat actually has the audacity to turn *left*! *Now* what do you do? Obviously, something's got to give. But what? The theory or the rat? Let me give you a hint: The rat wasn't wrong. In fact, in this context, the rat is *never* wrong. All it takes is *one* disconfirming piece of evidence, one ugly fact, and an entire theory can topple. In short, it's time to revise your theory to account for this new (albeit very unwelcome) bit of truth. If not, the theory ultimately will die on the vine. In sum, belief perseverance notwithstanding, *the rat is always right.*

Glossary Terms

The following terms (or variations) are defined in the Glossary:

accommodation
antidote
attitude
behavior
belief
Belief Perseverance Effect
bias
cause
clinical
conscious
consequence
data
deductive reasoning
disorder
dynamics
e.g.
effect
efficacy
ego defense mechanism
empirical
erroneous
evaluation
existence
external
fact

hypothesis
inductive reasoning
intentionality
internal
knowledge
logic
objective
personality
personality disorder
phenomenon
prediction
psychotherapy
rational
reasoning
reframe
repression
schema
scientific
skepticism
subsequent
tautologous reasoning
theory
trait
truth
unconscious

Notes

[1] For further experimental studies on belief perseverance, see Anderson, Lepper, and Ross (1980) and Lepper, Ross, and Lau (1986).

[2] These examples were drawn directly from my own experiences in a variety of settings, including classrooms, therapy sessions, clinical case conferences, and media broadcasts.

[3] For a comprehensive discussion of how belief perseverance appears to have been related to the development and current status of Freudian theory, I recommend Hans Eysenck's, *Decline and Fall of the Freudian Empire* (1985).

XXVI. *The Hindsight Bias: Predicting a Winner after the Race Is Finished*

Life is lived forwards, but understood backwards.
—SØREN KIERKEGAARD*

Anything seems commonplace, once explained.
—DR. WATSON**

A first-rate theory predicts; a second-rate theory forbids;
and a third-rate theory explains after the event.
—ALEKSANDER ISAAKOVICH KITAIGORODSKII

The *Hindsight Bias,* also known as the *I-knew-it-all-along phenomenon* (see Fischoff, 1975), refers to our tendency to believe that we would have foreseen how something turned out, after learning the outcome. In retrospect, events appear to us as obvious, predictable, or even unavoidable and inevitable. In other words, we tend to overestimate or exaggerate what we could have anticipated. It is one thing to explain after the fact why a particular horse won the race; it is quite another matter to predict beforehand which horse will win. Postdiction is easy; prediction is difficult.

In a classic example of the Hindsight Bias, the proverbial "Monday morning quarterback" can tell you, with astonishing confidence and precision, what his opponent was planning, what his team should have foreseen, and

*1813–1855
**In Arthur Conan Doyle's *Sherlock Holmes*

what could have been done to win the game—but, of course, all in retrospect. You may have experienced the Hindsight Bias yourself when reading a detective novel or seeing a mystery movie. Once the solution has been revealed, it seems glaringly obvious. Again, hindsight is always 20/20.

The Hindsight Bias is particularly problematic for "psychohistorians" who perform "psychological autopsies" on famous personalities (see Runyan, 1981) and for clinical psychologists who write retrospective case studies on their clients. In both instances, the investigator begins by already knowing what there is to "predict" (that is, how the person actually turned out). With this knowledge in hand, the investigator can proffer extensive and detailed after-the-fact (*post hoc*) explanations that, of course, confirm his theory and carry almost no risk of being disproven. Thus, irrespective of the writer's theoretical orientation, hindsight virtually guarantees a valid and infallible "explanation."

As an illustration of the Hindsight Bias, consider the following scenario. Suppose that, as you are browsing through the newspaper, you spot an interesting obituary about a great humanitarian, a man who dedicated his life to helping the downtrodden and the needy. He donated millions of dollars to charitable organizations, he provided food and shelter to the homeless, and he built schools, libraries, and hospitals for underprivileged children. You read further that his own childhood was exceptionally traumatic. He grew up in abject poverty, he witnessed the brutal murder of his father, and he watched helplessly as his mother slowly and painfully succumbed to cancer. Why did this man become such an altruist? It would be easy (perhaps even obvious) to explain his accomplishments in terms of his attempts to overcome or to compensate for the events of his childhood, by giving to others all of the things that he wished had been given to him.

Now, imagine the same scenario, but with one crucial difference: Suppose that, instead of becoming a humanitarian, he ended up becoming a serial killer, a man who was responsible for abducting, molesting, and murdering over a dozen elderly widows. How might we explain this outcome? Suddenly, the same past events (namely, his childhood poverty, his father's murder, and his mother's protracted and fatal illness) take on a completely different meaning. In fact, the very factors that in the first scenario ostensibly created an altruist, in the second scenario produced a psychopath. The outcome of his life now can "obviously" be explained in terms of his repressed rage, displaced aggression, and symbolic revenge . . . thanks to the Hindsight Bias.

The Hindsight Bias has been demonstrated empirically in numerous research studies (e.g., Fischoff, 1975, 1982; Fischoff & Beyth, 1975; Slovic & Fischhoff, 1977; Wood, 1979), all of which confirm that events seem far less obvious and predictable beforehand than in hindsight, and that knowing a result makes it seem inevitable. For example, when people are informed of the outcome of a historical event or a psychological experiment, it appears to be less surprising to them than it is to people who are asked to guess the outcome.

In this context, let's examine Stanley Milgram's (1963, 1974) experiments on obedience to authority, which are perhaps the most famous and controversial studies ever conducted in the field of psychology. To summarize briefly his basic experimental design, Milgram led the research subjects (all of them adult males) to believe that they were participating in an investigation on the effects of punishment on learning. As part of the experiment, the subjects were instructed to administer painful electric shocks to another subject every time he gave a wrong answer. (In fact, no real shocks were given, and the "other subject" actually was an accomplice[1] of the experimenter.) As the experiment progressed, the experimenter ordered the subjects to deliver more and more intense levels of shock. The accomplice, meanwhile, protested vehemently and screamed in agony. When the shocks seemed to reach fatal levels, the accomplice stopped responding entirely. Milgram's primary (dependent) variable of interest was the magnitude of shock that each subject would administer. The astonishing results were that nearly two-thirds of the subjects were fully obedient to the experimenter's orders, delivering the maximum "fatal" level of 450 volts.

Milgram subsequently performed a number of variations on this experiment, one of which entailed the use of female subjects. What effect do you think the sex of the subjects might have had on their degree of obedience? In the space below, indicate your best guess as to the outcome, *before reading any further.*

_____

_____

_____

_____

_____

As it turned out, the female subjects were substantially *more* obedient than were their male counterparts, with over 90% of them delivering the maximum shock level. Now, as an exercise, briefly offer your explanation for the underlying cause(s) of this result. In light of your prior prediction, how "obvious" or "unsurprising" does the outcome seem to you?

_____

_____

_____

_____

_____

Did you theorize that the female subjects were more obedient than male subjects because women in our culture are socialized to be more compliant toward authority figures? If so, you were mistaken, but not for the reason you might think. Actually, I must confess that I was less than honest in presenting to you the true results of this experiment, which did not turn out the way I indicated. In point of fact, the female subjects were significantly *less* obedient than were the male subjects, with most of them refusing to administer even the minimal levels of painful shock. Now that you know the actual results, how might you explain the cause(s)? Does the outcome now seem more obvious?

Did you postulate that women tend to be less aggressive and more empathic than men; therefore, their resistance to shocking an innocent victim would be higher? Well, I hate to tell you this, but...that's right, I gave you false results again. (Please understand that I engaged in this bit of benign deception with the sole intention of allowing you to experience firsthand just how the Hindsight Bias can operate.)

By the way, the *real* outcome of the experiment revealed that the rate of obedience for women was virtually *identical* to that of men. (Honest.) How would you explain *this* result? Does it now seem somehow more obvious?

This exercise is similar to a common method of studying the Hindsight Bias, which consists of presenting purported research findings, which are opposite and contradictory, to two groups of subjects. For example, one group may be informed that scientific research supports the belief that "out of sight is out of mind," whereas the other group is told that scientific research supports the belief that "absence makes the heart grow fonder." As it turns out, people in *both* groups find whichever result they were given as unsurprising "common sense." Of course, the results appear to be common sense only in hindsight.

Thus, the problem with many "common sense" explanations is not that they are wrong, but that we tend to use them only *after* we already know the outcome. In other words, they *describe* or *justify* much better than they *predict* or *explain.* As the example above shows us, we can find a proverb to make nearly any result seem like common sense. Because so many outcomes in life are possible, we have proverbs (many of them contradictory) to account for any occasion. As the following table illustrates, you can always find a commonsensical proverb to "explain" why an event turned out the way it did, no matter *what* the outcome.

TABLE 26-1 Which Proverb in Each Pair Is "Only Common Sense"?[2]

"Out of sight is out of mind." (Arthur Hugh Clough)	"No evil can happen to a good man." (Plato)
"Absence makes the heart grow fonder." (Sextus Aurelius)	"Nice guys finish last." (Leo Durocher)
"Haste makes waste." (John Heywood)	"Let your conscience be your guide." (Alexander Pope)
"He who hesitates is lost." (Anonymous)	"Conscience doth make cowards of us all." (William Shakespeare)
"'Tis better to have loved and lost than never to have loved at all." (Samuel Butler)	"Honesty is the best policy." (English proverb)
"A taste of honey is worse than none at all." (Anonymous)	"Tell the truth and get your head bashed in." (Hungarian proverb)
"Birds of a feather flock together." (Anonymous)	"If at first you don't succeed, try, try again." (William Edward Hickson)
"Opposites attract." (Anonymous)	"It's no use beating a dead horse." (Anonymous)
"You're never too old to learn." (Anonymous)	"It's not whether you win or lose but how you played the game." (Grantland Rice)
"You can't teach an old dog new tricks." (Anonymous)	"Winning isn't everything—it's the only thing." (Vincent Lombardi)
"No man is an island." (John Donne)	"There is no proverb that is not true." (Cervantes)
"Every man is an island." (Thomas Wolfe)	"General notions are generally wrong." (Lady Mary Wortley Montague)
"Opportunity knocks but once." (Anonymous)	
"Look before you leap." (Samuel Butler)	

The Hindsight Bias thus sheds light on one of the most prevalent criticisms of the entire field of psychology, namely, that it is "only common sense" expressed in more sophisticated terms and technical language. Specifically, some people view psychological research as trivial because it merely documents the obvious.[3] But just how obvious, *really*, are the results of psychological research? Remember that we typically learn of such studies only *after the fact*. When viewed in hindsight, how could they, in the vast majority of cases, appear as anything else *but* obvious and inevitable?

Is there an antidote to the Hindsight Bias? Slovic and Fischoff (1977) apparently found one. Subjects in their investigation were informed of the results of a number of experiments. Some of the subjects were then asked, "Had the study worked out the other way, how would you explain it?" These subjects saw the actual results as much less inevitable than did those subjects who had not been instructed to imagine the opposite result.

The conclusion? The Hindsight Bias can deceive you into believing that you know more than you actually do; however, one way to reduce its effect is to imagine how you might explain a result that is *different* from the one that actually occurred.

Glossary Terms

The following terms (or variations) are defined in the Glossary:

antidote	knowledge
belief	phenomenon
bias	postdiction
clinical	*post hoc*
dependent variable	prediction
description	psychological
e.g.	psychology
effect	repression
event	resistance
experience	scientific
explanation	social
fact	subsequent
Hindsight Bias	theoretical
intent	theory

Notes

[1] In the parlance of social researchers, an experimental accomplice is also referred to as a *confederate*.

[2] Unfortunately, I was not able to verify (or in some cases even locate) the original sources for a number of these quotations. Which reminds me of another quotation that seems apropos: "The most valuable quotation will be the one for which you cannot determine the source. The source for an unattributed quota-tion will appear in the most hostile review of your work." (Fortunately, I *do* have the reference for this quote: Arthur Bloch, *Murphy's Law, Book Two*, 1980).

[3] In his excellent textbook, David Myers (1995) effectively applies critical thinking principles to examine this phenomenon, as well as other contemporary issues facing the field of psychology.

Part Five

Other Biases and Fallacies in Thinking

XXVII. *The Representativeness Bias: Fits and Misfits of Categorization*

We all know we are unique individuals, but we tend to see others as representative of groups.
—DEBORAH TANNEN*

If my theory of relativity is proven successful, Germany will claim me as a German and France will declare that I am a citizen of the world. Should my theory prove untrue, France will say that I am a German and Germany will declare that I am a Jew.
—ALBERT EINSTEIN**

If it walks like a duck, and quacks like a duck, then it just may be a duck.
—WALTER REUTHER***

In everyday life, we are frequently called upon to make rapid judgments in circumstances that do not lend themselves to thoroughness or accuracy. Consider the following scenarios:

> >At a job interview, you have a limited amount of time to figure out how to create the right impression.

*Quoted in Santrock, 1995
**Address, at the Sorbonne, quoted in *The Pocket Book of Quotations,* Davidoff, 1952
***1907–1970, attributed by William Safire, *Safire's Political Dictionary;* cited in *The New International Dictionary of Quotations,* Miner & Rawson, 1994

>After receiving an urgent telephone call, you might have to decide on the best way to break some bad news to a close friend.

>During a committee meeting, you may be required to expeditiously narrow down a large pool of candidates who are applying for a limited number of positions.

>In a therapy setting, you might be assigned the task of quickly conducting an intake interview and determining a clinical diagnosis.

An ideal strategy for making decisions in these situations (and countless others like them) would involve the opportunity to conduct a comprehensive and systematic analysis of the problem, collect relevant data, test various hypotheses, draw appropriate inferences, thoroughly evaluate the pluses and minuses of all possible outcomes, and arrive at the optimum conclusions before having to take final action.

Well, so much for the ideal. For obvious reasons, such a strategy is impractical in most real-life circumstances. We do not have the time, information, or resources (not to mention incentive) that would enable us to solve most problems in this manner.

How, then, *do* we proceed to make decisions in the face of varying degrees of uncertainty? Cognitive psychologists Amos Tversky and Daniel Kahneman (1974) theorized that people use a variety of mental shortcuts, rules of thumb, or *heuristics* that reduce complex and time-consuming tasks to more simple, manageable, practical, and efficient problem-solving strategies. We all have a repertoire of such shortcuts, which we tend to use automatically, without necessarily considering their accuracy or validity in each situation.

Unfortunately, these rules of thumb are double-edged swords. On the one hand, they permit highly efficient information processing and rapid solutions to the problem. In other words, they help us to make quick "seat-of-the-pants" decisions. However, they do so at the expense of thoroughness and precision. In essence, we trade off accuracy for speed (see Metathought XXX, Every Decision Is a Trade-Off). Thus, the price we pay for their efficiency can be bad or wrong judgments. Nevertheless, despite their drawbacks, heuristics are an extremely useful collection of strategies that greatly facilitate rapid information processing in the multitude of decisions—both large and small—we make every day.

Tversky and Kahneman (1973, 1982) identified a number of such shortcuts, including the *representativeness* heuristic and the *availability* heuristic (see Metathought XXVIII).[1] According to Tversky and Kahneman, representativeness is the most basic cognitive heuristic. Essentially, it involves judging the likelihood that something belongs to (that is, "represents") a particular category. Stated slightly more formally, representativeness is a method of estimating the probability that Instance *A* is a member of Category *B*.

We use the representativeness heuristic to identify phenomena in our environment by automatically and intuitively comparing the phenomenon (be it a person, object, event, or ideology) to our mental representation, *prototype,* or *schema* of the relevant category. In so doing, we are attempting to ascertain if there is a "match" on the basis of whether the phenomenon's features are similar to the essential features of the category. If there is a match, we conclude that we have successfully identified the phenomenon; if not, we continue our cognitive search.

One of our most common uses of the representativeness heuristic involves judging whether a person belongs to a specific group based on how similar he or she is to typical members of that group. As an exercise, consider the following personality sketch (from Tversky & Kahneman, 1974): "Steve is very shy and withdrawn, invariably helpful, but with little interest in people, or in the world of reality. A meek and tidy soul, he has a need for order and structure, and a passion for detail."

Now, if you were asked to guess Steve's occupation, which of the following would you select: farmer, trapeze artist, librarian, salvage driver, or surgeon? (Indicate your answer by circling the appropriate job title.)

Approximately how long did it take you to reach your decision? _____

On what basis did you arrive at this conclusion? What method or rationale (if any) did you employ?_____

_____

_____

_____

_____

_____

Before we discuss your response, let's examine an "optimal" approach to solving this problem. With no constraints placed on your time or resources, you could (although I'm not quite sure why you'd ever *want* to) systematically calculate the statistical probabilities that Steve is a member of each occupation. In so doing, you would need to acquire, organize, and analyze extensive data on the comparative frequencies of job membership as well as the correlations between these occupations and particular personality characteristics.

Needless to say, such an endeavor would be thoroughly impractical and unquestionably not worth the costs involved. Fortunately, the representativeness heuristic provides a relatively quick, simple, and painless alternative.

Back to the exercise. If you are like most research participants, you reached your decision very quickly with the use of the representativeness heuristic. Specifically, you were likely to have surmised that Steve is a librarian. Why? Because the description of his personality (Instance *A*) most closely resembles the characteristics stereotypically associated with librarians (Category *B*).

Consider a few more illustrations. The representativeness heuristic could, in like manner, lead you to conclude that Jill (*A*) is an actress because she behaves like your stereotype of an actress (*B*). Or that Jack (*A*) belongs to a fraternity because he looks like your prototypical fraternity member (*B*). Or that Barbara (*A*) is a therapist because her demeanor is similar to your schema of a therapist (*B*). Or that Joe (*A*) is an alcoholic because his appearance matches your conception of an alcoholic (*B*).

In addition to identifying people, we also use the representativeness heuristic for identifying objects (model of automobile, flavor of food, style of art), events (recreational, romantic, dangerous), ideologies (religious, philosophical, political), or even as a means of assigning causal explanations to actions (random, unintentional, malevolent). As you can readily see, this simple act is fundamental to all subsequent inferences and behaviors: Before any other cognitive task can be addressed, we must first answer the question, "What is it?"

As an exercise in identifying and exploring the nature and content of your own cognitive schemata, select three social categories (e.g., sex, race, ethnicity, occupation, religion, political affiliation, and so on) for which you happen to have fairly well-defined attitudes, beliefs, or impressions. Now, describe in detail the specific content (i.e., your personal perceptions) of each schema. Next, try to determine the schema's etiology (origin) and development. Last, try to recall (or imagine) an occasion where you came across an instance that clearly was inconsistent with (i.e., did not "fit") your schema. How did (might) you respond? What happened (might happen) to the schema itself?

Social Schema 1: _____

Content: _____

_____

_____

_____

Etiology and development: _____

_____

_____

_____

Your response to schema-inconsistent event: _____

_____

_____

_____

Social Schema 2: _____

Content: _____

_____

_____

_____

Etiology and development: _____

_____

_____

_____

Your response to schema-inconsistent event: _____

_____

_____

_____

_____

Social Schema 3: _____

Content: _____

_____

_____

_____

Etiology and development: _____

_____

_____

_____

Your response to schema-inconsistent event: _____

_____

_____

_____

Systematic Sources of Error

Although in most instances the representativeness heuristic yields quick and relatively accurate results, it sometimes produces systematic errors in information processing. We shall refer to this effect as the *Representativeness Bias*. There are numerous factors that can cause the Representativeness Bias (see Metathought XIV, Multiple Pathways of Causation), the most significant of which are enumerated and discussed below. Fortunately, most of them can be ameliorated by becoming sensitive to their presence and taking appropriate corrective measures (see Fiske and Taylor [1984] for a comprehensive discussion).

1. Our use of representativeness gives rise to faulty judgments when our initial prototypes are inaccurate, biased, or incomplete. In these instances, we are attempting to classify phenomena by comparing them to invalid schemata. To continue with the examples described above, ask yourself just how accurate are your prototypes of librarians, actresses, fraternity members, therapists, alcoholics, or any other group of people. To the extent that any given stereotype is erroneous (as they all, to some degree, are), the result could be a mistake in judgment. In the same way, if a therapist compares a client's presenting symptoms (*A*) to his or her inaccurate clinical schemata (*B*), a misdiagnosis is all but inevitable.

2. Other critical sources of error leading to the Representativeness Bias are due to the failure to take into account relevant statistical information, such as *base rates, sample size,* and *chance probability.* First, we tend to underuse or even ignore base-rate information (that is, data pertaining to the actual frequency of events in a particular group). Instead, we are prone to reach decisions primarily on the basis of how well any given phenomenon *resembles* our own subjective conceptions of the category. Referring back to the previous example, suppose you discover that Steve lives in a small, rural town where most of the residents are chicken farmers. Clearly, your judgment that he is a librarian should be modified by these facts. Unfortunately, however, such vital base-rate information often is overlooked or disregarded when we rely principally on the similarities we believe to exist, for instance, between personality characteristics and group membership.[2] As a consequence, in comparing instances (*A*) to categories (*B*), we run the risk of allowing perceived similarities to obscure genuine differences (see Metathought VII, the Similarity–Uniqueness Paradox). In other words, we tend to overvalue similarities while undervaluing the actual distribution of likelihood.

3. The Representativeness Bias can also result from our insensitivity to the effects of sample size. Research has shown us, time and time again, that estimates that are derived from large samples are more reliable than estimates derived from small samples. Nevertheless, when forming judgments, we typically do not take this principle into account. As a consequence, despite the fact that data collected from small samples cannot be counted on as trustworthy predictors of a population's characteristics, we are prone to commit the error of overgeneralizing from too small a sample. To illustrate this concept mathematically, even though 7 out of 10 looks like better odds than 60 out of 100, the more reliable indicator is the 60 out of 100.

4. Our misconceptions about what "chance events" ought to look like can also produce the Representativeness Bias. In particular, when we are confronted with an exceptionally rare or extraordinary event (for instance, an unusual winning or losing streak, uncanny coincidence, or bizarre behavior), we might be tempted to conclude that it was due to an extraordinary cause. Yet, as discussed in the Spectacular Explanation Fallacy (Metathought XIX), chance alone predicts the occasional occurrence of extraordinary events. Thus, it would be an error to conclude that an unusual phenomenon (*A*) is *necessarily* indicative of anything other than statistical probability (*B*).

5. Last, consider how your own *motivational biases,* personal wishes, or desires for something to fit (or not fit) a particular category may bias your perceptions and subsequent judgments. Thus, even though there may be a match between an instance and a category, if you don't want it to exist, you would be less likely to perceive it. Similarly, if you do want there to be a match, you would be more inclined to "see" one, whether or not it actually exists (see Metathought XXIII, the Assimilation Bias).

For example, let's say that you have a client in your psychotherapy practice of whom you are especially fond (or, in the vernacular of clinical psychology, toward whom you have developed a *"positive countertransference"*). You may, as a consequence, have a tendency to inadvertently minimize, or even overlook, the severity of her psychological problems. In such an instance, when faced with the question of determining her clinical diagnosis, your use of the representativeness heuristic could result in a significant (and potentially costly) mistake. In particular, by relying primarily on your own idiosyncratic impressions (rather than a structured, systematic assessment of specific diagnostic criteria), you run the risk of unintentionally allowing your positive feelings toward your client to distort, obstruct, or otherwise bias your clinical perceptions and judgment. Thus, you may fail to see, for instance, that her symptoms match the criteria for a diagnosis of schizophrenia. In this way, the Representativeness Bias yields a *"false negative"* diagnostic error (that is, not perceiving a problem that actually does exist).

Your personal, motivational biases can also produce the opposite outcome. Suppose that you have a client whom you especially *dislike* (aka *"negative countertransference"*). Even on a good day, you find her to be nothing short of irritating, obnoxious, belligerent, and just plain rude. Here, you may be prompted to come up with a diagnostic label that best explains away her odious demeanor (and thereby also reduce your own sense of frustration). Needless to say, your clinical perceptions and judgment in this process are liable to be adversely distorted by your negative feelings toward her. Thus, you may quickly, easily, (and perhaps unconsciously) see a match between your client's behavior and a diagnosis of, let's say, Borderline Personality Disorder, irrespective of whether or not she actually meets the clinical criteria. In scenarios of this type, the Representativeness Bias produces a *"false positive"* diagnostic error (that is, perceiving a problem that does not actually exist).

Before concluding this Metathought, one final point deserves mention. Despite all of the problems, pitfalls, and liabilities associated with the use of cognitive heuristics, we persist in relying on them as an integral component of our decision-making processes. Why? One of the main reasons is that, on the whole, they provide us with more right answers than wrong ones. Moreover, even in those circumstances where they are incorrect, the results typically are inconsequential.

One significant exception, however, can occur in relation to our usage of prototype categories about particular groups of people, based on, for example, their race, sex, culture, nationality, religion, or even clinical diagnosis. When viewed in this context, such group-related schemata are equivalent to stereotypes. Thus, when heuristics such as representativeness are utilized with respect to these categories, extreme caution is advised. As history has repeatedly demonstrated, stereotyping can have far-reaching and potentially harmful social consequences, not the least of which include prejudice, bigotry, and discrimination...outcomes that are far from inconsequential.

Glossary Terms

The following terms (or variations) are defined in the Glossary:

attitude	heuristic
availability heuristic	i.e.
base rate	ideology
behavior	intuition
belief	judgment
bias	mental
category	motivational bias
causal	negative countertransference
cause	perception
chance	personality
clinical	personality disorder
cognitive	phenomenon
concept	positive countertransference
consequence	probability
correlation	psychological
countertransference	psychology
criteria	psychotherapy
critical	random
data	reliability
decision	Representativeness Bias
description	representativeness heuristic
diagnosis	schema
disorder	social
e.g.	Spectacular Explanation Fallacy
effect	stereotype
erroneous	subjective
etiology	subsequent
evaluation	symptom
event	unconscious
explanation	validity
fact	

Notes

[1] It should be noted that these are not the only heuristics that people employ in reaching decisions under conditions of uncertainty. Others include the *simulation* heuristic (Kahneman & Tversky, 1982) and the *anchoring and adjustment* heuristic (Tversky & Kahneman, 1974). In addition, the social perceiver also utilizes idiosyncratic heuristics that apply to the individual's particular life circumstances (see Fiske & Taylor, 1984).

[2] For the results of a study that investigated people's perceptions of the relationships between personality characteristics and occupational role schemata, see Levy, Kaler, and Schall (1988).

XXVIII. The Availability Bias: The Persuasive Power of Vivid Events

One picture is worth a thousand words.
—ANONYMOUS

When a dog bites a man, that is not news.
But when a man bites a dog, that is news.
—JOHN B. BOGART*

For we must make no mistake about ourselves:
we are as much automaton as mind.
—BLAISE PASCAL**

As a means of introducing this Metathought, try to give your best estimates for the following questions:

1. What are the odds of sustaining a fatal accident traveling by car as compared to traveling by commercial airplane?
2. What percentage of deaths in the United States each year are caused by accidents and what percentage by cardiovascular diseases (such as heart attacks and strokes)?
3. What are the relative frequencies of deaths annually due to tornados, versus accidents, versus asthma?

---

*1845–1921, quoted in Frank M. O'Brien, *The Story of the Sun;* cited in *The New International Dictionary of Quotations,* Miner & Rawson, 1994
**1623–1662, *Pensées:* 821

4. Which is more frequent in English, words that start with the letter *k,* or words that have *k* as their third letter?

5. What is the prevalence of persons who either are, or ever have been, in psychotherapy?

6. What are the rates of psychopathology (such as depression, anxiety, or substance abuse) in the general population?

7. How common is the use of the insanity defense in courtroom trials?

Setting aside for the moment the actual answers to these questions, consider the cognitive processes you utilized reaching your conclusions. How, specifically, did you go about arriving at your estimates for each question? Did you notice any similarity in the mental strategies you employed?

If you are like most people in this way, your estimates probably were determined primarily on the basis of how *easily* or *quickly* specific instances of each question came to mind. And what types of incidents are more likely to stand out in memory? In general, events that create the most powerful impressions are those that are particularly vivid, dramatic, important, personally relevant, or otherwise salient to us. We are also prone to more quickly think of instances that are simply easy to imagine.

Unfortunately, however, the problem in relying on the ease with which events can be retrieved from memory for determining their likelihood is that our perceptions cannot necessarily be counted on as an accurate reflection of reality. Specifically, this strategy leads us to *overestimate* their actual occurrence, frequency, or distribution in the world.

Did you inadvertently succumb to this bias in answering any of the questions posed above? Let's examine each one in turn.

1. Few events are more disturbing than the graphic sights and sounds of a catastrophic airplane crash. Even a mere glimpse of these horrific images on the eleven o'clock news is likely to stamp in our minds a potent and indelible impression. Such tragic accidents, therefore, become easily accessible and readily available in our memory. As a consequence, many people erroneously jump to the conclusion that they are at greater risk when traveling by commercial airplane than by car. Yet, mile for mile, Americans are nearly *100 times* more likely to die in an automobile accident than in a commercial plane accident (Greenwald, 1986).

2. Despite the fact that cardiovascular diseases cause *ten times* as many deaths as accidents (50% versus 5%), most people overestimate the relative frequency of accidents. Why? Because accidents, compared to more common causes of death, are so much more startling, vivid, and therefore, memorable (see Slovic, Fischoff, & Lichtenstein, 1976).

3. When people are asked to estimate the frequency of deaths from a number of causes, they typically overestimate the rare and sensational instances (for example, deaths due to accidents or tornados), while underestimating the less dramatic but more frequent instances (for instance, deaths due to asthma). In point of fact, however, asthma causes *sixteen times* more deaths than accidents and about *twenty times* more deaths than tornados (see Slovic, 1987).

4. Most people choose the *k*-initial words, despite the fact that *k* is three times more likely to appear as the third letter. Why? According to Tversky and Kahneman (1974), it is *easier* to retrieve words from memory by their initial letter than by their third one, the consequence of which is a biased estimate of their frequency.

5. In responding to this question, your thoughts probably turned automatically to the number of people you personally know who are, or who have been, psychotherapy clients. Now, if you happen to be a mental health professional, a graduate student in psychology, an undergraduate psychology major, or even someone who is "psychologically-minded," the chances are that you know quite a few people who have, at some point, been in therapy. Further, you also are more likely to *notice* and *remember* instances of such persons. Conversely, if your area of study, practice, or interest is essentially unrelated to psychology, you are less likely to know (or perhaps be aware of) many people who are in therapy. Either way, you would be prone to arrive at a biased judgment (*overestimation* in the former case, *underestimation* in the latter case), based on the relative ease (or difficulty) with which instances of persons in therapy come to mind.

6. Your strategy for estimating the frequency of different forms of psychopathology also was very likely to have been a function of specific examples that, for various reasons, happened to stand out in your memory. In addition to direct knowledge of individuals from your personal and professional relationships who exhibit psychological problems, what other sources of information influenced your judgment? Did you consider the omnipresent and virtually inescapable barrage of psychological phenomena in the popular media? Take a few moments to reflect on the potential power of feature films; news broadcasts; television talk shows; radio call-in programs; disease-of-the-week, made-for-TV movies; documentaries; docudramas; newspaper and magazine articles; televised courtroom trials; and self-help books, not to mention advertising in the form of public service announcements; television and radio commercials; and billboards and print ads, to name but a few.

Because the media's very existence is, to a large extent, predicated on grabbing and holding our attention, instances of psychopathology typically are presented in a manner that ranges from the dramatic and engrossing, to the rare and unusual, to the sensationalistic and shocking: in a word, *memorable*. All of this leads us to overestimate its frequency in the general population. For the same reasons, we almost certainly would underestimate the incidence of "nonpathological," "normal," or "healthy" (whatever that might be) instances of human behavior—none of which is particularly newsworthy, entertaining, or otherwise useful for the vast majority of media purposes.

7. Popular opinion notwithstanding, the insanity defense—"not guilty by reason of insanity"—is utilized very infrequently. Over time, it has been invoked in less than 2 percent of courtroom cases (Fersch, 1980), in fewer than 1 out of 400 homicide trials, and even more rarely in nonhomicide trials (Rosenhan & Seligman, 1995). Further, it has been successful in many fewer cases than that (Rosenhan & Seligman, 1995). Why then, do people typically overestimate the extent to which the insanity defense is employed? This misconception is attributable primarily to the notoriety surrounding high-visibility cases in which it has been exposed to widespread public scrutiny. Certainly one of the most notorious cases in point was the trial of John W. Hinckley, Jr., who, on June 21, 1982, was found to be not guilty by reason of insanity in his attempted assassination of former President Ronald Reagan. Here again we see how vivid, although rare, events can exert a disproportionate influence on our estimates of their actual frequency.

You will recall from our discussion of the Representativeness Bias (Metathought XXVII) that, because we are limited in our capacity to process complex information, we utilize mental shortcuts or *heuristics* to simplify the world and thereby reach expedient solutions. In other words, we tend to focus on rapid and efficient, rather than slow and accurate, understanding.

The specific cognitive strategy demonstrated in the above examples has been termed the *availability heuristic* (Tversky & Kahneman, 1973) because it refers to the process of drawing on instances that are easily accessible or "available" from our memory. This heuristic helps us to answer questions concerning the frequency ("How many are there?"), incidence ("How often does something happen?"), or likelihood ("What are the odds that something will occur?") of particular events.

If examples are readily available in memory, we tend to assume that such events occur rather frequently. For instance, if you have no trouble bringing to mind examples of *X*, you are likely to judge that it is common. By contrast, if it takes you awhile to think of examples of *X*, you are prone to conclude that it is uncommon. In sum, when an event has easily retrieved instances, it will seem more numerous than will an equally frequent category that has less easily retrieved instances.

As is the case with the representativeness heuristic, very little cognitive work is needed to utilize the availability heuristic. Further, under a great many circumstances, the availability heuristic provides us with accurate and dependable estimates. After all, if examples easily come to mind, it usually is because there are many of them.

Unfortunately, however, there are a number of biasing factors that can affect the availability of events in our memory without altering their actual occurrence. Problems arise when this strategy is used, for instance, to estimate the frequency or likelihood of rare, though highly vivid, events as compared to those that are more typical, commonplace, or mundane in nature. When our use of the availability heuristic results in systematic errors in making such judgments, we may refer to this as the *Availability Bias.*

Perhaps the single most important factor underlying the Availability Bias is our propensity to underuse, discount, or even ignore, relevant base-rate information (that is, data about the actual frequency of events in a particular group) and other abstract statistical facts in favor of more salient and concrete, but usually less reliable, anecdotal evidence. As a consequence, personal testimonials, graphic case studies, dramatic stories, colorful tales, intriguing narratives, eye-catching illustrations, vibrant images, extraordinary occurrences, and bizarre events all are liable to slant, skew, or otherwise distort our judgments.

To cite one example, Borgida and Nisbett (1977) found that when students were faced with the task of forming impressions of a potential classroom instructor, they were more influenced by a few personal testimonies than by a comprehensive statistical summary of many students' ratings of the teacher. In the study, subjects (students) were informed that the average rating by 112 students for a Learning and Memory course was between "very good" and "excellent." Subsequently, some subjects also heard two or three students from the course express their feelings directly ("I thought the course was too simplistic..."). Now, statistically speaking, the subjects should simply have combined these few additional personal testimonies with the much larger data pool, the net effect of which would have been virtually inconsequential. Such was not, however, the case. In fact, the very small number of student testimonials actually had *more impact* on subjects' perceptions than the statistically summarized ratings of a substantially larger group of students. As this study so clearly demonstrates, a mere dollop of vivid information is capable of completely eclipsing and overshadowing more reliable but less "personal" statistical data.

Another significant problem related to the Availability Bias concerns our proclivity to *overgeneralize* from a few vivid examples, or sometimes even just a single vivid instance. This error in inductive reasoning (see Metathought XX) is responsible, at least in part, for the phenomenon of *stereotyping.*

In general, how do we formulate our beliefs about particular groups of people, whether racial, cultural, national, religious, political, occupational, or any other category? We typically base our impressions on observations of specific members of the group. But *which* members? By and large, our attention is drawn to the most conspicuous, prominent, or salient individuals. We then are prone to overgeneralize from these few extreme examples to the group as a whole, the result of which is a role schema (see Metathought XXIII, the Assimilation Bias) or stereotype. In this way, the Availability Bias leads us to perpetuate vivid but false beliefs about the characteristics of a wide variety of groups in our society.

Fortunately, there are a number of strategies you can employ to mitigate against the Availability Bias. First, whenever you are faced with the task of estimating the frequency or likelihood of an event, be careful not to rely on the ease or speed with which relevant examples come to mind. Instead, make a conscious effort to seek out and utilize base-rate information or other pertinent statistical data in reaching your conclusions. Suppose, for instance, that you are attempting to determine the prevalence of various types of psychopathology in the general population (as in question (6) above). In this case, a wise course of action would be to consult well-designed epidemiological research studies,[1] which are unquestionably more reliable sources of information than one's own "top of the head" impressions.

Second, take anecdotal evidence not with a grain but with several large shakers of salt. Although personal testimonies and dramatic case studies may be very persuasive, remember that they are not inherently trustworthy indicators of fact. Further, clinicians should exercise extreme caution when evaluating the results of any psychological assessment techniques that are highly reliant on the observer's subjective impressions and interpretations (such as the House-Tree-Person or other projective drawing tests), in contrast to tests that are empirically validated on appropriate research populations.

Third, resist the temptation to overgeneralize from a limited selection of instances or events. Don't forget that the best basis for generalizing is not from the exceptional, though vivid, cases one finds at the extremes, but rather from a representative sample of cases.

In conclusion, we tend to be more persuaded by an ounce of anecdotal evidence than by a pound of reliable statistics. Although vivid and dramatic events can make for appetizing fiction, they are ultimately unsatisfying to those with a taste for reality.

Glossary Terms

The following terms (or variations) are defined in the Glossary:

abstract	data
affect	disease
attribution	effect
Availability Bias	empirical
availability heuristic	erroneous
base rate	evaluation
behavior	event
belief	existence
bias	fact
category	heuristic
cause	inductive reasoning
cognitive	interpretation
concrete	judgment
conscious	knowledge
consequence	mental

mind	psychotherapy
normal	reliability
observation	Representativeness Bias
opinion	representativeness heuristic
perception	schema
phenomenon	stereotype
projective test	subjective
psychological	subsequent
psychology	vivid

Notes

[1] Examples of such research would include the comprehensive investigations of Myers and associates (1984), Robins and associates (1984), and Regier and associates (1988).

XXIX. The Insight Fallacy: To Understand Something Isn't Necessarily to Change It

It is naive to expect that, by telling people what we think we see
they are doing, we will enable them to stop doing it.
—R. D. LAING*

Recollection without affect almost
invariably produces no result.
—JOSEF BREUER AND SIGMUND FREUD**

One of our most prevalent and enduring societal myths is that once we can *understand* a problem, it will automatically *solve* the problem. In other words, people have a tendency to assume that insight alone invariably produces useful change.

Why is this an invalid assumption? Let us take, as a rather obvious example, the problem of removing kidney stones. We may understand perfectly well how kidney stones are created. And this knowledge might be very useful in helping us to design interventions that prevent the formation of kidney stones. But the knowledge itself doesn't inherently solve the problem of kidney stone removal; unfortunately, all the insight in the world can't dissolve or extract a kidney stone!

Within the field of psychology, nowhere is the Insight Fallacy more apparent than in psychotherapy. Many persons—therapists, clients, and the public

**The Politics of the Family*, 1969
***Studies on Hysteria*, 1895

alike—cling to the alluring yet unproven belief that by understanding a psychological problem, it will somehow spontaneously resolve itself: "If I can only figure it out, then I'll feel better and it will go away."

As an illustration, suppose that you are a client in psychotherapy. And after undergoing month after year after decade of intensive analysis, taking batteries of psychological tests, interpreting your unconscious dynamics, recognizing your recurring life themes and patterns, correlating your current situation with your past situations, seeing the connection between your parents' behavior and your behavior, attending dozens of weekend self-growth workshops, reading innumerable self-help books and magazine articles, you finally turn to your therapist and say something akin to:

"Doc, I entered therapy because I felt so abandoned/abused/abusive/acrophobic/addictive/aggressive/agitated/agoraphobic/alexithymic/alienated/alone/ambivalent/angry/anxious/apathetic/avoidant/bashful/betrayed/bitter/borderline/bored/catatonic/claustrophobic/codependent/compulsive/competitive/confused/crazy/critical/cruel/dangerous/defensive/delusional/dependent/depersonalized/depressed/deprived/desperate/detached/devastated/discontented/discouraged/disillusioned/disordered/disorganized/disoriented/dissatisfied/dissociated/distressed/disturbed/dumb/dysfunctional/emotional/emotionless/empty/enmeshed/evil/explosive/fake/fearful/frightened/furious/grandiose/guarded/guilty/helpless/hostile/histrionic/hopeless/hydrophobic/hypermanic/hypersomnic/hypochondriacal/hypomanic/hyposomnic/impatient/impulsive/inadequate/incompetent/indecisive/indifferent/immature/inferior/insecure/insomnic/irritable/isolated/jealous/judgmental/lonely/lost/maladjusted/malcontented/manic/manipulative/masochistic/miserable/misunderstood/narcissistic/needy/nervous/neurotic/numb/obsessive/odd/overcontrolled/overresponsible/oversensitive/oversocialized/pained/panicky/paranoid/passive/passive–aggressive/pessimistic/phobic/phony/powerless/pressured/psychotic/rebellious/rejected/repressed/revengeful/sad/sadistic/screwed-up/selfish/shy/split-off/stressed/stubborn/stuck/stupid/suicidal/suspicious/tense/terrified/tormented/tortured/toxic/trapped/troubled/unattractive/uncontrolled/undersocialized/unfeeling/unhappy/unlovable/unloved/unreal/unstable/unsuccessful/victimized/weird/worried/xenophobic/yearning/zoophobic.

And now I can honestly say that I truly understand *why* I feel so abandoned/.../zoophobic.

But, Doc, the problem is that I *still feel* abandoned/.../zoophobic. And I still don't know what to *do* about it."

In presenting this hypothetical (and obviously exaggerated) vignette, I certainly am not suggesting that explanations are worthless; or, as others have concluded, that insight is "the booby prize of life." In fact, I would like to underscore the value of insight in psychotherapy by enumerating three of its most useful attributes.

Benefits of Insight

First, gaining insight into the causes of a problem can, in itself, provide us with a source of relief or comfort simply by stripping away the mystique that frequently shrouds unexplained phenomena. Once we discover a rational basis or explanation for the occurrence of a problem, it is likely to feel more manageable; thus, *insight empowers by demystifying.*

Second, insight can be a critical first step toward adopting specific problem-solving strategies. If the causes of a problem can be identified, we may be in a better position to select a particular course of action to alleviate the situation. To take an example, consider a person who enters psychotherapy because she is plagued by chronic and unremitting depression. No matter what she's tried, she's been completely unable to break free of her intransigent misery. In the course of therapy, however, she gains the insight that her depression is due primarily to unresolved (and heretofore unrecognized) grief over the numerous losses—both literal and symbolic—that she has experienced in her life. Armed with this knowledge, the therapist may then design and implement specific therapeutic techniques that help her to adaptively and appropriately mourn these losses, thereby lifting her shroud of depression.

Third, insight can function as the "psychological glue" that consolidates and integrates one's thoughts, feelings, behavior, and experiences into a meaningful new whole, thereby resulting in more stable and long-lasting change. Once the person is able to explain, understand, or otherwise make sense of himself and his situation, this knowledge becomes internalized and therefore more enduring. As a consequence, the client is better able to translate (or generalize) the gains he has achieved in therapy into his future relationships and life challenges. In this context, insight can serve as a vital final step in the therapy process.

Limitations and Drawbacks of Insight

These advantages notwithstanding, problems can arise when people fail to recognize the *limits* of what insight is able to provide. Specifically, a number of clinical orientations (such as Freudian psychoanalysis and other psychodynamic approaches) have come under heavy fire for their fundamental belief that intellectual insight is a *sine qua non* (that is, an essential and indispensable ingredient) of successful therapy. Critics not only question the validity of this underlying assumption, they also point to the absence of clear empirical evidence that insight is, in fact, a necessary component of therapeutic effectiveness (see Corey, 1991).

As a consequence, numerous alternative orientations have emerged that discount (or even dismiss outright) the role of insight in clinical practice, some of which include: behavior therapies (systematic desensitization, progressive relaxation, biofeedback, flooding, aversive conditioning); strategic and structural family therapies; experiential psychotherapies (Gestalt therapy, psychodrama, movement therapy, art therapy, music therapy); and hypnotherapy—none of which relies fundamentally on achieving insights or understanding to produce significant and effective change.

Moreover, some people have gone so far as to argue that emphasizing insight can be *counterproductive*, even *detrimental,* to therapeutic progress. They maintain that extensive searching for cognitive insight allows both clients and therapists to avoid feeling unpleasant (yet essential) emotions, and instead to hide behind the comfort and apparent safety of logic, reason, and rationality. Unfortunately, then, it actually may hinder clients' progress by encouraging them to make excessive use of the ego defense mechanisms of *intellectualization, rationalization,* and *isolation of affect* (see A. Freud, 1936). Although this outcome may succeed in temporarily blocking out their anxiety, it does so at the expense of cutting themselves off further from their feelings, as well as falsifying, distorting, or denying reality. Taken to its extreme, seeking insight becomes an empty exercise in intellectual futility, which can exacerbate the client's problems by isolating them into the "neck-up" region of emotional dissociation. Thus, winning the battle of insight may, ironically, contribute to losing the war of genuine therapeutic success.

To summarize, insight can be a useful, even indispensable, tool to solve problems and to alleviate human suffering. However, we must continually remember to recognize the *limits* of insight, and therefore seek to explore additional avenues of change. For certain people, with certain problems, in certain situations, insight may be sufficient or necessary. For others, it may be sufficient *and* necessary. But for some, it is neither.

Exercises: Exploring the Limits of Insight

These exercises are intended to help you identify and examine the limits of insight. The following list encompasses a wide range of problems. In responding to the exercises, you may draw on this list or supply your own original examples. (Note that these groupings are purely for convenience and for purposes of this exercise.)

—*emotional problems* (depression, anxiety, guilt, anger, jealousy, loneliness, irritability, panic)

—*psychological problems* (phobias, insomnia, paranoia, sexual dysfunctions, hypochondriasis, schizophrenia, repressed traumatic memories)

—*behavioral problems* (delinquency, criminality, child abuse, spousal abuse, sexual abuse, violence, self-mutilation, suicidality)

—*compulsion problems* (drinking, drugs, gambling, shopping, overeating, working, studying, exercising)

—*interpersonal problems* (arguments, mistrust, dependence, miscommunication, rebelliousness, victimization)

—*medical problems* (flu, infections, headaches, bone fractures, allergies, hypertension, ulcers, AIDS, cancer)

1. a. Identify and describe some problems from your own life experience for which gaining insight into their causes directly served to solve the problems.

_____

_____

_____

_____

_____

1. b. What do these types of problems have in common?

_____

_____

_____

_____

_____

2. a. Identify and describe some problems from your own life experience for which gaining insight into their causes did *not* directly serve to solve the problems.

_____

_____

_____

_____

_____

2. b. What do these types of problems have in common?

_____

_____

_____

_____

_____

3. What *differences* do you see in the types of problems you have identified in Question (1) as compared to Question (2)?

_____

_____

_____

_____

_____

4. Can you think of instances or conditions for which insight is *sufficient* (that is, insight alone can solve the problem)?

_____

_____

_____

_____

_____

5. Can you think of instances or conditions for which insight is *not sufficient* (that is, insight alone cannot solve the problem)?

_____

_____

_____

_____

_____

6. Can you think of instances or conditions for which insight is *necessary* (that is, the problem cannot be solved without insight into its causes)?

_____

_____

_____

_____

_____

7. Can you think of instances or conditions for which insight is *not necessary* (that is, the problem can be solved without insight into its causes)?

_____

_____

_____

_____

_____

Glossary Terms

The following terms (or variations) are defined in the Glossary:

affect	insight
assumption	Insight Fallacy
attribution	intellectualization
behavior	interpersonal
behavior therapy	interpretation
belief	isolation of affect
cause	knowledge
chronic	logic
clinical	myth
cognitive	phenomena
consequence	psychoanalysis
correlate	psychodynamic therapy
critical	psychological
dysfunction	psychology
emotion	psychotherapy
empirical	rational
experience	rationalization
explanation	reasoning
fact	repression
fallacy	unconscious
family therapy	validity
Gestalt therapy	value
hypothetical	vignette

P a r t **Six**

Conclusions

XXX. *Every Decision Is a Trade-Off: Take Stock of Pluses and Minuses*

*In order for something to become clean,
something else must become dirty.*
—ARTHUR BLOCH*

Eternal vigilance is the price of liberty.
—WENDELL PHILLIPS**

DRUMMOND: *Gentlemen, progress has never been a bargain. You've
got to pay for it. Sometimes I think there's a man behind a counter
who says, "All right, you can have a telephone; but you'll have to give
up privacy, the charm of distance. Madam, you may vote; but at a
price; you lose the right to retreat behind a powder-puff or
a petticoat. Mister, you may conquer the air; but the birds will
lose their wonder, and the clouds will smell of gasoline!"*
—JEROME LAWRENCE and ROBERT E. LEE***

Every decision, activity, or event involves some kind of a trade-off. For each of our choices, the outcome has both pluses and minuses: For everything that we get, we give something up; for everything that we give up, we get something in return. You never get something for nothing, or nothing for something. When making a decision, therefore, it is wise to take stock of the advantages and the disadvantages—the benefits and the costs—of *all* your alternatives.

Murphy's Law, Book Two, 1980
**From the speech *Public Opinion* in 1852; cited in *The Pocket Book of Quotations*, Davidoff, 1952
***Inherit the Wind*, 1955

After weighing them out, you will be in a much better position to decide your course of action.

Remember that whatever choice you make leaves all others behind. Even something so simple as choosing to make a left turn, for example, entails forfeiting your choice to turn right. If you go to sleep, you give up staying awake. If you listen to music, you give up silence. Put another way, you *can* have your cake *and* eat it too, but if you do, then you *can't* have either one alone.

Should you have that extra scoop of ice cream? Should you buy a new coat? Should you take the day off from work? Should you start an exercise regimen? Should you stop smoking? Should you end a painful romantic relationship? Should you enter psychotherapy? Should you terminate psychotherapy? Should you go to graduate school? Should you change careers? Should you move to a new city? Should you get married? Should you have children? Should you retire from your job? Some decisions may be easy, some may be difficult, but they *all* involve making trade-offs.

"To Diagnose or Not to Diagnose?"

A vivid illustration of this Metathought is provided by the perennially heated debate in the mental health field over the practice of classifying, labeling, or diagnosing people with psychological problems. Here we see, once again, that taking a stand on *either* side of the issue entails both costs and benefits.

Arguments for the Use of Diagnostic Categories

1. By serving as the language currency of the mental health profession, diagnostic categories enable us to *communicate* more effectively with one another (Spitzer, 1975).

2. Diagnostic classifications permit clinicians and investigators to conduct controlled *research* into the causes and outcomes of mental disorders (American Psychiatric Association, 1987).

3. Diagnoses can guide the type and course of clinical *treatment* (Spitzer & Wilson, 1975). For example, in the case of a diagnosed phobia, systematic desensitization is a likely treatment of choice. For Bipolar ("manic-depressive") Disorder, lithium carbonate typically is indicated. For Major Depressive Disorder, a combination of cognitive psychotherapy and antidepressant medication might be most effective.

4. Diagnostic classifications help to *bring order out of chaos,* in that we are better able to organize phenomena in the world by naming them. In the course of a typical clinical intake interview, for example, the therapist is inundated with an overwhelming quantity and diverse array of information, much of which can be summarized and systematized with the use of clinical diagnoses.

5. Using diagnostic categories *sharpens our skills of perception* by bringing into focus what we might otherwise have overlooked. The mere act of naming something makes it stand out more distinctly from its context; thus, by having specific terms for different phenomena, we can more effectively discriminate among them.[1] As an illustration, consider the fact that Eskimos have over a dozen words for identifying and differentiating various types of snow (Carroll, 1956). Similarly, the Yiddish language contains a plethora of terms that refer to many types of fools, nerds, and jerks (Rosten, 1968).[2] Analogously, our use of specific diagnostic terms may help us better recognize different types of mental disorders.

6. Our use of diagnostic categories provides us with greater *scientific objectivity* and a concomitant reduction in our reliance on vague and subjective impressions, perceptions, and interpretations.

7. Diagnoses can serve as a reminder for clinicians to maintain a *professional distance* from their patients.

8. In order to provide *financial reimbursement,* most insurance carriers and managed care organizations require clinicians to submit formal clinical diagnoses of their patients.

Arguments against the Use of Diagnostic Categories

1. The use of diagnostic categories *depersonalizes* and *dehumanizes* the person to whom the label is attached (Rosenhan, 1973). Put another way, such labeling promotes "I–It" rather than "I–Thou" interpersonal relationships (Buber, 1958).

2. Despite claims to the contrary, psychiatric diagnoses are *unscientific* or *pseudoscientific.* Specifically, they frequently are statistically unreliable (Rosenhan, 1973), and they appear to be more a reflection of societal or political mores, creeds, and values than they are of objective fact. Szasz (1960, 1987), in fact, goes so far as to view diagnoses essentially as psychiatrists' "Index of Prohibited Behaviors." As noted by R. D. Laing (1975), the use of diagnostic labeling in many cases tells us much more about the person assigning the label than about the person who is being labeled.[3]

3. Once someone has received a diagnostic label, we tend to view that individual in a significantly different manner (Farina, 1982; Rosenhan, 1973). In particular, the labels create *biased preconceptions* that pathologize our subsequent perceptions and interpretations of the person's behavior (see Metathought XXIII, the Assimilation Bias).

4. Diagnostic categories are *stigmatizing labels,* which, once attached to people, follow them around for the rest of their lives and adversely influence others (relatives, friends, employers, government agencies) with whom they come into contact (see Link, Cullen, Frank, & Wozniak, 1987; Page, 1977).

5. A diagnostic label can become analogous to the proverbial *procrustean bed,* within which the client is metaphorically stretched to fit into the category.

6. Psychiatric diagnoses can result in a *self-fulfilling prophecy* (Metathought XXIII) in that they may actually elicit the very behaviors they are attempting to describe.

7. Diagnostic categories foster the use of *false dichotomies* (Metathought V) in our conceptualizations of people's behavior.

8. The use of psychiatric diagnoses encourages treating people as *helpless patients,* rather than as responsible human beings (Szasz, 1974).

"To Metathink or Not to Metathink?"

As a final illustration of this Metathought, let us turn to an evaluation of this book's principal content: the Metathoughts themselves. In a sense, the Metathoughts may be seen as cognitive schemas. As such, they provide the same benefits—and, of course, are subject to the same liabilities—inherent in all schematic processing (see discussion in Metathought XXII).

More specifically, in terms of their advantages, they

>significantly reduce or eliminate a wide variety of systematic biases, errors, and mistakes in thinking;

>improve the clarity of thinking and the accuracy of solutions;

>open pathways to new perspectives and alternative points of view;

>promote and facilitate innovative and creative approaches to problem-solving;

>serve as a foundation for identifying other as-yet-unidentified cognitive errors (that is, new Metathoughts), as well as their antidotes.

As for their disadvantages, their use

>requires more time and effort (particularly at first);

>involves greater complexity at the cost of simplicity;

>is likely to result in increased ambiguity;

>can leave you feeling frustrated or confused;

>may be impractical or inappropriate in some situations.

In sum, like all other choices, the acceptance or rejection of the ideas in this book entails costs and benefits. Thus, once you have made the effort to study, understand, and apply these Metathoughts in your life, take stock of their pluses and minuses. Once having weighed them, you will be able to make an informed choice as to your course of action. Either way, ultimately the decision is yours.

Exercise: Evaluating Trade-Offs

Read through the following hypothetical questions and select three that are of particular interest or relevance to you. Then, for each question list all of the "pluses" and "minuses" that you can think of (use additional paper if necessary). After taking stock of the pros and cons, see in which direction your decision is leaning.

Should you decide
—To go on a diet?
—To repair your broken television set?
—To purchase a motorcycle?
—To drink alcohol?
—To use drugs?
—To stay out late?
—To get a dog?
—To buy insurance?
—To cheat on your taxes?
—To accept financial assistance from your parents?
—To use deception as part of your research investigation?
—To conduct your research study in the laboratory or in the field?
—To have regular medical check ups?
—To always tell the truth in your relationships?
—To engage in unprotected sex?

Question 1 _____

Pluses   Minuses

Conclusion _____

Question 2 _____

Pluses   Minuses

Conclusion _____

Question 3 _____

Pluses   Minuses

Conclusion

Glossary Terms

The following terms (or variations) are defined in the Glossary:

ambiguous	interpretation
analogous	mental
antidote	metaphor
behavior	objective
bias	perception
category	phenomena
clinical	preconception
cognitive	procrustean bed
cognitive–behavioral therapy	psychological
concept	psychotherapy
decision	reliability
diagnosis	schema
dichotomous variable	Self-Fulfilling Prophecy
disorder	subjective
evaluation	subsequent
event	thinking
fact	treatment
hypothetical	truth
hypothesis	vivid
interpersonal	

Notes

[1] This may be seen as an extension of Whorf's (1956) hypothesis of linguistic relativity, which states in essence that language influences thought. Thus, for example, because different cultures have different languages, they have different ways of thinking about the world.

[2] As noted by Arthur Naiman, author of *Every Goy's Guide to Common Jewish Expressions* (1981), "Yiddish has more words for this concept than any other ten languages put together." A sampling from this veritable cornucopia of descriptors includes: *kuni lemmel, narr, nayfish, nebbish, nudnik, putz, schmuck, shlemiel, shlimazl, shlump, shmageggie, shmendrik, shmo, shnook, yutz,* and *zhlub.*

[3] For a satirical perspective on this theme, I refer you to my essay on "Pervasive Labeling Disorder" (Levy, 1992), which appears in Appendix 1.

E p i l o g u e

Concluding Meta-
Metathoughts

A conclusion is the place where you got tired of thinking.
—ARTHUR BLOCH*

Throughout this book I have sought to abide by the educational tenet that knowledge is sterile and meaningless without application. For each Metathought principle, therefore, I have cited practical applications in the form of "real-world" examples, illustrations, anecdotes, clinical vignettes, and contemporary social problems and issues.

This final chapter presents some closing thoughts about the Metathoughts (or "meta-Metathoughts"), focusing primarily on the application of this book as a whole to the differing needs of psychology students, teachers, clinicians, and researchers. Before we begin, however, please take note of the following brief but important caveat:

> *The applicability and usefulness of the Metathoughts are limited only by the creativity, imagination, and resourcefulness of the user. The following recommendations, then, should be seen as a starting point, not the last word. Your own individual contributions will be the key ingredients that can infuse the contents of this book with unique characteristics and new life.*

As an analogy, think of the Metathoughts as a collection of specialized tools for working on a diverse array of problems. When faced with a new task, one of your initial steps, naturally, would be to select the right tool (or tools)

*Murphy's Law, Book Two, 1980

for the job. An effective method of accomplishing this goal is to systematically sort through your inventory of Metathoughts, retaining the ones that apply to the problem at hand and setting aside those that don't. Obviously, the greater your familiarity, experience, and practice in working with these tools, the more proficient you will become, both in minimizing your expenditure of time and energy, and maximizing the accuracy, quality, and utility of your results.

Tools of Critical Thinking also may be seen as a pragmatic reference guide—not meant for rote memorization or rigid adherence—but rather for "trouble-shooting" errors, biases, and pitfalls in thinking. As such, you may wish to keep this book alongside your other useful references (dictionary, thesaurus, writing manual), all within reach for quick and easy access.

Because different Metathoughts are pertinent to various circumstances, your time would be well spent on a brief review of this book whenever you find yourself facing a new task or a change in the subject of your work. Examples would include studying a new topic in school, teaching a different course, or evaluating the outcome of a research investigation.

More generally, you might find it beneficial to periodically peruse the book's contents as a means of refreshing, refining, or "tuning up" your critical thinking skills. (The Summary and Antidote Table is especially useful for this purpose.) This practice will enhance your ability both to identify and to solve problems in thinking.

With respect specifically to psychology, the Metathoughts encompass a broad spectrum of perspectives, topics, and units of analysis: from philosophical to scientific, theoretical to empirical, conceptual to applied, descriptive to explanatory, normal to pathological, individual to interpersonal, biochemical to social, nomothetic to idiographic, historical to contemporary, legal to moral.

They are intended to assist you, for instance, in your efforts to describe, define, and differentiate psychological phenomena, to identify the strengths and weaknesses in various schools of psychological thought, to evaluate the usefulness of psychological theories, to recognize and improve on errors and biases in our cognitive processes, and to open up new avenues of exploration and insight. Thus, they may be employed to critically evaluate everything from sophisticated, empirically based research studies published in scientific and scholarly journals to the latest claims, trends, and topics touted in the self-help literature or reported in the popular media.

In addition to these general guidelines, the remainder of this chapter focuses on how *Tools of Critical Thinking* can be utilized to address the particular needs of five specific groups: psychology students, psychology classroom instructors, psychotherapists, psychological researchers, and students and instructors in other fields of study. What follows, then, is a compendium of suggestions, ideas, and recommendations for applying *Tools of Critical Thinking* to various people, in various contexts, and for various purposes.

To the Psychology Student:

You will find that ideas in this book are applicable throughout your schooling, from your first undergraduate introductory psychology course all the way to the final class of your doctoral degree. In a sense, the book will accompany your intellectual growth, with different Metathoughts emerging as especially relevant at various stages of your academic and professional development.

This book should be consulted whenever you seek a deeper and more comprehensive understanding of any issue or problem. In particular, the Metathoughts are ideally suited for any assignments in which you are instructed to "think critically" about a specific topic. You now have at your disposal the tools with which you can effectively review, evaluate, analyze, and critique books, journal articles, research studies, lectures, workshops, debates, or media presentations. Once you have your topic, peruse the Metathoughts, and select your tools. (Or your *weapons,* as the case may be.)

To the Psychology Classroom Instructor:

Tools of Critical Thinking can be utilized with great effectiveness as a supplementary text in a variety of both undergraduate and graduate psychology courses.[1] Of course, this book is ideal for any courses devoted specifically to critical thinking, problem-solving, or logic.

In the classroom context, the Metathoughts themselves can be used in a variety of ways. First, when beginning a new class, devote some time to presenting a didactic lecture on the Metathought principles that are relevant to the content of the course. Augment the examples from this book with those from your own and from your students' experiences. Inform students that, as the course progresses, you will be drawing on the Metathoughts to critically evaluate specific topics. Alert them, further, that you will be calling on them to do the same.

Second, demonstrate the process of critical thinking to your students by functioning as a role model. That is, don't just *tell* them how to think critically, but *show* them as well. Specifically, utilize the pedagogic technique of "thinking aloud," whereby one verbalizes every phase of problem-solving, step by step, from beginning to end. For instance, you would, speaking in the present tense, identify a problem, establish your goal, decide on a course of action, select the relevant Metathought(s) and provide your rationale for doing so, apply the Metathought to the problem, and reach your conclusion. Further, you could speculate what your conclusions might have been *without* applying any tools of critical thinking. This use of vicarious learning is both an extremely effective and efficient method of instruction, in that it places students in a minimal risk situation in which the process of critical thinking is simultaneously displayed and demystified. Further, it demonstrates vividly not only that critical thinking *can* be achieved, but also *how* it can be achieved.

Third, after having role-modeled this process, you can ask your students to follow suit. This technique provides direct experience and practice for students, allows for your immediate feedback, and increases their sense of competence and efficacy.

Fourth, design in-class and homework assignments that require students to apply tools of critical thinking. You might, for example, instruct them to write a paper in which they utilize the Metathoughts in their analysis of a relevant issue of their own choosing. Or you may elect to assign the topic yourself. Some examples, depending on the subject of the course, could include, "What are the problems in defining psychopathology?"; "How should we treat mental illness?"; "Is alcoholism a disease?"; "What accounts for psychological differences between men and women?"; "Why do people stereotype others?"; or any other real-world issues of concern. You might also have students use the Metathoughts in a critique of a published article (anything from a scientific journal to a "pop psych" magazine) or a media broadcast (such as radio psychology call-in programs or televised courtroom trials).

Fifth, utilize the Metathoughts yourself as part of your course preparations. They are especially useful for presentations that call for critical analyses of particularly complex or controversial topics.

To the Psychotherapist:

It is interesting to note that one of the most widely utilized and most effective approaches in modern clinical practice, cognitive therapy, is devoted primarily to identifying and correcting errors in the thought processes of clients in treatment. With meticulous precision, the clinician zeroes in on, confronts, and attempts to modify the client's erroneous assumptions, faulty belief systems, biased schemata, distorted perceptions, flawed logic, misattributions, overgeneralizations, and unfounded conclusions.

How ironic, then, that in many cases it is the *clinicians themselves* who unknowingly fall prey to these same errors. Yet very little, if any, attention is focused on teaching therapists how to examine and improve their own cognitive processes. To rectify this situation, it is vital that clinicians learn to regularly subject their own cognitions to the same kind of close scrutiny and appropriate modifications that are afforded to their clients.

The Metathoughts are a very useful means by which this critical goal can be achieved. For the student intern, as an example, clinical supervision and practicum courses would be excellent arenas in which to utilize these tools to address issues related to the therapist's own personal biases (countertransference) on an individual, case-by-case basis. For the professional clinician who is already in independent practice, this book can function as a vehicle of continuing education, to be intermittently studied and applied throughout one's career.

To the Psychological Researcher:

This book can be of tremendous use to you at every stage of your investigations, for a diverse array of purposes, and for virtually every type of research methodology: theoretical to empirical, basic to applied, descriptive to experimental, retrospective to prospective, and micro to macro levels of analysis.

The Metathoughts provide direct guidance in helping to ensure that your research is comprehensive, logically consistent, internally and externally valid, and accurately described. Further, they both alert you to and supply you with remedies to common research pitfalls; they assist you in exploring alternate hypotheses and perspectives; and they provide a path for creative solutions to difficult and complex problems.

In particular, they improve your ability to create and evaluate theories, test hypotheses, utilize deductive and inductive reasoning, select research topics, review background literature, conceptualize and measure psychological variables, collect and analyze data, understand statistical interactions, differentiate correlation and causation, examine and determine directions of causation, gauge probability, interpret results, generalize findings, and communicate conclusions. In addition, they help you to identify and ameliorate specific research problems pertaining to reactivity, expectancy effects, demand characteristics, and systematic biases in assimilation, belief perseverance, confirmation, and hindsight.

Note that all thirty Metathoughts have been grouped into conceptual categories, such as Explaining Phenomena, Investigating Phenomena, and Common Misattributions, each of which is relevant for different stages of conducting research. The intent of this thematic organization is to provide a framework that maximizes the likelihood that each and every set of issues will be addressed, explored, and resolved in a manner that is systematic and comprehensive.

Last, you can use the Metathoughts as a kind of "check list" to evaluate and critique the work of other researchers, as well as your own. In this way, you might identify, and hopefully rectify, potential weaknesses or flaws in your work *before* somebody else does.

To Students and Instructors in Other Fields of Study:

As I indicated in the Preface, although the examples I've presented are drawn almost entirely from psychology, the basic principles delineated and examined in this book are both flexible and robust enough to be readily applied to numerous other fields, such as education, law, philosophy, communication, medicine, business, economics, history, anthropology, sociology, political science, journalism, and even the arts. One need only adapt the book's basic framework to a new content area and then supply the relevant examples. In this way, *Metathoughts for Psychology* can be modified to become, for instance, *Metathoughts for Business, Metathoughts for Communication,* or *Metathoughts for Law.* In short, while the Metathoughts are relatively universal and constant, the applied topics are essentially interchangeable.

Final Meta-Metathoughts

Thomas Szasz once remarked, "I don't have the answer to every one of life's problems. I only know a stupid answer when I see one" (quoted in Miller, 1983). In like manner, the Metathoughts won't necessarily provide you with correct solutions to all of the questions that you will ask or that will be asked of you. Nevertheless, cultivating your skills of critical thinking certainly will, at the very least, enable you more easily and consistently to identify and discard "the stupid ones," thereby freeing your time, energy, and resources for more productive endeavors.

Of course, trade-offs are both inevitable and inescapable. In using these thought principles it is essential, therefore, to prepare yourself for their costs as well as their benefits. In particular, they can lead to conclusions that are more complex, intricate, ambiguous, and tentative than you ever bargained for. On the other hand, the more obstinately you search for simplistic, clear-cut answers to the innumerable problems in this world, the more likely you are to end up with nothing more than a bloodied head from having blindly and repeatedly bashed it against a wall.

Glossary Terms

The following terms (or variations) are defined in the Glossary:

ambiguous	critical thinking
analogy	data
assimilation	deductive reasoning
assumption	description
belief	didactic
bias	disease
category	efficacy
causation	empirical
clinical	erroneous
cognitive	evaluation
cognitive therapy	experience
cognitive–behavioral therapy	experiment
correlation	external validity
countertransference	idiographic
critical	inductive reasoning

Insight Fallacy
intent
interpersonal
interpretation
knowledge
logic
measure
mental illness
meta
nomothetic
normal
pedagogic
perception
phenomena
pragmatic
probability
psychological

psychology
psychotherapy
reactivity
reasoning
schema
scientific
social
theoretical
thinking
treatment
universal
utility
variable
vicarious
vignette
vividness

Notes

[1] Some courses for which this text is particularly appropriate include Introductory Psychology, Abnormal Psychology (Psychopathology), Research Methods and Design, Social Psychology, Theories and Methods of Psychotherapy, Theories of Personality, Clinical Psychology Practicum, Psychological Testing and Assessment, Multicultural Psychology, Law and Ethics in Psychology, and Seminars on Contemporary Problems and Issues in Psychology.

Metathoughts Summary and Antidote Table

I. The Evaluative Bias of Language

Summary

In describing phenomena, particularly social phenomena, the language that people use invariably reflects their own personal values, biases, likes, and dislikes. As a consequence, descriptions can reveal at least as much about the *observer* as they do about the *observed*.

Antidotes

1. Remember that descriptions, especially concerning personality, can never be truly objective, impartial, or neutral.
2. Acknowledge how your own personal values and biases influence the descriptive language that you use.
3. Avoid presenting your value judgments as objective reflections of truth.
4. Recognize how other people's use of language reveals their own values and biases.

II. The Reification Error

Summary

It is a mistake in reification to treat an abstract, hypothetical concept (*construct*) as if it were a tangible, concrete thing (*object*). Constructs, in contrast to objects, are not directly measurable or quantifiable. This principle is particularly relevant to the delineation and evaluation of Construct (Type C) Theories and Event (Type E) Theories.

Antidotes

1. Learn to differentiate between abstract constructs and physical objects.
2. In particular, don't make the mistake of treating a construct as if it were an object.
3. Remember that constructs are *created*, not "discovered."
4. Evaluate Event (Type E) Theories in terms of their *accuracy;* evaluate Construct (Type C) Theories in terms of their *utility.*

III. Multiple Levels of Description

Summary

The same phenomenon can be described at different levels of analysis. In particular, an event can be described both at a *physical* level and at a *conceptual* level. Because these levels occur *simultaneously,* they do not, strictly speaking, *cause* each other. Thus, "biological" and "psychological" are two different ways of describing the same simultaneous event. Further, every psychological event has a biological correlate, but not every biological event has a psychological correlate.

Antidotes

1. Remember that the same event can be described at different levels of analysis, the most basic of which are the *physical* and the *conceptual* levels.
2. When analyzing a phenomenon, first *identify* the various levels at which it can be described, then *select* the most appropriate level(s) of description for purposes of your analysis.
3. Be aware of how these levels relate to each other. In particular, because they occur *simultaneously,* their relationship is *not causal.* Thus, don't make the mistake of concluding that once you've located a biological *correlate* to a psychological event, you have therefore discovered its biological *cause.*
4. Moreover, don't equate biological *correlates* with biological *diseases;* remember that *differences* are not, *per se,* valid proof of *disease.*
5. Be extremely cautious when addressing the logically senseless question, "Is the person's problem physical *or* mental?"

IV. The Nominal Fallacy and Tautologous Reasoning

Summary

Naming a phenomenon does not, *per se, explain* the phenomenon. Nevertheless, we may fool ourselves into believing that, once we've invented a special label (such as a psychological diagnosis) for someone's behavior, we have therefore explained the behavior. The Nominal Fallacy typically involves tautologous reasoning, which is a circular pseudo-explanation that, despite its appearance, is essentially void of useful information.

Antidotes

1. Don't confuse a *name* with an *explanation.*
2. Remember that labeling any particular behavior (such as with a clinical diagnosis) does not automatically explain the behavior.
3. Learn to identify tautologous (circular) reasoning, and to extricate yourself from its web.
4. Remind yourself that, although tautologies may have the *appearance* of being logical, they are, in fact, an invalid method of reasoning, explanation, and proof.

V. Differentiating Dichotomous and Continuous Variables

Summary

Dichotomous phenomena can be classified into either of two, mutually exclusive *categories*. Continuous phenomena, in contrast, can be placed somewhere along a particular *dimension,* depending on their frequency or magnitude. Thus, dichotomous variables are a matter of classification (*quality*), whereas continuous variables are a matter of degree (*quantity*). The problem is that people have a tendency to dichotomize variables that, more accurately, should be conceptualized as continuous.

Antidotes

1. Learn to differentiate between variables that are dichotomous versus those that are continuous.
2. Avoid the tendency to "dichotomize" continuous phenomena.
3. Remember that most person-related phenomena (especially psychological constructs) lie along a continuum; thus, it is both artificial and inaccurate to group them into categories.

VI. Consider the Opposite

Summary

In order to understand any given phenomenon, its theoretical polar opposite should also be addressed and explored. To contrast a phenomenon with its opposite is to provide definition to both terms. Polar opposites depend on each other for their very conceptual existence; without one, its opposite ceases to exist.

Antidotes

1. When seeking to define or understand a phenomenon, take the time to consider and explore its theoretical polar opposite.
2. When you are working on a problem and find yourself stuck at a conceptual dead end, gain a new perspective on the issue by considering the opposite. Specifically, in addition to asking "What *is* it?" also pose the questions, "What *isn't* it?" and "What's its *opposite*?"

VII. The Similarity–Uniqueness Paradox

Summary

All phenomena are both *similar to* and *different from* each other, depending on the dimensions or sorting variables that have been selected for purposes of evaluation, comparison, and contrast. No phenomenon is *totally identical* or *totally unique* in relation to other phenomena. The degree of similarity or uniqueness revealed between any two events is a function of the *points of critical distinction* (PCD).

Antidotes

1. When comparing and contrasting any two phenomena ask yourself, "In what ways are they similar?" *and* "In what ways are they different?"
2. Before beginning your evaluation, ask yourself, "What is the *purpose* of this analysis? What am I trying to find out?" Asking these questions will help you to choose the most appropriate and relevant dimensions and sorting variables.
3. Carefully and judiciously select the dimensions on which you will evaluate various phenomena. Recognize that the dimensions you select will ultimately determine the degree of "similarity" or "uniqueness" displayed between the two phenomena.
4. Despite what may appear to be an overwhelming number of similarities between two events, always search for and take into account their differences; conversely, regardless of what may seem to be a total absence of commonalities between two events, search for and take into account their similarities.
5. Don't allow yourself to be swayed by individuals who maintain that, "These events are *exactly* the same," or "You can't compare these events because they have absolutely *nothing* in common."
6. Keep these principles in mind whenever you are asked any "compare-and-contrast" type questions.

VIII. The Naturalistic Fallacy

Summary

The frequency of an event does not inherently determine its moral value or worth. What is common, typical, or normal isn't necessarily good; what is uncommon, atypical, or abnormal isn't necessarily bad. Conversely, what is common isn't necessarily bad, and what is uncommon isn't necessarily good.

Antidotes

1. Don't make the mistake of equating statistical frequency with moral value. Thus, if most people do something, that does not intrinsically make it right; if most people do not, that does not therefore make it wrong. In like manner, if most people do something, that does not make it wrong; if they do not, that does not make it right.
2. Learn to differentiate *objective descriptions* from *subjective prescriptions*. Specifically, don't confuse one's *description* of what "is" or "isn't" with one's *prescription* of what "should" or "shouldn't" be.

IX. The Barnum Effect

Summary

Barnum statements are "one-size-fits-all" personality interpretations that are true of practically all human beings, but that don't provide distinctive information about a particular individual. Thus, the problem with Barnum statements isn't that they are *wrong;* rather, because they are so generic, universal, and elastic, they are essentially *useless*.

Antidotes

1. Learn to differentiate Barnum statements from person-specific descriptions and interpretations.
2. Be aware of the limited utility inherent in Barnum statements. Specifically, remember that, although Barnum statements have validity about people in general, they fail to reveal anything distinctive about a *particular* individual.
3. Whenever feasible and appropriate, make it a point to reduce the Barnum Effect by qualifying personality descriptions and interpretations in terms of their *magnitude* or *degree*.

X. Correlation Does Not Prove Causation

Summary

A *correlational* relationship between events does not prove that there is a *causal* relationship between them. Although a correlation enables us to make *predictions* from one variable to another, it does not provide an *explanation* as to *why* the events are associated. Further, it does not permit us to draw unequivocal conclusions as to the source or direction of causes and effects.

Antidotes

1. Remember that the presence of a correlation is not, in itself, proof of causation.
2. Keep in mind that correlations enable us to make *predictions* from one event to another; they do not, however, provide *explanations* as to *why* the events are related.
3. When a correlation is observed, consider all possible pathways and directions of causation. For example, if Event *A* and Event *B* are correlated, does *A* cause *B*? Does *B* cause *A*? Do *A* and *B* cause each other? Does *C* cause *A* and *B*?

XI. Bi-Directional Causation

Summary

In contrast to unidirectional causation, when Event *A* causes Event *B*, in bi-directional causation Event *A* and Event *B* are linked in a circular or *causal loop,* in which each is both a cause and an effect of the other. In such instances, the pathway of causation is a "two-way street."

Antidotes

1. Don't assume *a priori* that the causal link between two variables is a unidirectional "one-way street."
2. When investigating directions of causation, consider the possibility that the variables are linked in a *causal loop;* that is, each might be both a cause and an effect of the other.

3. Remember that in a case of bi-directional causation, which variable appears to be the "cause" and which variable appears to be the "effect" may depend entirely on the point at which you happen to enter the causal loop.

XII. Multiple Causation

Summary

Any given event can be, and typically is, the result of *numerous* causes. It is therefore invariably an oversimplification to assume that there is *only one determinant* of any phenomenon as complex as human behavior.

Antidotes

1. In attempting to explain why an event occurred, don't limit your search to *one* cause. Instead, explore *multiple* plausible causes, *all* of which may be responsible for producing the effect.
2. When faced with an *either/or* question, always consider the possibility that the answer might be *both/and*.

XIII. Degrees of Causation

Summary

In a case of multiple causation, the causal factors are likely to vary in the degree to which each of them is responsible for producing the effect. Not all causes are of the same importance, magnitude, or weight: Some causes are "more equal" than others.

Antidotes

1. In situations involving multiple causation, remember that causation usually is a matter of *degree*. Remind yourself that causal factors typically differ as to their relative weight; in other words, not all causes are equal.
2. Attempt to assess the proportion that each cause contributes to the outcome.
3. Make an active effort not to disregard, rule out, or dismiss automatically those causes with less apparent relative weight, one of which may be analogous to the proverbial straw that broke the camel's back.

XIV. Multiple Pathways of Causation

Summary

The same event may be produced by different, independent causal routes or pathways. In other words, different antecedent conditions can lead to the same outcome. Multiple Pathways may apply both to the *etiologies* of various problems, as well as to their *solutions*.

Antidotes

1. When attempting to explain a phenomenon, consider all possible pathways of causation that might be *independently sufficient* to produce the same effect. In other words, on the road to your destination, always be on the lookout for alternate routes.
2. Don't assume *a priori* that similar outcomes must be the product of similar causes.
3. Keep in mind the possibility that an event may involve *both* Multiple Causation *and* Multiple Pathways of Causation.

XV. The Fundamental Attribution Error

Summary

In arriving at causal attributions to explain people's behavior, we have a tendency to overestimate the impact of their internal personality traits ("dispositions") and to underestimate the impact of their environmental circumstances ("situations"). This attributional error appears to be due to both *cognitive biases* and *motivational biases*.

Antidotes

1. Don't underestimate the power of external, situational determinants of behavior.
2. Remember that, at any given time, how people behave depends *both* on what they bring to the situation ("who" they are), *as well as* the situation itself ("where" they are).
3. Keep in mind that this attributional error can become *reversed,* depending on the perceiver's point of view. Specifically, while people are prone to underestimate the impact of others' situations, they tend to *overestimate* the impact of their *own* situations.
4. Be sure to take into account both cognitive *and* motivational biases that are responsible for producing these attributional errors.

XVI. The Intervention–Causation Fallacy

Summary

Our capacity to *change* an event does not necessarily prove what originally *caused* the event. Thus, we cannot draw valid conclusions about an event's etiology solely on the basis of how it responds to various interventions. As applied to psychopathology, the *Treatment–Etiology Fallacy* refers to arriving at the erroneous deduction that a favorable response to medical *treatment* is, in itself, conclusive proof of medical *disease*.

Antidotes

1. Remember that the factors that initially *caused* a problem may be entirely unrelated to the factors that might *solve* the problem.

2. Don't make the mistake of assuming that successful *treatment* is, in itself, valid and sufficient proof of *etiology.* In short, the *cure* doesn't necessarily prove the *cause.*
3. With respect to psychopathology, as counter-intuitive as it may seem, a positive response to medical treatment is *not* proof of medical disease.

XVII. The Consequence–Intentionality Fallacy

Summary

We have a propensity to assume that the *effect* of people's behavior reflects the *intent* of their behavior. However, consequences alone are not sufficient proof of intentionality. That is, we cannot determine others' intentions solely by the effects of their actions.

Antidotes

1. When attempting to understand or explain what motivated someone's behavior, remember that their intent cannot be ascertained solely on the basis of the consequences of their actions. In other words, the *effect* does not, in itself, prove the *intent.*
2. Make an active effort to consider other plausible causes or pathways of behavior, in addition to the ones implied directly by its consequences; in short, *consider alternative intents.*

XVIII. The "If I Feel It, It Must Be True" Fallacy

Summary

One's experience of emotional comfort or discomfort is not necessarily a valid gauge for differentiating what is true from what is false. Thus, subjective feelings of comfort may be prompted by a pleasing truth as well as by a pleasing falsehood. Similarly, feelings of discomfort may be due to an unpleasant truth as well as an unpleasant falsehood. Yes, the truth hurts; but so do lies.

Antidotes

1. Don't assume that truth or falsity are necessarily correlated with one's subjective feelings of comfort or discomfort. Thus, be careful not to confuse the degree of comfort/discomfort you are experiencing with the degree of truth/falsity inherent in a given observation, situation, or conclusion.
2. Remember that psychological or emotional discomfort does not always signal the discovery of a "painful truth."
3. Do not rely on your emotions as the sole barometer for distinguishing truths from falsehoods. There may be certainty in *what* you are feeling, but not necessarily in what it *"proves."*

4. Remember that what feels good isn't necessarily true, and what feels bad isn't necessarily false. Conversely, what feels bad isn't necessarily true, and what feels good isn't necessarily false.

XIX. The Spectacular Explanation Fallacy

Summary

When attempting to understand extraordinary events, we have a tendency to search for extraordinary explanations. Further, the more unusual or bizarre the events, the more likely we are to seek out bizarre causes—or even to create bizarre theories—to account for them. However, we typically overlook the fact that very ordinary causes can produce very extraordinary effects. In fact, pure chance alone predicts the occasional occurrence of extraordinary events. Thus, it is very normal for some events to appear very abnormal.

Antidotes

1. Don't assume that extraordinary *events* necessarily require extraordinary *explanations*.
2. Keep in mind that *very ordinary causes* are capable of producing *very extraordinary effects*.
3. Remember that statistical laws of probability predict the occasional occurrence of extraordinary events.
4. Whenever you are confronted with instances of human behavior that are particularly unusual, rare, spectacular, or odd make a deliberate effort to consider ordinary, commonplace, or mundane causes and explanations.

XX. Deductive and Inductive Reasoning

Summary

Two primary forms of reasoning are *deduction* and *induction*. Deductive reasoning involves inferring specific conclusions based on a general premise. Inductive reasoning involves inferring a general conclusion based on specific instances. Errors in deductive reasoning typically are due to erroneous premises and faulty logic. Errors in inductive reasoning are usually the result of overgeneralizing from biased, insufficient, or inappropriate observations.

Antidotes

1. Learn to differentiate between deductive and inductive reasoning.
2. Recognize that different types of problems call for different reasoning strategies. Thus, make your selection based on the nature and goal of the particular question, task, or situation.

3. In using deductive reasoning, be sure that your initial assumptions are correct and that your logic is sound.
4. When utilizing inductive reasoning, be careful not to hastily overgeneralize from an unrepresentative, inadequate, or otherwise flawed initial data base.

XXI. Reactivity

Summary

Reactivity refers to the phenomenon in which the mere act of *observing* an event can, in itself, *change* the event. Reactivity is particularly problematic in the study of human activity, in that it impedes our ability to accurately ascertain people's "true" behavior. Reactivity thus limits the extent to which researchers can safely generalize their findings.

Antidotes

1. Remember that measuring something, to some degree, changes it. In a nutshell, "to observe is to disturb."
2. Be constantly vigilant as to the presence and potential impact of reactivity. In particular, when conducting research, always take into account the specific ways and the degree to which reactivity presents a threat to the validity of your investigation.
3. Recognize that, even if the effects of reactivity cannot be entirely eliminated, they can (and should) be reduced. Thus, whenever feasible, actively search for and utilize unobtrusive, nonreactive, or minimally reactive measures.

XXII. The Self-Fulfilling Prophecy

Summary

The assumptions, attitudes, and beliefs that we hold toward other people can, with or without our intent, actually *produce* the very behaviors that we *expect* to find. Similarly, *our own* behavior may inadvertently be shaped by other people's expectations of us. In sum, expectations can generate their own reality.

Antidotes

1. In all of your social interactions, remember that expectations can, in themselves, create their own reality.
2. Make a conscious effort to become aware of your own expectations and the ways in which they may lead you to induce those very behaviors in others.
3. Don't forget that *your own behavior* is not immune to the influence of the self-fulfilling prophecy. Specifically, keep in mind that your behavior can be shaped by other's expectations of you.

4. In conducting research, initiate safeguards to reduce the potential impact of expectancy effects. This may be accomplished by, for example, keeping the experimenters unaware of (i.e., "blind" to) the specific purpose, goals, or hypotheses of the study.

XXIII. The Assimilation Bias

Summary

A *schema* is a mental structure that organizes our preconceptions, thereby providing a framework for understanding new events and future experiences. *Accommodation* means to modify our schema to fit incoming data; *assimilation,* in contrast, means to fit incoming data into our schema. In general, we are more prone to assimilate than to accommodate, even if this entails altering or distorting the data. Thus, assimilation can profoundly bias our perceptions of reality.

Antidotes

1. Don't underestimate the extent to which your *prior* beliefs, knowledge, and expectations (schemata) can affect your *current* experience, impressions, and perceptions.

2. Try to become as aware as possible of schemata that are important to you; awareness of schemata increases your ability to modify them.

3. Experiment with temporarily lowering or altering your "perceptual filters" or "schema-colored glasses" by attempting to understand someone *else's* subjective (phenomenological) experience.

4. Learn to *differentiate* your use of *assimilation* versus *accommodation,* particularly when you are faced with a discrepancy between your beliefs (schemas) and the information (data). Beware of the general tendency to assimilate, rather to than accommodate.

5. *Prod yourself to accommodate* when, out of habit, reflex, or just sheer laziness, you would typically be inclined to automatically assimilate. Strive toward flexibility; guard against "hardening of the categories."

XXIV. The Confirmation Bias

Summary

The manner in which we seek answers to our questions frequently tends to be biased. Specifically, we more actively seek out information that will confirm our prior beliefs and expectations than information that might refute them. In short, we are prone to be biased collectors of evidence; as a consequence, we are more apt to find only what we seek.

Antidotes

1. Be aware that the ways in which you search for evidence, such as the questions that you ask, may lead you to arrive selectively only at those conclusions that corroborate your initial beliefs.
2. Make it a point to actively seek out evidence that could, in principle, disconfirm your prior expectations.

XXV. The Belief Perseverance Effect

Summary

We have a tendency to stubbornly cling to our beliefs, sometimes even in the face of disconfirming evidence. This is especially likely to occur when we feel personally invested in our beliefs. Thus, when these beliefs are challenged, we feel impelled to protect them, almost as if we were protecting ourselves. One consequence of this phenomenon is that it generally requires much more compelling evidence to *change* our beliefs than it did to *create* them in the first place.

Antidotes

1. Keep an open mind to different, and especially challenging, points of view.
2. Remind yourself (and others as well) to think carefully about how you evaluate evidence and to monitor your biases closely as you formulate your conclusions.
3. Make it a point to actively *counterargue* your preexisting beliefs. That is, ask yourself directly in what ways your beliefs might be wrong. One specific method of doing so is to *consider the opposite.*
4. When faced with a discrepancy between your beliefs and the facts, resist the natural tendency to assume that your beliefs are right and the facts must somehow be wrong.

XXVI. The Hindsight Bias

Summary

We tend to overestimate the extent to which events could have been anticipated, foreseen, or expected. In retrospect, outcomes appear to us as obvious, predictable, or even unavoidable; however, in reality, they are far less so beforehand. Because knowing a result makes it seem inevitable, hindsight creates an illusion of predictability. Postdiction is easy; prediction is difficult.

Antidotes

1. Remember that, in retrospect, nearly any outcome seems obvious.
2. Be careful not to overestimate what could have been predicted or foreseen. Although hindsight is 20/20, foresight frequently is shrouded in obscurity.
3. Recognize the limitations of after-the-fact "explanations" that, by their very nature, can't be disproven.
4. When attempting to understand an event, imagine how you might explain a result that is different from the one that actually occurred.

XXVII. The Representativeness Bias

Summary

In order to identify any given phenomenon (such as a person, object, event, or ideology), we automatically and intuitively compare the phenomenon to our mental representation, *prototype,* or *schema* of the relevant category. Although this cognitive shortcut (or *heuristic*) generally produces accurate results, errors can occur as a result of faulty prototypes, failure to take into account pertinent statistical data (such as base rates, sample size, and chance probability), or when motivational dynamics bias our search.

Antidotes

1. In situations when you are likely to utilize the representativeness heuristic, make a conscious effort to consider the possibility that the prototype in question might be inaccurate, biased, or incomplete.
2. Take into account relevant statistical information, such as base rates, samples sizes, and chance probability.
3. Beware of the natural tendency to overestimate the degree of similarity between phenomena and categories.
4. Recognize that your personal attitudes about phenomena and prototypes can bias your comparisons and subsequent judgments.

XXVIII. The Availability Bias

Summary

We utilize the *availability* heuristic whenever we attempt to assess the frequency or likelihood of an event on the basis of how quickly or easily instances come to mind. Thus, vivid examples, dramatic events, graphic case studies, and personal testimonies, in contrast to statistical information, are likely to exert a disproportionate impact on our judgments. In this way, anecdotes may be more persuasive than factual data.

Antidotes

1. When estimating the frequency or probability of an event, remind yourself not to reach a conclusion based solely on the ease or speed with which examples can be retrieved from your memory.
2. Whenever feasible, utilize base rates and other relevant statistical information.
3. Resist the temptation to generalize from a few, vivid anecdotal examples.

XXIX. The Insight Fallacy

Summary

Our ability to *understand* something does not necessarily enable us to *change* it. Specifically, insight into the cause of a problem does not invariably solve the problem. Moreover, an overemphasis on insight may be counterproductive or even detrimental. In sum, despite its virtues, insight may be the booby prize of life.

Antidotes

1. Recognize the *limits,* as well as the benefits, of what insight can provide.
2. Don't make the mistake of assuming that if you can *understand* a problem, then that will automatically *solve* the problem.
3. Keep in mind that, in some situations, insight is neither necessary nor sufficient for bringing about change.
4. Actively explore alternative methods of change that do not rely solely on insight.

XXX. Every Decision Is a Trade-Off

Summary

All events, activities, and outcomes are comprised of both pluses and minuses, advantages and disadvantages, upsides and downsides. Thus, every decision involves a trade-off of some kind. Although decisions vary in terms of their content, complexity, and importance, they all entail trade-offs. Of course, the costs and benefits in the "ledger" may not turn out to be equitably balanced, but they always exist and therefore should be identified, examined, and weighed in your decision-making process.

Antidotes

1. Come to terms with the reality that *any* decision you make will *always* involve a trade-off of some kind.
2. Before making a decision, *take stock* of the pluses and minuses of all your alternatives.
3. Weigh the trade-offs, and then act accordingly.

A Proposed Category
for the Diagnostic
and Statistical Manual
of Mental Disorders (DSM):
Pervasive Labeling Disorder[1]

The purpose of this essay is to propose a new diagnostic category for inclusion in the American Psychiatric Association's *Diagnostic and Statistical Manual of Mental Disorders,* better known as the DSM. As noted in a recent edition (American Psychiatric Association, 1987), the DSM should be viewed as "only one still frame in the ongoing process of attempting to better understand mental disorders." The category proposed here represents a significant contribution to the composition of the next still frame by focusing on one of the most ubiquitous, yet least recognized, of all mental disorders.

409.00 Pervasive Labeling Disorder

Diagnostic Features

The essential features of this mental disorder are: (1) an uncontrollable impulse, drive, or temptation to invent labels and to apply them to other people, (2) a repetitive pattern of trying to fit people into preconceived categories, (3) an increasing sense of fear or inadequacy before committing the act, (4) an experience of overwhelming triumph or relief at the time of committing the act.

Manifestations of the disorder appear in many situations, but are especially likely to occur when the person with Pervasive Labeling Disorder (PLD) feels uncomfortable around other people. The person then spontaneously assigns a label to others, thus viewing them as "types," rather than as human beings. Because the disorder serves to control other people and to keep them at a distance, it provides the person with the temporary illusion of both superiority and safety.

Associated Features

People with PLD frequently display marked signs of arrogance, smugness, grandiosity, and a sense of personal entitlement. They exhibit an especially condescending attitude toward others who do not share this mental disorder.

These persons derive immense pride from inventing seemingly incisive and articulate (yet ambiguous and indecipherable) pseudoscientific neologisms. When called on to explain the precise meaning of these newly created labels, however, they typically display peculiar speech characteristics and inappropriate communication patterns, including: catatonic silence; stammering and cluttering; verbal perseveration on the label, coupled with poverty of content of speech; and psychomotor agitation, such as engaging in beard-stroking, head-shaking, or eye-rolling behaviors.

Persons with PLD operate under the fallacious belief that, by having named something, they have therefore explained it (i.e., **Delusional Disorder, Nominal Type**). Research indicates that many persons with PLD are exceptionally adept at seeing in other people the flaws they cannot see in themselves.

Prevalence

PLD is widespread throughout all sectors of society, but many people have found a means to obtain reinforcement for this disorder in socially acceptable ways by becoming psychiatrists, psychoanalysts, psychologists, astrologists, Scientologists, evangelists, cult leaders, authors of self-help books, politicians, and interview guests on radio and television shows.

Specific Culture and Age Features

Despite its prevalence, the disorder typically is not recognized until the person has attained a position of social power.

Course

Recovery from PLD rarely occurs once the person's annual income exceeds six figures.

Complications

Because persons with chronic, intractable, and severe cases of PLD are incapable of achieving and maintaining any type of human bonding, they rarely have any real friends.

Predisposing Factors

Vulnerability to this disorder is directly correlated with the extent to which one has a fear of one's own feelings. When PLD is found in psychotherapists, it typically serves to mask their deeply hidden and nagging fears that they haven't the faintest idea as to how to actually help their patients.

Differential Diagnosis

Obsessive Compulsive Personality Disorder, Social Phobia, and **Delusional Disorder (Grandiose Type)** are related to, and therefore sometimes difficult to distinguish from, **Pervasive Labeling Disorder.** To ensure diagnostic validity, flipping a coin, tossing the *I Ching,* or utilizing the Eenie-Meenie-Meinie-Moe (EM³)method is recommended.

Subtypes and Specifiers

409.01 With Narcissistic Personality Features. This category should be used for the person with PLD whom you think has too much self-esteem.

409.02 With Codependent Personality Features. This category should be used for the person with PLD whom you think has too much empathy.

409.03 With Histrionic Personality Features. This category should be used for the person with PLD whom you think is too emotional.

409.04 With Schizoid Personality Features. This category should be used for the person with PLD whom you think is not emotional enough.

409.05 With Neurotic Personality Features. This category should be used for the person with PLD whom you think worries too much.

409.06 With Antisocial Personality Features. This category should be used for the person with PLD whom you think doesn't worry enough.

409.07 With Borderline Personality Features. This category should be used when the person with PLD is disliked intensely by others, especially unsuccessful psychotherapists.

409.08 With Adult-Child-of-Alcoholic Personality Features. This category should be used when the person with PLD came from parents who, in any way whatsoever, did not satisfy each and every one of his or her needs as a child.

409.09 With Resistant Personality Features. This category should be used when the person with PLD doesn't do what you want him or her to do.

409.10 With Cognitive Slippage Features. This category should be used for the person with PLD whom you can't understand, but don't want to admit it.

409.11 With Transference Features. This category should be used for psychotherapy patients with PLD who have any feelings whatsoever about their therapist.

409.12 With Countertransference Features. This category should be used for psychotherapists with PLD who have any feelings whatsoever about their patients.

Notes

[1] This article originally appeared in the *Journal of Humanistic Psychology* (Levy, 1992).

Selected Answers to Chapter Exercises

I. The Evaluative Bias of Language

Suggested Responses from the Perspective of Person B:

obstacle—*challenge*
problem—*issue*
issue—*learning opportunity*
failure—*learning experience*

terrorist—*freedom fighter*
murder—*sacrifice*
handout—*subsidy*
conformity—*pro-solidarity*
hostage—*detainee*
brainwashed—*enlightened*

perversion—*alternative lifestyle*
slut—*promiscuous*
promiscuous—*sexually liberated*
idiot savant—*autistic savant*
retarded—*developmentally disabled*
developmentally disabled—*developmentally challenged*

anal retentive—*tidy*
egocentricity—*self-esteem*
thought disordered—*creative*
irresponsible—*spontaneous*
psychotic—*eccentric*
catatonic—*reserved*
codependent—*empathic*

rationalization—*rationale*
resistance—*autonomy*
defense mechanism—*coping strategy*

psychotherapy—*counseling*
therapy patient—*client*
psychiatric institution—*treatment center*

Dependent Personality Disorder—*loyal*
Avoidant Personality Disorder—*cautious*
Paranoid Personality Disorder—*vigilant*
Narcissistic Personality Disorder—*self-confident*
Histrionic Personality Disorder—*colorful*
Obsessive–Compulsive Personality Disorder—*meticulous*

II. The Reification Error

Answers to Chapter Exercise:

humor: (C)
laughter: (E)

tearfulness: (E)
sadness: (C)

smiling: (E)
happy: (C)

nervous: (C)
fidgety: (E)

restless: (E)
anxious: (C)

energy: (C)
activity: (E)

talkative: (E)
extraverted: (C)

quiet: (E)
introverted: (C)

personality type: (C)
blood type: (E)

muscular strength: (E)
ego strength: (C)

disordered psyche: (C)
disordered desk: (E)

housing complex: (E)
inferiority complex: (C)

drunkenness: (E)
alcoholism: (C)

heartburn: (E)
heartache: (C)

rotten egg: (E)
rotten attitude: (C)

sea sickness: (E)
love sickness: (C)

broken dream: (C)
broken nose: (E)

lost toothbrush: (E)
lost soul: (C)

healthy outlook: (C)
healthy spleen: (E)

free will: (C)
motionless: (E)
love: (C)
disorganized: (E)
heavy: (E)
self-concept: (C)
self-actualization: (C)
deviant: (E)
unseen: (E)
hepatitis: (E)
schizophrenia: (C)
repression: (C)
intuition: (C)
suicide: (E)

V. Differentiating Dichotomous and Continuous Variables

Answers to Exercise:

conscious–unconscious: (C)
feminine–masculine: (C)
gun fired–gun not fired: (D)
optimist–pessimist: (C)
married–single: (D)
present–absent: (D)
emotionally secure–emotionally insecure: (C)
published–not published: (D)
airborne–grounded: (D)
day–night: (C)
good mood–bad mood: (C)
licensed–unlicensed: (D)
honest–dishonest: (C)
morning person–evening person: (C)
neurotic–nonneurotic: (C)
mailed–unmailed: (D)

subjective–objective: (C)
alcoholic beverage–nonalcoholic beverage: (D)
successful basketball shot–unsuccessful shot: (D)
psychological trait–psychological state: (C)
tenured–untenured: (D)
"Type A" personality–"Type B" personality: (C)
guilty verdict–not guilty verdict: (D)
power on–power off: (D)
addicted–not addicted: (C)
therapeutic–nontherapeutic: (C)

XII. Multiple Causation

Suggested Answers to Exercise on the Multiple Causes of Overeating:

C_1 love the taste of food
C_2 severe hunger
C_3 extreme nervousness
C_4 "stuff down" unwanted feelings
C_5 fill internal void of loneliness
C_6 long-term habit pattern
C_7 learned response/positive reinforcement
C_8 parental role modeling
C_9 compensation for unfulfilled love
C_{10} poor impulse control
C_{11} avoidance of intimacy
C_{12} cannabis intoxication
C_{13} substitute for mother's love
C_{14} self-destructive displacement of anger
C_{15} struggle for exertion of control
C_{16} symbolic act of rebelliousness
C_{17} psychological regression to infancy
C_{18} fear of food unavailability
C_{19} attempt at self-nurturance
C_{20} low self-esteem
C_{21} fixation at oral stage
C_{22} sublimation of sex

$\rightarrow$ E (Overeating)

XIV. Multiple Pathways of Causation

Causal Pathways Pertaining to the Etiology of Anxiety:

>the ingestion of drugs (such as caffeine, cocaine, or amphetamines);

>withdrawal from drugs (such as alcohol, sedatives, or opiates);

>physical illness (such as hyperthyroidism, pheochromocytoma, or hypercortisolism);

>fear of actual external events (also known as "reality anxiety," such as an angry King Cobra that corners you in your tent);

>fear of anticipated external events (such as social rejection or disapproval);

>fear of losing control over your own potentially destructive impulses (also known as "neurotic anxiety," such as being overwhelmed by powerful sexual or aggressive drives);

>fear of your own self-judgment, self-criticism, or guilt (also known as "moral anxiety");

>prior learning (such as by classical conditioning, operant learning, or vicarious learning);

>ontological insecurity and fear of existential nothingness.

XXIV. The Confirmation Bias

Additional "Leading" Questions That Are Likely to Confirm a Diagnosis of Paranoia:

"Do you sometimes doubt the sincerity of other people's intentions?"

"Do you believe that people may say one thing to your face and something else behind your back?"

"If somebody unexpectedly goes out of their way to do something exceptionally nice for you, are you inclined to wonder about their motives?"

"When people make an exaggerated effort to reassure you, does that sometimes only serve to make you feel even more concerned or suspicious?"

"Have you ever found that co-workers, friends, or family members weren't as loyal to you as they had led you to believe?"

"Do you sometimes get the feeling that others may have the desire to hurt or demean you in some way?"

"Do you ever feel the need to be on guard to prevent others from manipulating, exploiting, or taking advantage of you?"

"Have other people ever tried to hold you back from succeeding?"

"Have you noticed others being jealous of your talents, skills, or achievements?"

"Have you ever felt betrayed by someone whom you trusted?"

"When someone insults or injures you, might you sometimes be inclined not to forgive and forget?"

"Have you noticed that other people often don't take responsibility for the harm that they inflict on others?"

"Do you find that you can sometimes be overly sensitive to criticism?"

"Do you ever experience feelings of tension, apprehension, or worry?"

Additional "Non-leading" Questions That May Disconfirm a Diagnosis of Paranoia:

"How often do your suspicions turn out to be confirmed by actual proof, evidence, or facts?"

"What are your reasons for mistrusting others?"

"How frequently have you, in fact, been betrayed by others?"

"Can you name some specific instances when your suspiciousness was warranted?"

"Are you in a position of power or authority that might tempt others to manipulate, exploit, or take advantage of you?"

"Why might others be jealous of you?"

"For what reasons might others begrudge your achievements?"

"What special or unique talents do you have that others might envy?"

"What specific reasons have you had for questioning the loyalty of co-workers, friends, or family members?"

"Do you have valid reason to be jealous of your spouse?"

"Has your spouse ever given you cause to doubt her/his word or question her/his loyalty?"

"Have others, whom you do trust, ever told you that your suspicions, fears, or concerns are excessive or unreasonable?"

"In general, to what degree would you say that you are wary of other people's motives?"

"Compared to most other people, how pronounced are your feelings of tension, apprehension, or worry?"

Glossary

Author's Note: I have written this glossary with three explicit goals in mind:

1. To provide you with an easily accessible reference source for learning the meanings of a wide range of important terms and concepts;
2. To maximize the book's conceptual, as well as stylistic, consistency and continuity;
3. To communicate to you my thoughts and ideas in the most efficient way possible. In light of the fact that so many terms in psychology are subject to multiple meanings and interpretations, I felt that it was particularly important to clarify my use of them.

Guide to the Glossary:

>*n* = noun

>*vb* = verb

>*adj* = adjective

>*pl* = plural

>*sg* = singular

>*syn* = synonym

>*cf.* ("compare with") points out other terms that are either opposite to or, in some cases, difficult to distinguish from, the term in question.

>"see" is used to refer you to additional terms that are conceptually related to the original term.

>Terms appearing in **bold typeface** (or variations) are cross-referenced in the Glossary.

>Last, to locate the exact placement of terms in the text itself, please refer to the Subject Index.

abnormal   That which deviates from what is typical, common, or statistically average; (*cf.* **normal**).

abstract   (*adj*) Considered apart from **physical existence** or tangible **events; theoretical** or **hypothetical; (*cf.* **concrete**).

acausal   To occur in the absence of a proposed **explanation** or **cause.**

accommodation   A **cognitive** process by which people adapt to their environment by modifying their preexisting **beliefs** or **schemas** to incorporate new information and **experiences; (*cf.* **assimilation**).

Actor–Observer Bias   An error in **attribution** by which a person **perceiving** his or her own **behavior** tends to overestimate the impact of situational factors (**i.e.,** to assign **external attributions**), but an observer overestimates the impact of that person's **dispositional** characteristics (**i.e.,** to assign **internal attributions**).

acute   Of or pertaining to any **disorder** characterized by a sudden onset, a sharp rise in severe **symptoms,** and relatively brief duration; (*cf.* **chronic**).

affect   1. (*n*) The **observable** expression of **subjectively experienced** feelings or **emotions.** 2. (*vb*) To **cause** an **effect.**

ambiguous   (*adj*) The characteristic of being vague, obscure, or open to more than one definition, meaning, or **interpretation.**

analogous   (*adj*) Similar, alike, or parallel in a way that permits the drawing of an **analogy.**

analogy   (*n*) A systematic comparison of one **phenomenon** to another, with the **inference** that if they are similar in some respects, they probably will be similar in others; a proposed relation, correspondence, or parallel; (see **metaphor**).

antecedent   That which precedes an **event,** occurrence, or condition, whose relationship may or may not involve **causality;** (*cf.* **subsequent**).

antidote   A remedy to prevent or counteract an adverse **effect;** (see **treatment**).

a posteriori   Derived by or based on **inductive reasoning, factual** evidence, **empirical** examination, direct **experimentation,** or **sensory experience,** rather than presupposed **assumptions, preconceptions,** or **deductive reasoning;** (*cf.* **a priori**).

a priori   Formed or conceived beforehand; a presupposed **assumption** derived by **deductive reasoning,** rather than from **factual** evidence, **empirical** examination, direct **experimentation,** or **sensory experience;** (*cf.* **a posteriori**).

ascribe   (*vb*) To **infer, attribute,** assign, or conjecture a **cause,** quality, or source.

assimilation   A **cognitive** process by which people adapt to their environment by modifying new information and **experiences** to fit into their preexisting **beliefs or** schemas; (*cf.* **accommodation**); (see **Assimilation Bias**).

Assimilation Bias   The propensity to resolve discrepancies between preexisting **schemas** and new information in the direction of **assimilation** rather than **accommodation,** even at the expense of distorting the information itself.

assumption   A statement, supposition, or **premise** that is accepted as **true** without prior proof or demonstration; (see **a priori**).

attitude   A relatively stable **cognitive–emotional–behavioral** predisposition to **respond** in a particular way to various **phenomena,** including people, objects, **events,** situations, issues, and ideas.

attribution   1. The process of determining or assigning **causation** to an **event,** usually a person's **behavior;** (see **internal attribution, external attribution, Fundamental Attribution Error**). 2. Using available information to draw an **inference, interpretation,** or reach an **explanation.** 3. **Ascribing** characteristics, features, or qualities.

Availability Bias   Any condition where the **availability heuristic** produces systematic errors in **thinking** or information processing, typically due to highly **vivid** although rare **events.**

availability heuristic   A **cognitive** strategy for quickly estimating the frequency, incidence, or **probability** of a given **event** based on the ease with which such instances are retrievable from memory; (see **heuristic, representativeness heuristic**).

Barnum Effect   A **phenomenon** describing people's willingness to accept uncritically the **validity** of **Barnum statements.**

Barnum statement   Any **generic,** "one-size-fits-all" **personality interpretation** about a particular individual that is true of practically all human beings; (see **Barnum Effect**).

base rate   **Data** pertaining to the **normal** frequency with which an **event,** such as a **disease** or **disorder,** occurs in a particular group or the general population.

behavior An **observable** action or **response** emitted by an organism.

behavior theory (behaviorism) A **theoretical** orientation in **psychology** that focuses on **observable, measurable behavior,** rather than **mental** processes, and stresses strict adherence to **empirical** evidence and the **scientific method.**

behavior therapy A group of approaches to **psychotherapy** founded on the **scientific** principles of **behaviorism,** learning **theory, reinforcement,** and classical and operant conditioning; (see **cognitive–behavioral therapy**).

belief A conviction held with confidence, trust, or faith that a particular **phenomenon** (person, thing, or idea) is **true** or real.

Belief Perseverance Effect The tendency to cling stubbornly to one's **beliefs,** even in the face of contradictory or disconfirming evidence.

bias A prejudicial inclination or predisposition that inhibits, deters, or prevents impartial **judgment;** (see **cognitive bias, motivational bias**).

bi-directional causation A mutual, **reciprocal** relationship between two **variables** wherein each is both a **cause** and an **effect** of the other; (*syn* **causal loop**); (*cf.* **uni-directional causation**).

bifurcate To divide into two parts or branches.

category A defined division in a system of classification, or **taxonomy,** in which **phenomena** sharing common attributes can be grouped.

causal (*adj*) Of or pertaining to **cause.**

causality (*syn* **causation**).

causal loop (*syn* **bi-directional causation**).

causation A situation in which a given **cause** produces an **effect;** a cause-and-effect relationship between **variables;** (*syn* **causality,** determinism); (see **bi-directional causation, uni-directional causation**).

cause 1. (*n*) A circumstance, action, or **event** that necessarily brings about a particular result; (*syn* **determinant**); (see **causa-**

tion). 2. (*vb*) To create or produce an **effect.**

cf. Compare with (from the Latin, *confer*).

chance 1. The occurrence of an **event** in the absence of a discernable, **observable,** or demonstrable **cause;** an apparently **random** outcome. 2. To happen without **intent** or design. 3. The likelihood or **probability** of an event.

chronic Of or pertaining to any **disorder** characterized by a slow onset and prolonged duration or frequent recurrence; (*cf.* **acute**).

clinical 1. Of or pertaining to the direct **observation,** study, and **treatment** of clients or patients. 2. Emotionally detached, impersonal, or **objective.**

Clinical Orientation Assimilation Bias (COAB) A psychotherapist's inclination to **perceive, interpret,** and **explain** clients' **symptoms** principally (or exclusively) in terms of his or her own **clinical schema** or **theoretical** orientation, irrespective of its actual relevance or suitability; (see **assimilation, Assimilation Bias**).

cognition 1. A general term referring to the **mental** activity of **thinking;** the **psychological** process by which people become aware and acquire **knowledge.** 2. A discrete piece of information; a thought; (*cf.* **emotion**).

cognitive Of or pertaining to **cognition.**

cognitive–behavioral therapy (CBT) An approach to **psychotherapy** in which the principles of **behaviorism** are applied both to the individual's **behaviors** and **cognitions;** (*cf.* **behavior therapy, cognitive therapy**).

cognitive bias Any systematic error in **attribution** that derives from limits that are inherent in people's **cognitive** abilities to process information; (*cf.* **motivational bias**); (see **Fundamental Attribution Error**).

cognitive therapy An approach to **psychotherapy** that focuses on the client's **thinking** processes, with emphasis on identifying and correcting faulty **belief**

systems, irrational **expectations,** distorted **perceptions,** rigid or **biased schemata,** flawed **logic, erroneous attributions,** overgeneralizations, and unfounded conclusions.

concept   A general or **abstract** idea that combines several elements to form a **mental** impression, typically derived through the process of **induction.**

concrete   (*adj*) The quality of being tangible, **physical, observable,** or directly **measurable;** consisting of mass or material substance; (*cf.* **abstract**).

conditioned response (CR)   In classical conditioning, a learned **response** to a previously **neutral stimulus;** (see **unconditioned stimulus, unconditioned response, behaviorism**).

conditioned stimulus (CS)   In classical conditioning, an originally neutral **stimulus** that, after paired association with an **unconditioned stimulus,** is effective in eliciting a **conditioned response;** (see **unconditioned response, behaviorism**).

Confirmation Bias   The tendency, **intentional** or unintentional, to selectively search for and gather evidence that is consistent with, and therefore supports, one's **preconceptions,** prior **beliefs,** and **expectations.**

connotation   (*n*) The implied or suggested meaning of a word, symbol, or **event;** (*cf.* **denotation**).

connote   (*vb*) (*cf.* **denote**); (see **connotation**).

conscious   1. (*adj*) The **mental** state of being aware, attentive, or cognizant. 2. (*adj*) Having **intent** or **intentionality.** 3. (*n*) A **theoretical construct** referring to the part of the **mind** that is responsible for the organism's awareness; (*cf.* **unconscious**).

consciousness   The state of being **conscious.**

consequence   1. The result, outcome, or **effect** of a given **cause.** 2. A conclusion derived through **logic.**

Consequence–Intentionality Fallacy   The **erroneous belief** that the **effect** of a

person's **behavior,** in itself, proves the **intent** of the behavior.

construct   (*n*) A **concept** that is **mentally** conceived or constructed by combining **sensory** impressions or **empirical data;** an **abstract, theoretical** model that is not directly **observable, measurable,** or testable; (*cf.* **event**).

Construct (Type C) Theory   A type of **theory** whose proposed **explanation** cannot be directly **observed** or **measured;** thus, even under ideal conditions, a Type C Theory is never provable or refutable; (*cf.* **Event Theory**).

Contiguity–Causation Error   The **erroneous** conclusion that a **causal** relationship exists between two **events** solely on the basis of **temporal contiguity;** (see **parataxic reasoning**).

continuous variable   Any **variable** that lies along a dimension, range, or spectrum, rather than in a discrete **category,** that can theoretically take on an infinite number of **values** and is expressed in terms of quantity, magnitude, or degree; (*cf.* **dichotomous variable**).

correlate   1. (*n*) A **phenomenon** that accompanies, is associated with, or is related to another **phenomenon;** (*syn* **correlation**). 2. (*vb*) To establish a mutual or **reciprocal correlation** between two or more **variables.**

correlation   A statistical **measure** of the degree to which **variables** are related to or associated with each other, whereby changes in one variable are systematically accompanied by changes in the other variable; (see **orthogonal**).

counterintuitive   Running contrary to **expectation** or common sense.

countertransference   A distorted **perception,** usually **unconscious,** on the part of the psychotherapist toward a client based on his or her prior relationship **experiences;** the perception may be favorable (**positive countertransference**) or unfavorable (**negative countertransference**); (*cf.* **transference**).

criteria   (*pl*) (see **criterion**).

criterion (*sg*) 1. A standard by which an **evaluation, judgment, decision,** or classification can be attained. 2. An independent **external measure** against which a test can be **validated.**

critical 1. Characterized by careful, exact, and comprehensive **evaluation** and **judgment.** 2. The quality of being essential, vital, or integral; a point that is crucial or definitive. 3. A derogatory, disparaging, or fault-finding **attitude** or **behavior.**

critical thinking (*vb*) An active and systematic **cognitive** strategy to examine, **evaluate,** and understand **events,** solve problems, and make **decisions** on the basis of sound **reasoning** and **valid** evidence. More specifically, critical thinking involves: maintaining an **attitude** that is both open-minded and **skeptical;** recognizing the distinction between **facts** and **theories;** striving for factual accuracy and **logical** consistency; **objectively** gathering, weighing, and synthesizing information; forming reasonable **inferences, judgments,** and conclusions; identifying and questioning underlying **assumptions** and **beliefs;** discerning hidden or implicit **values; perceiving** similarities and differences between **phenomena;** understanding **causal** relationships; reducing logical flaws and personal **biases,** such as avoiding oversimplifications and overgeneralizations; developing a tolerance for uncertainty and **ambiguity;** exploring alternative perspectives and **explanations;** and searching for creative solutions; (see **metathinking**).

data (*pl*) A collection of **facts,** information, or **empirical** evidence; a body of **measurements** gathered in the conduct of research.

datum (*sg*) (see **data**).

decision The act of making a choice, **judgment,** or arriving at a solution; (*cf.* **evaluation**).

deduction A form of **reasoning** that involves drawing an **inference** from a general premise to a specific conclusion; (*cf.* **induction**).

deductive reasoning (*cf.* **inductive reasoning**); (see **deduction**).

defense mechanism (see **ego defense mechanism**).

delusion A false **belief** that is firmly maintained as **true,** despite obvious and incontrovertible evidence to the contrary; a diagnostic **criterion** for certain **psychotic disorders.**

denial An **ego defense mechanism** by which the individual reduces his or her **emotional** discomfort by **unconsciously** refusing to accept, or even **perceive,** a **psychologically** painful reality.

denotation (*n*) The literal or explicit meaning of a word, symbol, or **event;** (*cf.* **connotation**).

denote (*vb*) (*cf.* **connote**); (see **denotation**).

dependent variable 1. In an **experiment,** the **variable** whose **value** is determined or **caused** by the manipulation, **treatment,** or **independent variable;** (*syn* outcome, **measure, response**). 2. In nonexperimental settings, a test, **observation,** or measure.

description An **objective** report or account of observed **phenomena,** without **inference, interpretation, explanation,** or **value judgment;** (*syn* **descriptor**); (*cf.* **prediction, evaluation**).

descriptor (*syn* **description**).

determinant (*syn* **cause**).

diagnosis The process of determining, identifying, and classifying the nature of a specific **disorder** or **disease** on the basis of its signs and **symptoms;** (see **differential diagnosis**).

Diagnostic and Statistical Manual of Mental Disorders (**DSM**) The American Psychiatric Association's official system of classification for **psychological disorders;** (see **mental illness, psychopathology**).

dichotomous variable Any **variable** that can be placed into either of two discrete and mutually exclusive **categories;** (*cf.* **continuous variable**).

didactic Designed to impart information, teach, or instruct.

differential diagnosis The process of distinguishing between **diagnoses** on the basis of an individual's particular **symptoms** or complaints.

dilemma A predicament involving two or more mutually exclusive or incompatible alternatives that seemingly defies a satisfactory solution; a conflict comprised of opposing **values** or **motives.**

dimension A range, scope, or spectrum on which a **continuous variable** can be placed; the degree, magnitude, or extent of a particular **phenomenon; (*cf.* category, dichotomous variable).**

disease Strictly defined, an **abnormal** or **pathological somatic** condition, **disorder,** or illness involving serious impairment in **physical** functioning. By extension, defined **metaphorically** as any abnormal **psychological** condition involving serious impairment in functioning; (see **psychopathology, symptom, syndrome**).

disorder A **pathological** or psychologically distressing state of body or **mind; (*cf.* disease**); (see **psychopathology, symptom, syndrome**).

displacement An **ego defense mechanism** by which the individual redirects and discharges **repressed** aggressive or sexual impulses on substitutive objects or people that are **perceived** as less threatening or dangerous than those that originally aroused the conflict.

disposition An individual's relatively stable and enduring constellation of **psychological** (**personality**) and **physical** (biological) **traits** or characteristics; one's **internal** attributes (as opposed to **external** circumstances, situations, or **events**).

DSM (see **Diagnostic and Statistical Manual of Mental Disorders**).

dynamics 1. The action of **psychological** forces, mechanisms, or **motivations.** 2. Pertaining to change, or that which initiates change. 3. Underlying or **unconscious causes.**

dysfunction Impairment, disturbance, or disruption in **normal physical** or **psychological** functioning.

effect (*n*) The inevitable result, **consequence,** or outcome of a preceding **casual event;** (see **causation, internal validity**).

efficacy 1. A term in **clinical psychology** referring to the effectiveness or efficiency of **psychotherapy treatment.** 2. An individual's perceived ability to exert influence and control over his or her outcomes.

e.g. For example (from the Latin, *exempli gratia*).

ego defense mechanism A collection of self-protective **psychological** processes, usually **unconscious,** whose function is to reduce anxiety by denying, falsifying, or distorting reality.

ego-dystonic Referring to aspects of a person's own thoughts, feelings, or **behavior** that are **perceived** as unacceptable, undesirable, or inconsistent with the individual's self-concept; (*cf.* **ego-syntonic**).

ego-syntonic Referring to aspects of a person's own thoughts, feelings, or **behavior** that are perceived as acceptable, desirable, or consistent with the individual's self-concept; (*cf.* **ego-dystonic**).

emotion A strong **subjective** feeling state (such as anger, sadness, happiness, or fear), accompanied by **somatic** changes; (see **affect**).

empirical Based on **objective measurement,** naturalistic **observation,** direct **experience,** or **experimental** procedures, without explicit regard for any particular **theory** or philosophical orientation; capable of being verified or disproven by analyzing and testing evidence, **facts,** or other **quantified data; (*cf.* theoretical, hypothetical, abstract**).

erroneous To be false, mistaken, or wrong.

et al. And others (from the Latin, *et alia*).

ethics Moral principles or standards for human conduct in the pursuit of aims or goals; **prescriptions** for **behavior** based on personal or professional **values** (**e.g.,** good versus bad, moral versus immoral, acceptable versus unacceptable).

etiology The study of origins and **causes,** usually pertaining to **disease.**

evaluation The act of determining or appraising the relative worth, importance, or **value** of a person, object, **event,** or other **phenomenon;** the most fundamental **dimension** underlying **perception** and impression formation; (*cf.* **judgment, description, explanation, inference, interpretation**).

event An **observable, measurable,** or **empirical phenomenon;** any **physical** occurrence; (*cf.* **construct**).

Event (Type E) Theory A type of **theory** whose proposed **explanation** is, in principle, **measurable;** thus, given the proper circumstances, a Type E Theory is provable, and therefore refutable; (*cf.* **Construct Theory**).

existence A state of being; reality as presented in **experience;** (see **ontological**).

existentialism A philosophy centered on the analysis of **existence,** the nature of the human condition, and the search for meaning in life. Existentialism stresses **subjective phenomenology,** the active creation of **experience,** and the acceptance both of free will and personal responsibility in the individual's struggle to break free from the **causal** influences of biological and environmental determinism.

existential therapy A group of approaches to **psychotherapy,** founded on the philosophy of **existentialism** that focus on the uniqueness of each individual in the context of a here-and-now encounter. Emphasis is placed on those qualities that are distinctly human, such as the capacity for self-awareness, personal responsibility, and the freedom to determine one's own fate. **Treatment** goals typically include maximizing awareness, choices, authenticity, and personal growth.

expectation The anticipated outcome of a situation; (see **prediction, probability**).

experience 1. Any **event** through which one has lived. 2. **Observation,** participation, or learning derived from one's prior history or personal background that results in a state of enhanced **knowledge.** 3. The totality of one's immediate and **subjective perceptions,** current **phenomenological** awareness, or present **consciousness.**

experiment A **scientific** research method that enables the investigator to draw **valid** conclusions regarding **causal** relationships between various **phenomena.** More specifically, a procedure carried out under controlled conditions for the purpose of testing **hypotheses,** in which the investigator manipulates the **independent variable** (such as a **treatment**) while holding all other **variables** constant, thereby permitting him or her to assess its **effect** on the outcome **measure** or **dependent variable;** (see **internal validity, scientific method**).

explanation The process of making clear, accounting for, or providing the reasons for understanding various **phenomena;** (*cf.* **interpretation, evaluation, judgment, description, prediction**); (see **theory**).

external Situated or existing on the outside or exterior, usually of the body; (*cf.* **internal**).

external attribution **Ascribing** the **causes** of **behavior** to people's situational factors, such as their circumstances, surroundings, or environment; (*cf.* **internal attribution**); (see **Fundamental Attribution Error, Actor–Observer Bias**).

external validity The extent to which research findings in one setting can be safely related or generalized to other contexts, populations, or settings; (*syn* **generalizability, representativeness**); (*cf.* **internal validity**).

extraversion A fundamental **personality dimension** in which the individual is oriented toward, and derives gratification from, the **objective, external** world of people, things, and **events;** a general **psychological attitude** focusing on one's **social** and **physical** environment; (*cf.* **introversion**).

extravert An individual who displays characteristics of **extraversion.**

fact   Information or **datum** presented as having **objectively** demonstrable **existence;** an **empirically** observed **event;** something that is actual or real.

fallacious   A misleading or deceptive **inference** involving a **fallacy.**

fallacy   A mistaken **belief** based on **erroneous reasoning,** faulty **logic,** or an invalid **inference,** the result of which is a conclusion that is seemingly true, but actually false.

family therapy   A group of **interpersonal** approaches to **psychotherapy** founded on the principles of general systems **theory,** communications theory, and **psychodynamic** theory, which maintains that **behavior** can best be understood and changed in the context of a family system and that **symptoms** serve a function for the system.

fantasy   As an **ego defense mechanism,** the **mental** process whereby the individual escapes from anxiety-provoking reality by seeking gratification in imaginary **events,** activities, or achievements.

Fundamental Attribution Error   A **bias** in attempting to determine the **causes** of people's **behavior** which involves overestimating the influence of their **personality traits,** while underestimating the influence of their particular situations; that is, overutilizing **internal attributions** and underutilizing **external attributions;** (see **cognitive bias, motivational bias, Actor–Observer Bias**).

generalizability   The extent to which findings in one setting can be safely applied, related, or extrapolated to other contexts, populations, or settings; (*syn* **external validity, representativeness**).

generalization   1. A **universal concept** arrived at by **inductive** examination of particular instances; an **inference,** drawn inductively, about a whole **category** based on **experience** with a limited component of that category. 2. In the context of **behavior theory,** the tendency for **stimuli** that are similar to the original **conditioned stimulus** to elicit similar **responses.**

generic   1. General; not specific. 2. Relating to, or characteristic of, all members of a particular group, class, or **category;** (see **ubiquitous, universal**).

Gestalt psychology   The **scientific** study of human **perception.** A holistic, **phenomenological** approach that postulates that the **mind** actively and spontaneously seeks to organize, structure, or otherwise make sense out of **stimuli.** Because **behavior** is assumed to be a function of the individual's perceptions, the **critical** factor is seen as **subjective interpretation,** rather than "**objective**" reality. (From the German word *Gestalt,* which translates roughly as "shape" or "form," and is embodied in the Gestalt tenet that the perceived whole is greater than the sum of its parts.)

Gestalt therapy   An approach to **psychotherapy** founded on the principles of **existentialism,** Gestalt psychology, and **phenomenological** field **theory,** that focuses on the **concepts** of unity, closure, and wholeness of the person. The primary **treatment** goal is broadened awareness, attained through the exploration and integration of **cognitive, emotional, sensory,** and motoric (muscular) functions.

heuristic   1. (*n*) A **mental** shortcut or rule-of-thumb strategy for problem solving that reduces complex information and time-consuming tasks to more simple, rapid, and efficient judgmental operations, particularly in reaching **decisions** under conditions of uncertainty; (see **availability heuristic, representativeness heuristic**). 2. (*adj*) Serving to stimulate **thinking,** learning, investigation, discovery, or problem-solving.

Hindsight Bias   The tendency to overestimate or exaggerate what reasonably could have been anticipated or predicted, only after having learned the outcome; also known as the **I-knew-it-all-along phenomenon.**

Humanistic psychology   Referred to as the "third force" in **psychology** (after **psychoanalysis** and **behaviorism**), Humanistic psychology emphasizes people's positive virtues and focuses on higher human **motives** and **values,** such as self-enhancement, self-actualization, and the potential for growth. Although in agreement with many of the major tenets of **existentialism** (such as **subjective phenomenology,** free will, and personal responsibility), a **critical** exception is Humanistic psychology's fundamental **belief** in the innate goodness of human beings. Humanistic theorists view the individual, at his or her core, as rational, trustworthy, and intrinsically motivated to make **decisions** in the direction of healthy functioning, which they define as more than simply the absence of **disease.**

humanistic therapy   An approach to **psychotherapy** founded on the principles of **Humanistic psychology.** The therapy is client-centered and focuses on providing an atmosphere of genuineness, empathy, and unconditional positive regard so that the client's inherent actualizing **motives** may be permitted to emerge. Faith is placed in clients' ability ultimately to resolve their own problems. Maladjustment (**psychopathology**) is seen as arising primarily from obstructions to the client's intrinsic drive toward growth and an incongruence between what one wants to be (**i.e.,** "ideal self") and what one is (**i.e.,** "real self"); (*cf.* **existential therapy**).

hypothesis   1. A **predicted** relationship between **variables,** derived either from **observations** or a **theory,** that can be tested **empirically** to determine its accuracy. 2. A tentative statement, proposition, or **assumption** that expresses the relationship between **events,** for the purpose of investigation or argument. In contrast to theories, hypotheses do not seek an **explanation** of the underlying **causal** relationships between **variables;** (see **scientific method**).

hypothetical   1. Of or pertaining to a **hypothesis.** 2. **Abstract** or **theoretical.**

ideology   A system of ideas or **beliefs,** usually at the core of any particular social,

political, religious, philosophic, or economic orientation.

idiographic   1. Of or pertaining to that which is individual, particular, or **concrete.** 2. An approach to research emphasizing those aspects of **personality** that are distinctive and unique to each person; (*cf.* **nomothetic**).

i.e.   That is; that is to say (from the Latin, *id est*).

I-knew-it-all-along phenomenon   (*syn* **Hindsight Bias**).

independent variable   1. In an **experiment,** the **variable** whose manipulation **causes** a change in the **value** of the outcome **measure, response,** or **dependent variable;** (*syn* experimental **treatment**). 2. In nonexperimental settings, any condition or factor that is related to a particular outcome.

induction   1. A form of **reasoning** that involves drawing an **inference** from specific instances to a general conclusion; (*cf.* **deduction**). 2. (*syn* **projective identification**).

inductive reasoning   (*cf.* **deductive reasoning**); (see **induction**).

infer   (see **inference**).

inference   A conclusion derived implicitly or explicitly on the basis of prior premises, results, or other **data;** (see **deduction, induction**).

insight   1. A sudden and novel realization of a heretofore unknown explanation or solution to a problem. 2. Clinically, the extent of a client's awareness and understanding of his or her **psychological motives** and **dynamics.** 3. The result of **intuitive perception.**

Insight Fallacy   The **erroneous belief** that understanding the **cause** of a problem will automatically solve the problem.

intellectualization   An **ego defense mechanism** in which the individual analyzes a problem or conflict in remote, detached, **abstract,** or cerebral terms, while feelings and **emotions** are denied or ignored; (*cf.* **isolation of affect**).

intent   (see **intentionality**).

intentionality   A **mental** state involving a deliberate, willful, or **conscious** purpose, aim, or goal; volition; (*syn* **intent**).

internal   Situated or existing on the inside or interior, usually of the body; (*cf.* **external**).

internal attribution Ascribing the **causes** of **behavior** to people's **dispositional** factors, such as their **personality traits,** characteristics, or **attitudes;** (*cf.* **external attribution**); (see **Fundamental Attribution Error, Actor–Observer Bias**).

internal validity   In research, the extent to which a **cause** and **effect** relationship can be established between the **independent variable** and the **dependent variable,** free from contamination by extraneous or confounding **variables;** (*cf.* **external validity**).

interpersonal   Of or relating to **social phenomena;** that which exists between individuals; (*cf.* **intrapsychic**).

interpretation   1. A meaningful **explanation** of a **phenomenon** based on one's pre-existing conceptual **schemas,** models, **theories,** or **beliefs;** (*cf.* **description, prediction, evaluation**). 2. In **psychoanalysis,** the act of **explaining** the significance of a client's dream symbols, free associations, **parapraxes, resistances,** or other **behaviors** to promote **insight** and understanding (**i.e.,** to make the **unconscious, conscious**).

Intervention–Causation Fallacy   The mistaken **belief** that one's ability to modify an **event** inherently proves what originally **caused** the event; (see **Treatment–Etiology Fallacy**).

intrapsychic   Existing or taking place within the **mind** or **psyche;** (*cf.* **interpersonal**).

introversion   A fundamental **personality dimension** wherein the individual is oriented toward, and derives gratification from, the **subjective, internal** world of thoughts, **concepts,** and inner **experience;** a general **psychological attitude** focusing on one's **mental** processes; (*cf.* **extraversion**).

introvert   An individual who displays characteristics of **introversion.**

intuition   1. Direct or immediate **knowledge** or **insight,** without **intentional** effort, **rational** thought, or **conscious judgment.** 2. **Perception** by means of the **unconscious;** a strong premonition or hunch in the absence of **objective empirical** evidence.

isolation of affect   An **ego defense mechanism** in which the individual detaches, dissociates, or otherwise cuts off emotions from anxiety-arousing **events,** situations, or memories; (*cf.* **intellectualization**).

judge   (*vb*) (see **judgment**).

judgment   The act of forming an **opinion,** reaching a conclusion, or making a **decision** by comparing and **critically** evaluating two or more alternatives; (*cf.* **evaluation, inference, reasoning, interpretation**).

knowledge   Awareness or **understanding** of specific information acquired by **experience** or study; the sum of what has been **perceived,** discovered, or learned.

linear   1. A direct and orderly sequence, pattern, or arrangement. 2. Of or relating to a straight line; (*cf.* **nonlinear**).

logic   The study and process of the principles of **valid reasoning, inference,** and proof; (see **deduction, induction**).

measure/measurement   1. (*vb*) To ascertain, determine, or **evaluate** the quantity or magnitude of an entity by assigning a numeric **value** to a given **variable.** 2. (*n*) The **quantification** of a variable's **physical** properties, such as dimension, capacity, or amount. 3. (*n*) The comparison of an **observed phenomenon** or **event** with a standard scale. 4. (*n*) A test, scale, questionnaire, or other statistical device of quantification.

mental   Pertaining to the **mind** or processes associated with the mind; (see **psychological**).

mental disorder   (see **mental illness**).

mental illness   1. A term that is used traditionally to refer to a **clinical syndrome** characterized by significant distress, disability, and impairment in functioning, the violation of societal norms, and/or a markedly increased risk of suffering, over which the individual ostensibly has little or no control. 2. The metaphoric or alleged literal equivalent of **physical disease** or biological illness. 3. More broadly defined, any **disorder** or **dysfunction** of the **mind;** (see **psychopathology**).

meta Transcending; used with the name of a discipline to designate a new but related discipline designed to deal **critically** with the original one; **e.g.,** metacommunication, metatheory, meta-analysis, **metathinking.**

metaphor (*adj* metaphorical) A linguistic device or figure of speech whereby an **abstract concept** is expressed by means of **analogy** or symbolism.

metathinking The act of **thinking** about thinking; engaging in a **critical** analysis and **evaluation** of the thinking process; (see **critical thinking**).

metathoughts Literally, thoughts about thought; (see **metathinking, critical thinking**).

mind A **construct** referring to the organized totality of one's **psychological** or **mental** processes, including but not limited to **conscious** awareness, **unconscious dynamics,** thoughts, **emotions,** memories, **perceptions,** and **motives;** (*syn* **psyche**).

mood Predominant state of feeling or **emotion.**

motivation (*syn* **motive**).

motivational bias Any systematic error in **attribution** that derives from people's efforts to satisfy their own personal needs, such as the desire for self-esteem, power, or prestige; (*cf.* **cognitive bias**); (see **Fundamental Attribution Error**).

motive An impetus, **stimulus,** or drive, either **internal** or **external,** that **causes** an individual to act.

myth A widely accepted but false **belief.**

Naturalistic Fallacy An error in **thinking** whereby the individual confuses or equates **objective descriptions** with **subjective**

value judgments, in particular by defining what is morally good or bad solely in terms of what is statistically frequent or infrequent.

negative countertransference (*cf.* **positive countertransference**); (see **countertransference, transference**).

negative transference (*cf.* **positive transference**); (see **transference, countertransference**).

neurotic A **generic** and somewhat dated term referring to any relatively benign but enduring and distressing **psychological** or **emotional disorders,** such as those characterized by extreme anxiety, preoccupation with things that might go wrong, obsessions, compulsions, phobias, **somatic symptoms,** or excessive use of **ego defense mechanisms.** By definition, neurotic conditions are less serious than **psychotic** disorders (**i.e.,** reality testing is intact) and the symptoms are recognized by the individual as unacceptable or **egodystonic.**

neutral 1. Free of personal or **subjective bias;** not favoring or allied with any particular perspective in a conflict or dispute; fair, impartial, or **objective.** 2. In the context of the **measurement** of **values, attitudes,** or **beliefs,** a middle region between the extremes of two polar opposites.

Nominal Fallacy The mistaken **belief** that naming a **phenomenon,** in itself, **explains** the phenomenon. The Nominal Fallacy frequently involves the use of **tautologous reasoning.**

nomothetic 1. Pertaining to the formulation of general, **universal,** or **abstract** principles. 2. An approach to research that emphasizes those aspects of **personality** that are common to all persons; (*cf.* **idiographic**).

nonlinear 1. Absence of a direct and orderly sequence, pattern, or arrangement. 2. Not related or pertaining to a straight line; (*cf.* **linear**).

normal That which does not deviate markedly from what is typical, common, or statistically average.

objective 1. (*adj*) Existing in **fact** or in **physical** reality, based on **concrete events** that are independent of an observer. 2. (*adj*) Accessible to **observation** and free of **subjective bias,** such as personal **beliefs, values, opinions,** or **interpretations;** (see **neutral**). 3. (*n*) A goal, purpose, or aim.

observation The act of purposive and **intentional** examination of an **event,** particularly with the goal of gathering and organizing **data;** noting and recording an occurrence by means of **empirical measurement.**

ontological Pertaining to **existence** and the nature of being.

opinion A tentatively held **belief** that typically is open to modification; a point of view that is stronger than an initial impression but less strong than **factual knowledge;** (see **attitude, judgment, decision**).

orthogonal Pertaining to **phenomena** that are independent, conceptually unrelated, or statistically uncorrelated; (see **correlation**).

paradox A seemingly contradictory statement or idea that may nevertheless be true; (see **paradoxical intention, paradoxical intervention**).

paradoxical intention (*syn* **paradoxical intervention**).

paradoxical intervention (*syn* **paradoxical intention**) A **psychotherapy** technique in which the client is encouraged or instructed to engage in, or even exaggerate, the very **behaviors** for which he or she is seeking **treatment.** The primary rationale for this technique is to undermine the client's **resistance** to change by rendering it useless.

parapraxis (*pl* parapraxes) Any apparent "mistake" in **behavior** that is allegedly due to **repressed, unconscious motives;** commonly referred to as a "Freudian slip."

parapsychology The study of paranormal **psychological phenomena,** that is, **events** that seemingly cannot be accounted for in terms of known scientific principles or **theories;** examples include extrasensory perception (ESP), telepathy, psychokinesis, and clairvoyance.

parataxic reasoning A distortion of reality brought about by **inferring** a **causal** relationship between **events** that are actually independent or **orthogonal;** a kind of "magical thinking," frequently responsible for superstitious **behaviors,** in which **events** that occur close together in time are construed as causally linked; (see **Contiguity–Causation Error**).

pathological (*adj*) Strictly defined, that which pertains to an **abnormal somatic** or biological condition, **disease, disorder,** or illness involving serious impairment in **physical** functioning. By extension, defined **metaphorically** as pertaining to any abnormal **psychological** condition involving serious impairment in functioning; (see **psychopathology**).

pathology (*n*) (see **pathological**).

pedagogic Pertaining to the art, **science,** or profession of teaching.

perceive (*vb*) (see **perception**).

perception 1. An individual's **subjective** or **phenomenological** organization and **interpretation** of **sensory** information. 2. A **theoretical** intervening process or **variable** that links **physical stimuli** with the organism's unique **psychological** characteristics, such as past **experiences, schemas, beliefs, expectations, attitudes,** and **mood.** In this way, the meaning **ascribed** to an entity or **event** is determined by a synthesis of **stimulus** factors and organism factors.

per se By or in itself; as such; intrinsically.

personality An individual's unique pattern of **psychological** and **behavioral** characteristics that are relatively stable over time and across or within situations.

personality disorder A class of **psychological disorders** marked by enduring, inflexible, and maladaptive **personality traits** or characteristics that lead to persistent **subjective** distress or significant impairment in **social** functioning.

personality trait A fundamental and relatively permanent **psychological disposition,** characteristic, or **dimension** that underlies **personality** and that, in **theory,** accounts for both the systematic consistency and variability in an individual's **behavior.**

phenomena (*pl*) A broad term encompassing both **concrete events** and **abstract constructs;** (*sg* **phenomenon**).

phenomenon (*sg*) (see **phenomena**).

phenomenology (*adj* phenomenological) The **description** of one's immediate **subjective experience** and **perceptions** without analysis, **interpretation,** or **explanation.** Phenomenology is based on awareness and exploring the **conscious** (as opposed to the **unconscious**), with a minimum focus on **objective events** or **external, physical** reality.

physical The quality of being tangible, **concrete, observable,** or directly **measurable;** consisting of mass or material substance; (*cf.* **mental, abstract**); (see **somatic**).

point of critical distinction (PCD) A **conceptual** boundary delineating one **phenomenon** from another, before which point they are similar, and after which they are different.

positive countertransference (*cf.* **negative countertransference**); (see **countertransference, transference**).

positive transference (*cf.* **negative transference**); (see **transference, countertransference**).

postdiction A statement about an **event's** prior outcome, made **subsequent** to its actual occurrence; (*cf.* **prediction**); (see **description, explanation, Hindsight Bias**).

post hoc 1. After the fact; (Latin for "after this"). 2. A shortened form of *post hoc, ergo propter hoc* ("after this, therefore because of this"), referring to the **logical** error that because Event *B* follows Event *A*, then *B* must have been **caused** by *A*; (see **Contiguity–Causation Error**).

pragmatic The quality of being practical or realistic; concerned with **concrete facts,** **events,** or results rather than **abstract** ideas, processes, or **theories.**

preconception Any preexisting **belief, opinion, attitude, schema, theory,** frame of reference, or conclusion.

prediction A forecast about the likelihood or **probability** of an **event's** outcome made prior to its actual occurrence; (*cf.* **postdiction; description, explanation**); (see **expectation, Hindsight Bias**).

premise A proposition, supposition, or **assumption** on which an argument, **inference,** or conclusion is based; (see ***a priori***).

prescription A directive, order, endorsement, guideline, or injunction; any suggested or recommended course of action; (*cf.* **description, explanation**).

prima facie At first sight, view, or appearance, before closer inspection; apparent or on the surface.

probability 1. The likelihood that an **event** will occur. 2. In mathematical terms, a numeric **value** that corresponds with the degree of certainty in one's statistical estimate or **prediction.**

procrustean (procrustean bed) A **category, schema,** or pattern into which someone or something is arbitrarily forced, with no regard for individual differences or special circumstances.

projection An **ego defense mechanism** by which the individual reduces anxiety by **attributing** his or her own unacceptable (**ego-dystonic**) desires, **beliefs, traits,** or conflicts to others.

projective hypothesis An **assumption** underlying **projective tests** that proposes that when people are presented with an **ambiguous stimulus,** they will respond by automatically assigning or imposing (**i.e.,** "projecting") structure, organization, or meaning onto the stimulus, thereby revealing their **psychological dynamics,** both **conscious** and **unconscious.**

projective identification An **ego defense** mechanism involving the **unconscious splitting** and **projection** of one's own unacceptable (**i.e., ego-dystonic**) attributes such that they elicit those very

behaviors in another person; (*syn* **induction**); (see **Self-Fulfilling Prophecy**).

projective test Any **psychological** assessment technique based on the **projective hypothesis** that involves exposing the examinee to a relatively unstructured or **ambiguous stimulus,** and then soliciting his or her **perceptions.** Examples include the Rorschach Inkblot Test, the Thematic Apperception Test (TAT), house-tree-person (HTP) projective drawing test, and sentence completion tests.

psyche Of or pertaining to the **mind.**

psychoanalysis 1. As originally proposed by Sigmund Freud, a **theory** of **personality** that emphasizes primarily **unconscious motivations** and **repressed** sexual and aggressive conflicts. 2. An approach to **psychotherapy treatment** based on psychoanalytic theory, utilizing the techniques of free association, dream **interpretation,** and the analysis of **transference, resistance, ego defense mechanisms,** and **parapraxes;** (*cf.* **psychodynamic theory, psychodynamic therapy**).

psychodynamic theory A relatively broad group of **personality theories,** which, despite their differences, share common emphases on **unconscious motivations,** the influence of childhood **experiences** on adult **thinking** and **behavior, intrapsychic** tensions and conflicts, **ego defense mechanisms,** and conceptualizing the **mind** in terms of exchanges and transformations of psychic energy. (**Psychoanalysis** is one specific subset of psychodynamic theory.)

psychodynamic therapy A group of approaches to **psychotherapy** founded on the principles of **psychodynamic theory.** Specific goals and techniques vary, but typically include **interpretations,** the "working through" of **resistance** and **transference,** and the attainment of **insight** and understanding; in short, to make the **unconscious, conscious;** (*cf.* **psychoanalysis**).

psychological Of or pertaining to any **mental** and **behavioral** processes, including but not limited to thought, **emotion, attitude, perception,** memory, **motivation,** and intelligence.

psychological disorder (*syn* **psychopathology, mental disorder, mental illness**); (see **pathology, disease, dysfunction, symptom, syndrome, DSM**).

psychology The **scientific** study of **mental** and **behavioral** processes.

psychopathology 1. Any **psychological** or **emotional disorder;** (*syn* **mental disorder, mental illness**). 2. The **scientific** study of **psychological disorders.**

psychosis (*adj* **psychotic**) A severe **clinical syndrome** that broadly indicates gross impairment in reality testing.

psychotic (see **psychosis**).

psychotherapy The **treatment** of **mental** or **behavioral** problems by **psychological** methods. Commonly referred to as "therapy," particularly when modifiers are utilized to identify a specific **theoretical** orientation or **clinical** approach (**e.g., behavior therapy, cognitive therapy, cognitive–behavioral therapy, existential therapy, humanistic therapy, psychodynamic therapy, family therapy, Gestalt therapy**); (see **psychoanalysis, mental disorder, psychopathology**).

psychotropic (*adj*) Literally, **mind**-altering or **mood**-altering; usually as pertaining to medication; (*syn* **psychoactive**).

quantify To numerically express, determine, or **measure** the amount or quantity of an entity.

random The absence of any apparent or discernable order, direction, or purpose; occurring haphazardly or by **chance.**

rational (*adj*) Of or pertaining to **reasoning** and **logic,** rather than **emotion;** (*cf.* **rationalization**).

rationalization An **ego defense mechanism** involving the attempt to justify one's own **attitudes** or **behaviors** by making them appear to be reasonable, sensible, and **logical,** but which actually conceals, and is a pretext for, the true **motivation** of **unconscious** anxiety reduction; (*cf.* **rational**).

reaction formation An **ego defense mechanism** by which the individual copes with **repressed, ego-dystonic** wishes, impulses, or **attitudes** by **unconsciously** transforming them into their opposite, and therefore more acceptable, form.

reactive effect of testing A threat to a study's **external validity** wherein taking a pretest may modify research subjects' sensitivity to the subsequent **experimental treatment.**

reactive effects of experimental arrangements A threat to a study's **external validity** wherein the artificiality of the research setting, or the subjects' awareness that they are participating in a study, may significantly limit the extent to which a researcher may safely **generalize** the **effect** of the **experimental treatment** to people in nonexperimental settings.

reactivity A **phenomenon** wherein the conduct of research, in itself, affects the very entity that is being studied; the extent to which **measuring** something **causes** it to change.

reasoning The process of **thinking,** problem solving, or drawing **inferences** in a manner that is **rational,** logical, or coherent; (*cf.* **tautologous reasoning, parataxic reasoning**); (see **logic, deduction, induction**).

reciprocal (*adj*) 1. Of or pertaining to mutual influence, action, or exchange; (see **bi-directional causation**). 2. Inversely related; opposite.

reframing A **psychotherapy** technique involving a verbal redefinition of **dysfunctional** or undesirable **events** or **behaviors,** with the purpose of making them appear more positive, understandable, or controllable; (*syn* relabeling).

reification The act of treating an **abstract concept** or **theoretical construct** as if it were a **concrete event** or **physical** entity.

reify (*vb*) (see **reification**).

reinforcement The operation of strengthening the **probability** that a given

response will recur by the presentation of a rewarding **stimulus** or the removal of an aversive stimulus; (see **behaviorism**).

reliability (*adj* reliable) 1. The state of being dependable, trustworthy, or accurate. 2. An index of the extent to which a test or **measure** is consistent, either internally, over time, across observers, or between alternate forms; (*cf.* **validity**).

representativeness The extent to which findings in one setting can be safely related or generalized to other contexts, populations, or settings; (*syn* **external validity, generalizability**).

Representativeness Bias Any condition in which the **representativeness heuristic** produces systematic errors in **thinking** or information processing.

representativeness heuristic A **cognitive** strategy for quickly estimating the **probability** that a given instance is a member of a particular **category;** (see **heuristic, availability heuristic**).

repression An **ego defense mechanism** by which the individual reduces anxiety by **unconsciously** blocking out or forgetting particular thoughts, feelings, or memories, usually of a traumatic nature.

resistance 1. In **psychotherapy** (particularly **psychoanalysis**), the client's **unconscious** unwillingness to acknowledge or confront areas of **repressed** conflict. This may manifest itself in the form of unconscious opposition to, or deflection of, the therapist's probing questions or uncomfortable (but possibly accurate) **interpretations.** 2. The natural tendency of a living system (such as a family) to avoid, obstruct, or prevent changes (positive or negative) in its current homeostatic functioning, even if this involves the maintenance of distressing **symptoms** or the sabotage of **treatment.** 3. More broadly defined, an **interpersonal phenomenon** whereby one person declines or refuses to do what another person wants him or her to do; a **conscious,** willful, or deliberate act of defiance, disobedience, or rebelliousness.

response 1. A reaction to a **stimulus.** 2. Any **behavior,** whether overt or covert. 3. An answer or reply to a question; (see **dependent variable**).

schema (*pl* schemas, **schemata**) A **cognitive** structure or representation that organizes one's **knowledge, beliefs,** and past **experiences,** thereby providing a framework for understanding new **events** and future experiences; a general **expectation** or **preconception** about a wide range of **phenomena;** (see **stereotype**).

schemata (*pl*) (see **schema**).

science An organized and systematic body of **knowledge** and approach to the investigation of natural **phenomena,** as obtained and verified through the application of the **scientific method.** In contrast to philosophy, science requires that its procedures and conclusions satisfy the **criterion** of **empirical** proof.

scientific (*adj*) Of or pertaining to **science.**

scientific method A relatively standardized set of rules and procedures guiding the conduct of **science,** which rests on a foundation of **empirical** evidence and **valid reasoning.** Its essential features include: the use of known **facts, observations,** and **inductive reasoning** to construct **theories; deductive reasoning** to derive testable **hypotheses;** specific research methods (such as **experiments**) to collect **data;** statistical analyses to **evaluate** the results; sound **logic** to draw appropriate **inferences** and conclusions; and **critical thinking** principles to maximize **reliability, validity,** and usefulness.

Self-Fulfilling Prophecy A **phenomenon** whereby people's **attitudes, beliefs,** or **assumptions** about another person (or persons) can, with or without their **intent,** actually produce the very **behaviors** that they had initially **expected** to find.

semantic (*adj*) Of or pertaining to meaning, or the study of meaning, particularly as related to words and language.

sensory (*adj*) Of or pertaining to the five senses or to the neurological mechanisms involved in the process of sensation; (*cf.* **perception**).

shadow archetype Those components of people's own **personality** that are so repulsive, threatening, or frightening (**i.e.,** ego-dystonic) to them that they refuse to acknowledge their existence and, instead, **unconsciously project** these disowned characteristics onto other individuals.

skepticism (*adj* skeptical) An **attitude** of suspended **judgment,** uncertainty, or doubt that reflects an unwillingness to accept any statement or **belief** as **truth** in the absence of **empirical** evidence or other **valid** proof; (see **critical thinking**).

social Of or relating to **interpersonal events** or relationships.

somatic (*adj.; n* soma) Of or pertaining to the body.

Spectacular Explanation Fallacy The **erroneous belief** that extraordinary **events** are necessarily due to extraordinary **causes.**

splitting An **ego defense mechanism** by which the individual attempts to resolve **unconscious** conflict by **bifurcating** ambivalent **attitudes** and feelings into good versus bad **categories,** thereby failing to integrate the positive and negative qualities of the self or others into a cohesive whole.

stereotype A simplistic, overgeneralized, and relatively rigid **preconception** about a particular **social category** or group of people; (*syn* role **schema**).

stimuli (*pl*) (see **stimulus**).

stimulus (*sg*) Any **physical** or **psychological event** that **causes** a **response;** an impetus that prompts an organism to action; (see **motive, reinforcement, conditioned stimulus, unconditioned stimulus**).

subjective Existing solely within the individual's **mind,** personal **perceptions,** or private, **internal experience,** and incapable of direct, **external** verification; (*cf.* **objective**); (see **phenomenology**).

subsequent That which ensues or follows an **event,** occurrence, or condition, whose relationship may or may not involve **causality**; (*cf.* **antecedent**).

symptom   1. A **phenomenon** regarded as an indicator or manifestation of a medical **disease, psychological disorder,** or other **pathological** condition. 2. **Subjective perception** of illness, typically reported by the affected individual, rather than observed by the examiner; (see **syndrome**).

synchronicity   (*n; adj* **synchronistic**) An extraordinary or uncanny coincidence to which the person involved **ascribes** unique and significant meaning; a link between two **events** that is connected through their **subjectively experienced** meaning to the individual and that ostensibly cannot be explained or accounted for by the principles of direct **causation.**

syndrome   A cluster of related signs and **symptoms** that collectively characterize or constitute a particular medical **disease, psychological disorder,** or other **pathological** condition.

tautological reasoning   (see **tautologous reasoning**).

tautologous reasoning   Circular **reasoning** in which one conclusion rests upon another, which in turn refers back to the first. Tautologies involve the needless repetition of an idea, statement, or word, wherein the **phenomenon** is true by virtue of its **logical** form alone; thus, a tautology can never be falsified; (*syn* **tautological reasoning**).

taxonomy   Any classification system of **abstract** or **concrete phenomena,** based on their similarities and differences; (see **category, point of critical distinction**).

temporal   Of or pertaining to time.

temporal contiguity   Referring to the occurrence of one **event** immediately after or immediately before another event; two events that occur side by side in time; (see **Contiguity–Causation Error, parataxic reasoning**).

theoretical   1. Of or pertaining to **theory.** 2. **Abstract or hypothetical.**

theory   1. A proposed **explanation** of observed **events;** (see **Event Theory, Construct Theory**). 2. A systematic statement that sets forth the apparent relationships and underlying principles that make a domain of observable **phenomena** and **empirical** findings meaningful. In contrast to **hypotheses** (which seek to make **predictions** between **variables**), theories seek to explain the **causal** relationships between variables; (see **scientific method**).

thinking   The **mental** process of producing ideas; exercising the powers of intellect, **reasoning, logic, judgment, conception,** memory, or **inference;** (*syn* **cognition**).

trait   Any relatively enduring **physical** or **psychological** characteristic, feature, or **disposition;** (see **personality trait**).

transference   A distorted **perception,** usually **unconscious,** on the part of the client toward a psychotherapist based on his or her prior relationship **experiences;** the perception may be favorable (**positive transference**) or unfavorable (**negative transference**); (*cf.* **countertransference**).

treatment   1. In the **clinical** context, any medical or **psychotherapy** procedure whose purpose is to alleviate or eliminate a particular **disorder, disease,** or other related problem; (see **antidote, prescription**). 2. In research, an **experimental** condition or type of **independent variable.** 3. More broadly defined, the specific manner in which an individual regards, handles, deals with, cares for, or otherwise behaves toward another person.

Treatment–Etiology Fallacy   The **erroneous belief** that a favorable **response** to medical **treatment** is, in itself, proof of medical **disease;** (see **Intervention–Causation Fallacy**).

truth   1. The property of any statement or **belief** that is in accordance with **fact,** accuracy, or reality; (*syn* **veracity**). 2. The quality of being honest, candid, or sincere.

ubiquitous   (*adj*) Any **phenomenon** that is common, widespread, or omnipresent.

ubiquity (*n*) (see **ubiquitous**).

unconditioned response (UCR) In classical conditioning, an innate or unlearned **response** to an **unconditioned stimulus; (*cf.* conditioned response**); (see **behaviorism**).

unconditioned stimulus (UCS) In classical conditioning, any **stimulus** that elicits an unlearned or **unconditioned response**; (*cf.* **conditioned stimulus**); (see **behaviorism**).

unconscious 1. (*adj*) The **mental** state of being unaware or lacking in awareness. 2. (*adj*) A loss of consciousness. 3. (*adj*) According to **cognitive theorists,** information processing that is automatic, rapid, and essentially unintentional and out of awareness. 4. (*n*) According to **psychodynamic theorists,** that part of the **psyche** that is largely unknown, irrational, and **repressed,** but that nevertheless exerts a significant influence on people's **motivations, attitudes, perceptions, emotions,** and **behavior; (*cf.* conscious**).

uni-directional causation A relationship between two **variables** wherein one is the **cause** and the other is the **effect; (*cf.* bi-directional causation**).

universal Of or pertaining to that which is global, general, extensive, or omnipresent; (see **ubiquitous, generic**).

utility The quality of being useful; having practical relevance, **value,** or worth for some particular purpose; (*syn* **pragmatic**).

validity (*n; adj* valid) 1. The quality of being meaningful, correct, or well-grounded. 2. An index of the extent to which a test actually **measures** what it purports to measure; (*cf.* **reliability**); (see **internal validity, external validity**).

value 1. A material object or **social** principle that is held in high regard or **perceived** as desirable, worthwhile, or useful. 2. A numerical quantity that is assigned or is determined by calculation or **measurement.**

variable (*n*) 1. A characteristic, property, or attribute that may assume any one of a set of different qualities or quantities. 2. That which is capable of changing or being changed; (see **continuous variable, dichotomous variable**).

veracity The quality of being true, correct, **factual,** or real; (*syn* **truth**); (*cf.* **erroneous**).

vicarious 1. That which is learned or **experienced** indirectly by one person through another person via **observation,** proxy, or modeling. 2. Pertaining to or functioning as a substitute or surrogate.

vignette A short, **descriptive** sketch, synopsis, or narrative.

vivid Any property of a **stimulus** that produces a strong, intense, and usually immediate impact on one's attention, senses, or **perceptions;** characteristic of **events** that are dramatic, graphic, salient, striking, or otherwise memorable.

viz. Namely (from the Latin, *videlicet*).

References

American Psychiatric Association. (1987). *Diagnostic and statistical manual of mental disorders* (3rd ed., rev.). Washington, DC: Author.

American Psychiatric Association. (1994). *Diagnostic and statistical manual of mental disorders* (4th ed.). Washington, DC: Author.

Anastasi, A. (1988). *Psychological testing* (6th ed.). New York: Macmillan.

Anderson, C. A. (1982). Inoculation and counter-explanation: Debiasing techniques in the perseverance of social theories. *Social Cognition, 1,* 126–139.

Anderson, C. A., Lepper, M. R., & Ross, L. (1980). Perseverance of social theories: The role of explanation in the persistence of discredited information. *Journal of Personality and Social Psychology, 39,* 1037–1049.

Andreason, N. J. C., & Canter, A. (1974). The creative writer: Psychiatric symptoms and family history. *Comprehensive Psychiatry, 15*(2), 123–131.

Andreason, N. J. C., & Powers, P. S. (1975). Creativity and psychosis: An examination of conceptual style. *Archives of General Psychiatry, 32,* 70–73.

Angeles, P. A. (1981). *Dictionary of philosophy.* New York: Harper & Row.

Asch, S. (1946). Forming impressions of personality. *Journal of Abnormal and Social Psychology, 41,* 258–290.

Barber, J. W. (1971). *The book of 1000 proverbs.* New York: American Heritage Press. (Original work published 1876)

Bartlett, J. (1968). *Familiar quotations* (14th ed.). Boston: Little, Brown.

Bass, E., & Davis, L. (1988). *The courage to heal.* New York: Harper & Row.

Baumrind, D. (1983). Rejoinder to Lewis's reinterpretation of parental firm control effects: Are authoritative families really harmonious? *Psychological Bulletin, 94,* 132–142.

Berscheid, E. (1982). Attraction and emotions in interpersonal relationships. In M. S. Clark &

S. T. Fiske (Eds.), *Affect and cognition: The 17th Annual Carnegie Symposium on Cognition.* Hillsdale, NJ: Erlbaum.

Bertalanffy, L. von. (1968). *General systems theory: Foundation, development, applications.* New York: Braziller.

Bloch, A. (1980). *Murphy's Law, Book Two.* Los Angeles: Price/Stern/Sloan.

Borgida, E., & Nisbett, R. E. (1977). The differential impact of abstract vs. concrete information on decisions. *Journal of Applied Social Psychology, 7,* 258–271.

Breuer, J., & Freud, S. (1895). Studies on hysteria. In *The standard edition of the complete psychological works of Sigmund Freud* (Vol. 2). London: Hogarth Press, 1955.

Bruner, J. S., & Potter, M. C. (1964). Interference in visual recognition. *Science, 144,* 424–425.

Buber, M. (1958). *I and thou.* New York: Charles Scribner's Sons.

Buri, J. R., Louiselle, P. A., Misukanis, T. M., & Mueller, R. A. (1988). Effects of parental authoritarianism and authoritativeness on self-esteem. *Personality and Social Psychology Bulletin, 14,* 271–282.

Cacioppo, J. T., & Berntson, G. G. (1992). Social psychological contributions to the decade of the brain: Doctrine of multilevel analysis. *American Psychologist, 47*(8), 1019–1028.

Campbell, D. T., & Stanley, J. C. (1963). *Experimental and quasi-experimental designs for research.* Chicago: Rand McNally.

Cantor, N., & Mischel, W. (1977). Traits as prototypes: Effects on recognition memory. *Journal of Personality and Social Psychology, 35,* 38–48.

Cantor, N., & Mischel, W. (1979). Prototypes in person perception. In L. Berkowitz (Ed.), *Advances in experimental social psychology* (Vol. 12, pp. 3–52). New York: Academic Press.

Carroll, J. B. (Ed.). (1956). *Language, thought, and reality: Selected writings of Benjamin Lee Whorf.* New York: Wiley.

Carson, R. C. (in press). Aristotle, Galileo, and the *DSM* taxonomy: The case of schizophrenia. *Journal of Consulting and Clinical Psychology.*

Coopersmith, S. (1967). *The antecedents of self-esteem.* San Francisco: Freeman.

Corey, G. (1991). *Theory and practice of counseling and psychotherapy* (4th ed.). Pacific Grove, CA: Brooks/Cole Publishing.

Darley, J. M., & Fazio, R. H. (1980). Expectancy confirmation processes arising in the social interaction sequence. *American Psychologist, 35*, 867–881.

Davidoff, H. (1952). *The pocket book of quotations.* New York: Pocket Books.

Dickson, D. H., & Kelly, I. W. (1985). The "Barnum Effect" in personality assessment: A review of the literature. *Psychological Reports, 57*, 367–382.

Dukas, H., & Hoffman, B. (Eds.). (1979). *Albert Einstein: The human side.* Princeton, N.J.: Princeton University Press.

Ellis, A. (1984). Rational-emotive therapy. In R. Corsini (Ed.), *Current psychotherapies* (3rd ed., pp. 196–238). Itasca, IL: Peacock.

Ellis, A., & Bernard, M. E. (1985). What is rational-emotive therapy (RET)? In A. Ellis & M. E. Bernard (Eds.), *Clinical applications of rational-emotive therapy* (pp. 1–30). New York: Plenum Press.

Erdelyi, M. H., & Goldberg, B. (1979). Let's not sweep repression under the rug: Toward a cognitive psychology of repression. In J. F. Kihlstrom & F. J. Evans (Eds.), *Functional disorders of memory* (pp. 355–402). Hillsdale, NJ: Erlbaum.

Erikson, E. H. (1950). *Childhood and society.* New York: Norton.

Exner, J. E., Jr. (1990). *A Rorschach workbook for the comprehensive system* (3rd ed.). Asheville, NC: Rorschach Workshops.

Exner, J. E., Jr. (1993). *The Rorschach: A comprehensive system Volume 1: Basic foundations* (3rd ed.). New York: John Wiley & Sons.

Eysenck, H. J. (1957). *Sense and nonsense in psychology.* Harmondsworth, Middlesex, England: Pelican Books.

Eysenck, H. J. (1985). *Decline and fall of the Freudian empire.* London: Viking.

Farina, A. (1982). The stigma of mental disorders. In A. G. Miller (Ed.), *In the eye of the beholder.* New York: Praeger.

Fazio, R. H., Effrein, E. A., & Fallender, V. J. (1981). Self-perceptions following social interaction. *Journal of Personality and Social Psychology, 41*, 232–242.

Feldman, R. S., & Prohaska, T. (1979). The student as Pygmalion: Effect of student expectation on the teacher. *Journal of Educational Psychology, 71*, 485–493.

Feldman, R. S., & Theiss, A. J. (1982). The teacher and student as Pygmalions: Joint effects of teacher and student expectations. *Journal of Educational Psychology, 74*, 217–223.

Fersch, E. A. (1980). *Psychology and psychiatry in courts and corrections.* New York: Wiley.

Feshbach, S., & Weiner, B. (1986). *Personality* (2nd ed.). Lexington, MA: D. C. Heath.

Festinger, L. (1957). *A theory of cognitive dissonance.* Stanford: Stanford University Press.

Festinger, L., & Carlsmith, J. M. (1959). Cognitive consequences of forced compliance. *Journal of Abnormal and Social Psychology, 58*, 203–210.

Fischoff, B. (1975). Hindsight ≠ foresight: The effects of outcome knowledge on judgment under uncertainty. *Journal of Experimental Psychology: Human Perception and Performance, 1*, 288–299.

Fischoff, B. (1980). For those condemned to study the past: Reflections on historical judgment. In R. A. Shweder (Ed.), *New directions for methodology of social and behavioral science* (Vol. 4). San Francisco: Jossey-Bass.

Fischoff, B. (1982). For those condemned to study the past: Heuristics and biases in hindsight. In D. Kahneman, P. Slovic, & A. Tversky (Eds.), *Judgment under uncertainty: Heuristics and biases.* New York: Cambridge University Press.

Fischoff, B., & Beyth, R. (1975). "I knew it would happen"—Remembered probabilities of once future things. *Organizational Behavior and Human Performance, 13*, 1–16.

Fiske, S. T., & Taylor, S. E. (1984). *Social cognition.* Reading, MA: Addison-Wesley.

Forer, B. R. (1949). The fallacy of personal validation: A classroom demonstration of gullibility. *Journal of Abnormal and Social Psychology, 44,* 118–123.

Frank, L. K. (1939). Projective methods for the study of personality. *Journal of Psychology, 8,* 389–413.

Frankl, V. E. (1959). *Man's search for meaning: An introduction to logotherapy.* New York: Washington Square Press.

Freud, A. (1936). The ego and the mechanisms of defense. In *The writings of Anna Freud* (Vol. 2). New York: International Universities Press.

Freud, S. (1953). The interpretation of dreams. In J. Strachey (Ed. and Trans.), *The standard edition of the complete psychological works of Sigmund Freud* (Vol. 4–5, pp. 1–621). London: Hogarth Press. (Original work published 1900)

Freud, S. (1961). Civilization and its discontents. In J. Strachey (Ed. and Trans.), *The standard edition of the complete psychological works of Sigmund Freud* (Vol. 21, pp. 64–145). London: Hogarth Press. (Original work published 1930)

Freud, S. (1964). New introductory lectures. In J. Strachey (Ed. and Trans.), *The standard edition of the complete psychological works of Sigmund Freud* (Vol. 22, pp. 7–182). London: Hogarth Press. (Original work published 1933)

Greenwald, J. (1986, January 13). Is there cause for fear of flying? *Time,* pp. 39–40.

Haley, J. (1976). *Problem-solving therapy.* San Francisco, CA: Jossey-Bass.

Hamilton, D. L. (1979). A Cognitive–attributional analysis of stereotyping. In L. Berkowitz (Ed.), *Advances in experimental social psychology* (Vol. 12, pp. 53–81). New York: Academic Press.

Hamilton, D. L. (1981). *Cognitive processes in stereotyping and intergroup behavior.* Hillsdale, NJ: Erlbaum.

Heider, F. (1958). *The psychology of interpersonal relations.* New York: Wiley.

Higgins, E. T., & Bargh, J. A. (1987). Social cognition and social perception. *Annual Review of Psychology, 38,* 369–425.

Holden, C. (1980a). Identical twins reared apart. *Science, 207,* 1323–1325.

Holden, C. (1980b, November). Twins reunited. *Science, 80,* pp. 55–59.

Holmes, D. (1990). The evidence for repression: An examination of sixty years of research. In J. Singer (Ed.), *Repression and dissociation: Implications for personality, theory, psychopathology, and health* (pp. 85–102). Chicago: University of Chicago Press.

Horwitz, L. (1983). Projective identification in dyads and groups. *International Journal of Group Psychotherapy, 33,* 254–279.

Huesmann, L. R. (1982). Television violence and aggressive behavior. In D. Pearl & L. Bouthilet (Eds.), *Television and behavior: Ten years of scientific progress and implications for the 80's.* Washington, DC: U.S. Government Printing Office.

Huesmann, L. R., Lagerspetz, K., & Eron, L. D. (1983). Intervening variables in the television violence–aggression relation: Evidence from the two countries. *Developmental Psychology, 19,* 71–77.

Huxley, A. (1959). *Collected essays.* New York: Harper.

Jamieson, D. W., Lydon, J. E., Stewart, G., & Zanna, M. P. (1984). *Pygmalion revisited: New evidence for student expectancy effects in the classroom.* Paper presented at the meeting of the American Psychological Association.

Jamison, K. R. (1993). *Touched with fire: Manic-depressive illness and the artistic temperament.* New York: Free Press.

Jones, E. E., & Harris, V. A. (1967). The attribution of attitudes. *Journal of Experimental Social Psychology, 3,* 2–24.

Jones, E. E., & Nisbett, R. E. (1972). The actor and the observer: Divergent perceptions of the causes of behavior. In E. E. Jones et al. (Eds.), *Attribution: Perceiving the causes of behavior.* Morristown, NJ: General Learning Press.

Jung, C. G. (1953). Two essays on analytical psychology. In H. Read (Ed.) and F. C. Hull (Trans.), *The collected works of C. G. Jung* (Vol. 7, pp. 8–292). Princeton, NJ: Princeton University Press. (Original work published 1943)

Jung, C. G. (1959). Aion: Researches into the phenomenology of the self. In H. Read (Ed.) and F. C. Hull (Trans.), *The collected works of*

C. G. Jung (Vol. 9ii, pp. 3–269). Princeton, NJ: Princeton University Press. (Original work published 1951)

Jung, C. G. (1961). *Memories, dreams, reflections* (R. Winston & C. Winston, Trans.). New York: Random House.

Jung, C. G. (1969). Synchronicity: An acausal connecting principle. In H. Read (Ed.) and F. C. Hull (Trans.), *The collected works of C. G. Jung* (Vol. 8, pp. 421–519). Princeton, NJ: Princeton University Press. (Original work published 1952)

Jung, C. G. (1971). Psychological types. In H. Read (Ed.) and F. C. Hull (Trans.), *The collected works of C. G. Jung* (Vol. 6, pp. 3–555). Princeton, NJ: Princeton University Press. (Original work published 1921)

Kahneman, D., & Tversky, A. (1982). The simulation heuristic. In D. Kahneman, P. Slovic, & A. Tversky (Eds.), *Judgment under uncertainty: Heuristics and biases* (pp. 201–209). New York: Cambridge University Press.

Kaplan, H. S. (1974). *The new sex therapy: Active treatment of sexual dysfunctions.* New York: Brunner/Mazel.

Kelley, H. H. (1950). The warm-cold variable in first impressions of persons. *Journal of Personality, 18,* 431–439.

Kelley, H. H. (1967). Attribution theory in social psychology. In D. Levine (Ed.), *Nebraska Symposium of Motivation* (Vol. 15, pp. 192–240). Lincoln, NE: University of Nebraska Press.

Klayman, J., & Ha, Y-W. (1987). Confirmation, disconfirmation, and information in hypothesis testing. *Psychological Review, 94,* 211–228.

Klein, M. (1937). *The psycho-analysis of children* (2nd ed.). London: Hogarth.

Klein, M. (1946). Notes on some schizoid mechanisms. *International Journal of Psycho-Analysis, 33,* 433–438.

Kosko, B. (1993). *Fuzzy thinking: The new science of fuzzy logic.* New York: Hyperion.

Laing, R. D. (1967). *The politics of experience.* New York: Pantheon Books.

Laing, R. D. (1969). *The politics of the family and other essays.* New York: Pantheon Books.

Laing, R. D. (1970). *Knots.* New York: Random House.

Laing, R. D. (1975). In R. I. Evans (Producer) & R. Cozens (Director). *R. D. Laing's discussion with Richard Evans: Dilemma of mental illness* [Film]. University Park, PA: Penn State Audio-Visual Services.

Laing, R. D. (1976). *The facts of life: An essay in feelings, facts, and fantasy.* New York: Random House.

Lawrence, J., & Lee, R. E. (1955). *Inherit the wind.* New York: Random House.

Lepper, M. R., Ross, L., & Lau, R. R. (1986). Persistence of inaccurate beliefs about the self: Perseverance effects in the classroom. *Journal of Personality and Social Psychology, 50,* 482–491.

Lerner, M. J. (1970). The desire for justice and reactions to victims. In J. McCauley & L. Berkowitz (Eds.), *Altruism and helping behavior.* New York: Academic Press.

Levy, D. A. (1985). Optimism and pessimism: Relationships to circadian rhythms. *Psychological Reports, 57*(3), 1123–1126.

Levy, D. A. (1991, Spring). How to be a good psychotherapy patient. *Journal of Polymorphous Perversity, 8*(1), 17–19.

Levy, D. A. (1992). A proposed category for the diagnostic and statistical manual of mental disorders (DSM): Pervasive labeling disorder. *Journal of Humanistic Psychology, 32*(1), 121–125.

Levy, D. A. (1993, Spring). Psychometric infallibility realized: The one-size-fits-all psychological profile. *Journal of Polymorphous Perversity, 10*(1), 3–6.

Levy, D. A. (1994). Is the remedicalization of psychiatry good for the mental health field? No. In S. A. Kirk & S. D. Einbinder (Eds.), *Controversial issues in mental health* (pp. 160–176). Boston, MA: Allyn & Bacon.

Levy, D. A., & Erhardt, D. D. (1988). Stinks and instincts: An empirical investigation of Freud's excreta theory. *Journal of Irreproducible Results, 33*(5), 8–9.

Levy, D. A., Kaler, S. R., & Schall, M. (1988). An empirical investigation of role schemata: Occupations and personality characteristics. *Psychological Reports, 63,* 3–14.

Levy, D. A., & Nail, P. R. (1993). Contagion: A theoretical and empirical review and reconceptualization. *Genetic, Social, and General Psychology Monographs, 119*(2), 233–284.

Lewin, K. (1931). The conflict between Aristotelian and Galileian modes of thought in contemporary psychology. *Journal of General Psychology, 5,* 141–177.

Link, B. G., Cullen, F. T., Frank, J., & Wozniak, J. F. (1987). The social rejection of former mental patients: Understanding why labels matter. *American Journal of Sociology, 92,* 1461–1500.

Loftus, E. F. (1993). The reality of repressed memories. *American Psychologist, 48*(5), 518–537.

Loftus, E. & Ketcham, K. (1994). *The myth of repressed memory: False memories and allegations of sexual abuse.* New York: St. Martin's Griffin.

Lord, C. G., Lepper, M. R., & Preston, E. (1984). Considering the opposite: A corrective strategy for social judgment. *Journal of Personality and Social Psychology, 47,* 1231–1247.

Lord, C. G., Ross, L., & Lepper, M. (1979). Biased assimilation and attitude polarization: The effects of prior theories on subsequently considered evidence. *Journal of Personality and Social Psychology, 37,* 2098–2109.

Mahler, M. S., Pine, F., & Bergman, A. (1975). *The psychological birth of the human infant.* New York: Basic Books.

Mandler, G. (1975). *Mind and emotion.* New York: Wiley.

Maslow, A. (1970). *Motivation and personality* (2nd ed.). New York: Harper & Row.

McGuire, W. J., & Papageorgis, D. (1961). The relative efficacy of various types of prior belief defense in producing immunity against persuasion. *Journal of Abnormal and Social Psychology, 62,* 327–337.

Meehl, P. E. (1956). Wanted—A good cookbook. *American Psychologist, 11,* 262–272.

Meehl, P. E. (1973). Why I do not attend case conferences. In P. E. Meehl (Ed.), *Psychodiagnosis: Selected papers* (pp. 225–302). Minneapolis: University of Minnesota Press.

Milgram, S. (1963). Behavioral study of obedience. *Journal of Abnormal and Social Psychology, 67*(4), 371–378.

Milgram, S. (1974). *Obedience to authority.* New York: Harper & Row.

Miner, M., & Rawson, H. (1994). *The new international dictionary of quotations* (2nd ed.). New York: Signet.

Miller, J. (1983). *States of mind.* New York: Pantheon Books.

Myers, D. G. (1995). *Psychology* (4th ed.). New York: Worth Publishers.

Myers, J. K., Weissman, M. M., Tischler, G. L., Holzer, C. E., Leaf, P. J., Orvaschel, H., Anthony, J. C., Boyd, J. H., Burke, J. D., Kramer, M., & Stolzman, R. (1984). Six-month prevalence of psychiatric disorders in three communities: 1980 to 1982. *Archives of General Psychiatry, 41,* 959–967.

Naiman, A. (1981). *Every goy's guide to common Jewish expressions.* Boston, MA: Houghton Mifflin.

Napolitan, D. A., & Goethals, G. R. (1979). The attribution of friendliness. *Journal of Experimental Social Psychology, 15,* 105–113.

Nickerson, R. S., Perkins, D. N., & Smith, E. E. (1985). *The teaching of thinking.* Hillsdale, NJ: Erlbaum.

Page, S. (1977). Effects of the mental illness label in attempts to obtain accomodation. *Canadian Journal of Behavioral Science, 9,* 84–90.

Pascal, B. (1966). *Pensées.* (A. J. Krailsheimer, Trans.). Harmondsworth, Middlesex, England: Penguin Books.

Perls, F. S. (1969). *Gestalt therapy verbatim.* Lafayette, CA: Real People Press.

Piaget, J. (1948). *The moral judgment of the child.* New York: Free Press.

Piaget, J. (1952). *The origins of intelligence in children.* New York: International Universities Press.

Piaget, J. (1954). *The construction of reality in the child.* New York: Basic Books.

Piaget, J. (1970). Piaget's theory. In P. H. Mussen (Ed.), *Carmichael's manual of child psychology* (3rd ed., Vol. 1, pp. 773–847). New York: John Wiley.

Plomin, R., & Daniels, D. (1987). Why are children in the same family so different from one another? *Behavioral and Brain Sciences, 10,* 1–60.

Reason, J., & Mycielska, K. (1982). *Absent-minded? The psychology of mental lapses and everyday errors.* Englewood Cliffs, NJ: Prentice-Hall.

Regier, D. A., Boyd, J. H., Burke, J. D., Rae, D. S., Myers, J. K., Kramer, M., Robins, L. N., George, L. K., Karno, M., & Locke, B. Z. (1988). One-month prevalence of mental disorders in the United States. *Archives of General Psychiatry, 45*, 877–986.

Robins, L. N., Helzer, J. E., Weissman, M. M., Orvaschel, H., Gruenberg, E., Burke, J. D., & Regier, D. A. (1984). Lifetime prevalence of specific psychiatric disorders in three sites. *Archives of General Psychiatry, 41*, 949–958.

Roethlisberger, F. J., & Dickson, W. J. (1939). *Management and the worker.* Cambridge, MA: Harvard University Press.

Rosenhan, D. L. (1973). On being sane in insane places. *Science, 179*, 250–258.

Rosenhan, D. L., & Seligman, M. E. P. (1995). *Abnormal psychology* (3rd ed.). New York: Norton.

Rosenthal, R., & Fode, K. (1963). The effect of experimental bias on the performance of the albino rat. *Behavioral Science, 8*, 183–189.

Rosenthal, R., & Jacobson, L. (1968). *Pygmalion in the classroom: Teacher expectation and pupils' intellectual development.* New York: Holt, Rinehart, & Winston.

Ross, L. (1977). The intuitive psychologist and his shortcomings: Distortions in the attribution process. In L. Berkowitz (Ed.), *Advances in experimental social psychology* (Vol. 10). New York: Academic Press.

Ross, L. D., Amabile, T. M., & Steinmetz, J. L. (1977). Social roles, social control, and biases in social-perception processes. *Journal of Personality and Social Psychology, 35*, 485–494.

Ross, L. D., & Lepper, M. R. (1980). The perseverance of beliefs: Empirical and normative considerations. In R. A. Shweder (Ed.), *New directions for methodology of behavioral science: Fallible judgment in behavioral research.* San Francisco: Jossey-Bass.

Ross, L. D., Lepper, M. R., & Hubbard, M. (1975). Perseverance in self-perception and social perception: Biased attribution processes in the debriefing paradigm. *Journal of Personality and Social Psychology, 32*, 880–892.

Rosten, L. (1968). *The joys of Yiddish.* New York: Pocket Books.

Rowes, B. (1979). *The book of quotes.* New York: E. P. Dutton.

Runyan, W. M. (1981). Why did Van Gogh cut off his ear? The problem of alternative explanations in psychobiography. *Journal of Personality and Social Psychology, 40*, 1070–1077.

Ryle, G. (1949). *The concept of mind.* London: Hutchinson's University Library.

Santrock, J. W. (1995). *Life-span development.* Dubuque, IA: Wm. C. Brown Communications.

Sears, D. O., Peplau, L. A., & Taylor, S. E. (1991). *Social psychology* (7th ed.). Englewood Cliffs, NJ: Prentice-Hall.

Shaw, G. B. (1913). *Pygmalion: A romance in five acts.* New York: Random House.

Skov, R. B., & Sherman, S. J. (1986). Information-gathering processes: Diagnosticity, hypothesis-confirmatory strategies, and perceived hypothesis confirmation. *Journal of Experimental Social Psychology, 22*, 93–121.

Skrypnek, B. J., & Snyder, M. (1982). On the self-perpetuating nature of stereotypes about women and men. *Journal of Experimental Social Psychology, 18*, 277–291.

Slovic, P. (1987). Perception of risk. *Science, 236*, 280–285.

Slovic, P., & Fischhoff, B. (1977). On the psychology of experimental surprises. *Journal of Experimental Psychology: Human Perception and Performance, 3*, 544–551.

Slovic, P., Fischoff, B., & Lichtenstein, S. (1976). Cognitive processes and societal risk taking. In J. S. Carroll & J. W. Payne (Eds.), *Cognition and social behavior.* Hillsdale, NJ: Erlbaum.

Smith, M. B. (1978). Psychology and values. *Journal of Social Issues, 34*, 181–199.

Snyder, C. R., Shenkel, R. J., & Lowery, C. R. (1977). Acceptance of personality interpretations: The "Barnum Effect" and beyond. *Journal of Consulting and Clinical Psychology, 45*(1), 104–114.

Snyder, M. (1984). When belief becomes reality. In L. Berkowitz (Ed.), *Advances in Experimental Social Psychology* (Vol. 18). New York: Academic Press.

Snyder, M., & Swann, W. B., Jr. (1978). Behavioral confirmation in social interaction:

From social perception to social reality. *Journal of Experimental Social Psychology, 14,* 148–162.

Snyder, M., Tanke, E. D., & Berscheid, E. (1977). Social perception and interpersonal behavior: On the self-fulfilling nature of social stereotypes. *Journal of Personality and Social Psychology, 35,* 656–666.

Spitzer, R. L. (1975). On pseudoscience in science, logic in remission, and psychiatric diagnosis: A critique of Rosenhan's "On being sane in insane places." *Journal of Abnormal Psychology, 84,* 442–452.

Spitzer, R. L., & Wilson, P. T. (1975). Nosology and the official psychiatric nomenclature. In A. Freedman & H. Kaplan (Eds.), *Comprehensive textbook of psychiatry.* New York: Williams & Wilkins.

Storms, M. D. (1973). Videotape and the attribution process: Reversing actors' and observers' points of view. *Journal of Personality and Social Psychology, 27,* 165–175.

Sullivan, H. S. (1954). *The psychiatric interview.* New York: Norton.

Sullivan, H. S. (1956). *Clinical studies in psychiatry.* New York: Norton.

Sullivan, H. S. (1962). *Schizophrenia as a human process.* New York: Norton.

Szasz, T. S. (1960). The myth of mental illness. *American Psychologist, 15,* 113–118.

Szasz, T. S. (1974). *The myth of mental illness: Foundations of a theory of personal conduct* (rev. ed.). New York: Harper & Row.

Szasz, T. S. (1984). *The therapeutic state: Psychiatry in the mirror of current events.* Buffalo, NY: Prometheus Books.

Szasz, T. S. (1987). *Insanity: The idea and its consequences.* New York: Wiley.

Taylor, S. E., & Crocker, J. (1981). Schematic bases of social information processing. In E. T. Higgins, C. P. Herman, & M. P. Zanna (Eds.), *Social cognition: The Ontario Symposium* (Vol. 1, pp. 89–134). Hillsdale, NJ: Erlbaum.

Taylor, S. E., & Fiske, S. T. (1975). Point of view and perceptions of causality. *Journal of Personality and Social Psychology, 32,* 439–445.

Tellegen, A., Lykken, D. T., Bouchard, T. J., Jr., Wilcox, K. J., Segal, N. L., & Rich, S. (1988). Personality similarity in twins reared apart and together. *Journal of Personality and Social Psychology, 54,* 1031–1039.

Tversky, A., & Kahneman, D. (1973). Availability: A heuristic for judging frequency and probability. *Cognitive Psychology, 5,* 207–232.

Tversky, A., & Kahneman, D. (1974). Judgment under uncertainty: Heuristics and biases. *Science, 185,* 1124–1131.

Tversky, A., & Kahneman, D. (1982). Judgments of and by representativeness. In D. Kahneman, P. Slovic, & A. Tversky (Eds.), *Judgment under uncertainty: Heuristics and biases.* New York: Cambridge University Press.

Unger, R. K. (1983). Through the looking glass: No wonderland yet! (The reciprocal relationship between methodology and models of reality). *Psychology of Women Quarterly, 8,* 9–32.

Vokey, J. R., & Read, J. D. (1985). Subliminal messages: Between the devil and the media. *American Psychologist, 40,* 1231–1239.

Wakefield, J. C. (1992). The concept of mental disorder: On the boundary between biological facts and social values. *American Psychologist, 47*(3), 373–388.

Walster, E. (1966). Assignment of responsibility for an accident. *Journal of Personality and Social Psychology, 3,* 73–79.

Wason, P. C. (1960). On the failure to eliminate hypotheses in a conceptual task. *Quarterly Journal of Experimental Psychology, 12,* 129–140.

Weiner, B. (1980). A cognitive (attribution)–emotion–action model of motivated behavior: An analysis of judgment of help-giving. *Journal of Personality and Social Psychology, 39,* 186–200.

Whorf, B. (1956). *Language, thought, and reality.* Cambridge, MA: MIT Press.

Wood, G. (1979). The knew-it-all-along effect. *Journal of Experimental Psychology: Human Perception and Performance, 4,* 345–353.

Word, C. H., Zanna, M. P., & Cooper, J. (1974). The nonverbal mediation of self-fulfilling prophecies in inter-racial interaction. *Journal of Experimental Social Psychology, 10,* 109–120.

Zajonc, R. B. (1980). Feeling and thinking: Preferences need no inferences. *American Psychologist, 35,* 151–175.

Name Index

Subject Index

Note: *In addition to the cited pages, refer to the Glossary for definitions of key terms and concepts.*